Explore the World

 NELLES  GUIDE

PHILIPPINES

Authors:
Albrecht G. Schaefer, Wolf Dietrich,
Sylvia L. Mayuga, Roland Hanewald

An Up-to-date travel guide
with 154 color photos
and 12 maps

Dear Reader: Being up-to-date is the main goal of the Nelles series. Our correspondents help keep us abreast of the latest developments in the travel scene, while our cartographers see to it that maps are also kept completely current. However, as the travel world is constantly changing, we cannot guarantee that all the information contained in our books is always valid. Should you come across a discrepancy, please contact us at: Nelles Verlag, Schleissheimer Str. 371 b, 80935 Munich, Germany, tel. (089) 3571940, fax. (089) 35719430, e-mail: Nelles.Verlag@T-Online.de

Note: Distances and measurements, including temperatures, used in this guide are metric. For conversion information, please see the *Guidelines* section of this book.

LEGEND

★	Place of Interest	Tangalan	Place Mentioned in Text	
▨	Public or Significant Building	◪	International Airport	
■	Hotel	⊞	National Airport	
▨	Market, Shopping Center	♠	National Park	
✝	Church			
☾	Mosque	Mt. Apo 2956	Mountain Summit (Height in Meters)	
⚑	Buddhist Temple			
☀	Beach	\ 19 /	Distance in Kilometers	

▨▨▨	National Border
▨▨▨	Provincial Border
═══	Expressway
═══	Principal Highway
═══	Highway
═══	Provincial Road (mainly paved)
───	Secondary Road, Track, Path
───	Railway
──●──	Light Rail Transit System

PHILIPPINES
© Nelles Verlag GmbH, 80935 München
  All rights reserved

Third Revised Edition 2000
ISBN 3-88618-222-3
Printed in Slovenia

Publisher:	Günter Nelles	**Translation:**	Angus McGeoch, Jane Bainbridge, Mary Shields
Editor-in-Chief:	Berthold Schwarz	**Cartography:**	Nelles Verlag GmbH
Project Editor:	Albrecht G. Schaefer	**Color Separation:**	Reproline, München
Editor, English edition:	A. McGeoch	**Printing:**	Gorenjski Tisk

- T07 -

TABLE OF CONTENTS

FEATURES

GUIDELINES

MAP LIST

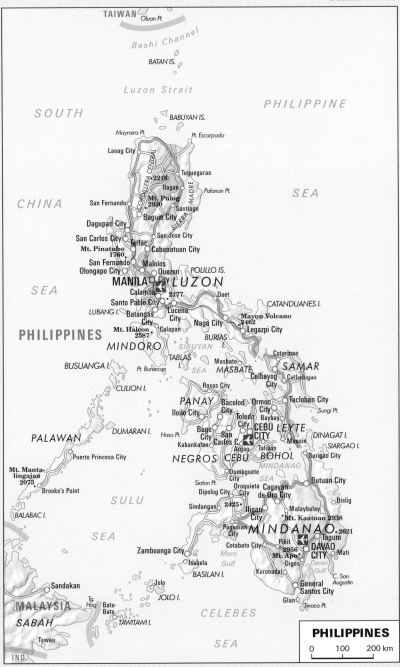

TAIWAN

Oluan Pt.

Bashi Channel

BATAN IS.

Luzon Strait

SOUTH

PHILIPPINE

BABUYAN IS.

Mayraira Pt.

Pt. Escarpada

Laoag City

CHINA

SEA

San Fernando

•2216

Tuguegarao

Ilagan

Mt. Pulog
2930

Palanan Pt.

Santiago

Dagupan City

Baguio City

SIERRA MADRE

CORDILLERA CENTRAL

San Carlos City

San Jose City

Tarlac

Cabanatuan City

Mt. Pinatubo
1760

San Fernando

Malolos

SEA

Olongapo City

Quezon

POLILLO IS.

MANILA City **LUZON**

Calamba

Santo Pablo City

•2177

Daet

CATANDUANES I.

LUBANG I.

Batangas
City

Lucena
City

Naga City

Mayon Volcano
•2462

PHILIPPINES

Mt. Halcon
2587

Calapan

Legazpi City

BURIAS

MINDORO

SIBUYAN

I.

SEA

Sea

BUSUANGA I.

TABLAS

Masbate

MASBATE

Catarman

I.

Pt. Buruncan

Calbayog
City

SAMAR

Catbalogan

Roxas City

Tacloban City

PANAY

Bacolod
City

Ormoc
City

CULION I.

DUMARAN I.

Iloilo City

Toledo
City

Baybay

Sungi Pt.

PALAWAN

Bago
City

San

CEBU
CITY

LEYTE

DINAGAT I.

Naso Pt.

Carlos C.

SIARGAO I.

Puerto Princesa City

Kabankalan

Argao

Talibon

Maasin

Surigao City

NEGROS

CEBU

BOHOL

Mt. Manta-
lingajan
2073

Dumaguete

MINDANAO

Brooke's Point

Siaton Pt.

Oroquieta

Cagayan

Butuan City

SULU

Dipolog City

de Oro City

Bislig

Sindangan

•2425

Malaybalay

SEA

Iligan
City

•**Mt. Kaatoan 2938**

BALABAC I.

Pagadian
City

MINDANAO•2621

Cotabato City

Pikit

Tagum

Zamboanga City

•2956

DAVAO

Mati

Sandakan

Isabela

Mt. Apo

CITY

BASILAN I.

Koronadal

Digos

Davao
Gulf

Jolo

Moro
Gulf

C. San
Augustin

MALAYSIA

Tg.
Hog.

JOLO I.

General

SABAH

Bato-
Bato

Santos City

Tawau

TAWITAWI I.

CELEBES

Glan

Tinaca Pt.

IND.

SEA

| **PHILIPPINES** | | |
| 0 | 100 | 200 km |

ISLANDS BETWEEN
EAST AND WEST

LAND AND PEOPLE

Many places in the world have been called "a land of contrasts," but of all the countries in South East Asia, it is the Philippines which most deserves this title. Here you will find idyllic palm-fringed islands, dazzlingly white beaches beside a turquoise blue sea, but also thundering volcanoes and typhoons that rage every year; fertile acres of paddy-fields, lush and impenetrable tracts of virgin forest, but also rivers like open sewers, and bare, scorched mountainsides; colorful, good-natured, rural fiestas next to smoke-belching factory chimneys; aboriginals living in an almost neolithic style, and asphalt jungles in the high-rise canyons; a fantastically affluent elite and hordes of poor crammed into overcrowded slums.

The geopolitical make-up of the Philippines – several thousand islands, with 13 regions, and 76 provinces under the umbrella of a single state – makes considerable demands on the imagination of a visitor from a relatively small and manageable country in, for example, Europe. The enormously fragmented nature of the country has had an influence on its history, culture and political development, which must not be underestimated.

The name is in itself significant and illustrates the dilemma of national identity which results from centuries of dependency. Even though the 300 years of Spanish colonial rule ended nearly a century ago, the Philippines still clings to the

name of the Spanish King, Philip II, who made this distant archipelago into a bastion of Christianity in Asia. Nevertheless, since the People's Power revolution of 1986 motivated the population to wear T-shirts with the slogan "I am proud to be a Filipino," an entirely new self-awareness has taken root in the inhabitants of "Philipp's Islands." Therefore this book we feel free to describe even the pre-Hispanic people of these islands as *Filipinos* and *Filipinas*.

Another equally ambitious world power stamped its colonial influence on the Philippines after the disintegration of the Spanish empire. The impact of only 50 years of American domination has left a deep impression, all in the name of progress, and in the cultural melting-pot of today it has survived in a more lasting way than has the Spanish legacy.

The superficially western elements encountered in these Far Eastern islands make them both attractive and deceptive to the visitor from Europe, America or Australia. At first one thinks one is on fairly familiar territory. Compared with the countries around them, the Philippines can calm one's fears of the mysterious orient. Almost everywhere people speak tolerably good American English, the cooking includes quite a number of western dishes, the majority of the population are nominally Christian, and the fact that traffic drives on the right, unlike most of Southeast Asia, is helpful to non-British tourists. And yet, the ancient Malay roots of Philippine society are still very much alive.

Tagalog is the native tongue of the Tagal people of central Luzon, but in 1937 it was given the status of national language – not without much protest from other major linguistic groups such as *Cebuano* and *Hiligaynon*, to name just two of the 87 langauges and dialects spoken in different parts of the country. Thus, in 1973 Tagalog, enriched with the vocabulary of several other regions, was

Previous pages: Mandaya women from Davao in festive costumes. Rice terraces at Banaue. T'boli-women, southern Mindanao. Left: Natural paradise in northern Palawan.

officially re-named *Filipino* or *Pilipino*. However, a certain local patriotism continues to govern communication in a country which has absorbed not only Indian, Arabic and even Persian influences, but also Chinese, Spanish and English vocabulary. For this reason, Pilipino is only making slow progress towards national acceptance.

Eight out of ten Filipinos are Catholic. Around 90 percent of the population are baptized Christians, of which significant groupings are the members of the *Iglesia Filipina Independiente* (Independent Chuch of the Philippines), which originated in 1902 after splitting from the Catholic church), and the almost equally large *Iglesia ni Cristo*, a prosperous denomination similar to American Protestantism. With Protestants making up four percent of the population (including former

Above: For a long time the people of north Luzon resisted the Spanish and Christianity. Today a church stands even in the Ifugao village of Batad.

President Ramos), Muslims a bare five percent, and Buddhists, Taoists and Hindus, only one percent, Philippine society continues to be strongly influenced by Catholic teachings.

Yet the life and character of most Filipinos have been shaped in many ways by the deep-rooted influence of earlier animistic traditions, even though these beliefs are today ostensibly followed only by ethnic minorities. Superstition is still rife and permeates daily life, though the fear and awe of nature-spirits have been swept aside by the desire for progress – at the expense of the environment.

There are many contradictions in the national character of the Filipinos, but they all share an attractive and endearing sociability, and a warm-hearted curiosity in anything that is foreign and different. Apart from the areas where there is tension between rebels and the military, and in the aggressively metropolitan Manila, a foreigner will generally feel quite at ease in the Philippines.

On the Edge of the Ring of Fire

One of the many delightful myths concerning the origins of the archipelago tells how a little bird had a hand in creating this land of many islands. According to legend, this creature, exhausted from endless flying, complained to the forces of nature that it lived quite alone between the sea and the sky, without even the smallest piece of land on which to rest. Cunningly the bird sowed the seeds of strife between the elements, which had hitherto avoided one another. By telling each one of the alleged evil intentions of the other, he unleashed a titanic conflict, in which the sea sent mountainous waves heavenwards and the sky hurled down fearful storms and huge showers of rock, which finally towered out of the sea. At last the wily bird found its longed-for resting-place and the newly created islands began to fill with life.

The Philippine archipelago is indeed fabulous; lying on the eastern edge of the South China Sea between longitudes 116° 55' and 127° 36' east and between latitudes 4° 23' and 21° 25' north of the equator it has islands of every size and shape, rising as atolls out of the turquoise blue water or towering skywards with rugged mountain ranges and mighty volcanoes, rising above the clouds; isles like paradise and bright coral reefs, evergreen rain-forest and sweeping plains. Some of the islands are so large that they are inhabited by several ehtnic groups. The vast majority of the islands which make up the archipelago are, however, mere suggestions of land – scarcely more than nesting sites – at high water only visible as sandbanks or rocky reefs. In 1939 zealous civil servants took on the task of counting every single island and the final total came to an impressive 7,107!

Only about 2,000 of the islands are inhabited, and some 2,700 have been given names over the centuries. This fragmented nation covers a total land area of 300,000 square kilometers, making it about as large as Italy or Poland. Virtually all of this (94 percent) is accounted for by just eleven islands – Luzon in the north, Mindanao in the south, Palawan in the southwest, and in between Mindoro, Masbate, Samar, Leyte, Panay, Negros, Cebu and Bohol, all the more remarkable, since the Philppines stretch 1,850 kilometers north to south, and 1,060 kilometers east to west. Apart from Vietnam, 960 kilometers away to the west, and the Pacific Ocean, with scarcely and land, in the east, the Asian neighbors are within easy reach and even within sight in good weather. From the northernmost island of the Philippines group, Y'ami, it is 150 kilometers to Taiwan; the Malaysian province of Sabah on Borneo is a short hop of 25 kilometers by sea from the southern tip of Palawan, while the northerly islands of Indonesia's Sulawesi group are only 60 kilometers from the southern point of Mindanao.

The islands of the Philippines form a sort of broken bridge across the East and Southeast Asian seas. There is no definite proof of the traditionally-held thought that the archipelago is the remains of a prehistoric land link between the Asian continent and Taiwan and Indonesia. In the Early Tertiary Period, about 55 million years ago, the islands which we know today as the Philippines were, so the theory goes, linked with Asia as one continuous sub-continent. The geologists' theories are supported by similarities in the plant and animal worlds, parallels in the geological structure, and by the relatively shallow sea, separating Asia and the Philippines. They are also served by the existence of the Mindanao Trench: 1,800 kilometers long and up to 10,540 meters deep, it runs along near the Pacific coast of the Philippines and could be said to prove that this was once the edge of the Asiatic land-mass.

Frequent movements of the earth's crust (the lithosphere), folding and uplift-

ing must have taken place to cause the extremely varied geomorphology of the archipelago. As a result, fossilized coral reefs and petrified sea creatures are found today in the mountains of the Philippines. According to geologists, there was a particularly restless period with intense volcanic activity some 50,000 years ago. Not until the glaciers of the last ice age melted 10,000 years ago and caused a global rise in the level of the oceans, was the continental shelf flooded, leaving the highest tips as islands above sea level.

Meanwhile, other researchers into the earth's history attribute the creation of this pattern of islands chiefly to the volcanic activity itself. They say there was no separation from the Asiatic land-mass, but rather that the islands were thrust upwards from the sea bed by powerful seismic and volcanic activity – rather as in the myth of the bird. And this subterranean restlessness is far from ended. The

Philippines are among the most geologically active regions in the world. They form part of the Pacific "ring of fire" and lie on a fault line in the earth's crust. The Phillipine Trench which, after the Mariana Trench south of Japan, is the second deepest ocean trench on the world's surface, is one of the areas of friction where the Eurasian and Indo-Australian tectonic plates are slowly colliding. This movement, which can only be measured as a few centimeters each year, nevertheless causes regular and sometimes devastating earth- and sea-quakes experienced in this part of the world. As recently as 1990 violent tremors laid waste large tracts of the northern Philippine town of Baguio and caused the death of nearly 1000 people. But far more feared by the islanders are the huge tidal waves which the tremors send thundering ashore along the coast of the islands.

One of the largest chains of volcanoes on earth runs through the islands of Southeast Asia. It was formed during the early movements of the earth's crust in

Above: Sinister beauty – Babuyan Claro, a volcano on the Babuyan Islands.

16

the Tertiary and Quarternary Periods. Out of a total of 200 volcanoes 94 have been active during the past 160 years, including at least 18 of the 37 volcanoes in the Philippines. There was a recent grim reminder of how suddenly this statistic can be altered: Mount Pinatubo, which until May 1991 had been dormant for 600 years and was only known to those living in its immediate vicinity, gave the latest demonstration of the powerful forces pent up in the earth beneath the Philippines. In a series of eruptions, which caused 300 deaths, the volcano hurled some 5 billion tons of rock and 19 million tons of sulphur dioxide as high as 24 kilometers into the atmosphere. Then in September 1992, avalanches of mud and eruptions of rock killed a further 100 people. Add to those the untold numbers of aboriginals who disappeared, and the million or so who were made homeless. The sulphurous fumes and clouds of ash thrown up by the erupting volcano will circle the earth for several years, as a thin layer of ice in the stratosphere. In the last few years there were repeated small eruptions.

Sunshine and Cyclones

The Philippines lie in the tropics, near the equator, and this dictates its climate. Generally speaking, the weather is hot, with high humidity and abundant rainfall. There are two seasons, both directly governed by the monsoons. From June until November the *Habágat* – the summer, southwest monsoon– reaches the Philippines and being laden with moisture, consequently produces the rainy season. The northeast monsoon, called *Amíhan* by the Filipinos, blows from December to May, initially bringing rather cool temperatures, but from March onwards, in the second part of the dry season, it becomes really hot. For the regions that lie along the Pacific coast the *Amíhan* brings a mild, oceanic climate but also heavy rainfall. The mountains, which for the most part run from north to south of the islands, act as a meteorological divide. This is particularly evident in the Central Cordillera in northern Luzon, where it can rain heavily on the eastern side of the mountains, while on the western slopes there is the most beautiful, dry weather for walking and climbing.

It is impossible to make any general statement about the climate overall, since in individual regions of this large and scattered archipelago there can be significant deviations. In parts of the western Visayas and in Mindanao the seasons often fail to abide by the calendar – it can rain during the dry season, and it can happen that in north Luzon it is raining down in stair-rods, while the people of the southern islands are gasping for the merest drop. It is certainly true that in the last fifteen years many over-long dry seasons have been recorded, which have caused real damage and a dangerous lack of drinking water in some regions. In Mindanao by early 1992 they had been waiting for nine months for rain – in an area which used to have rainfall throughout the year. Some of the blame for this is laid with *El Niño* – a phenomenon created by ocean currents and called "the holy child" because it usually occurs at Christmas time. The exceptional warming of the surface of the ocean in the eastern Pacific, possibly due to a moderation of the trade winds, thus causes changes in the temperature as far away as Southeast Asia and Australia.

In the meantime causes closer to home – one could say home-made causes – have been pin-pointed as affecting the environment of the Philippines. Careless large-scale tree felling in the rainforest, and extensive slash-and-burn clearing right up into the mountains, gives the soil scarcely any chance to store the precious groundwater, and leaves it exposed to dangerous erosion. When the dreaded typhoons sweep over the Philippines from

the western Pacific en route to the mainland of China, on very unpredictable courses in the period from June to December, the tracts of land that have been stripped bare can offer no resistance to their winds. On average, the Philippines have to endure 30 of these 300 kilometer-per-hour monsters every year. They give these *Bagyó* feminine names like "Meding" or "Oring," whereas storms in the western hemisphere can be of either sex – to the satisfaction of feminist groups. The Pacific coast of south Luzon and the mountains in the north are particularly hard hit, mainly in August and September, and the capital, Manila, is also affected every now and then.

Long experience of hurricanes has at least led to the establishment of an early-warning system which seems to function reasonably well, and architects are able to design buildings which are supposdly

Above: Devastating tidal waves in the wake of a typhoon. Right: Without plenty of water the farmers would be unable to grow rice.

"typhoon -proof." But Pacific typhoons have the oddity of changing course frequently and even turning around, so that the same place is hit twice. Even areas like Mindanao, the southwestern Visayas and Palawan, which are otherwise spared the hurricanes, can be battered by rogue winds that break away from the main storm. Typhoons always bring torrential rain, which can cause extensive flooding, collapsed bridges and landslides.

Nonetheless, the Philippines always need rain, to water the plains and mountain valleys where rice, the staple diet of the 72 million inhabitants, is cultivated. A minimum of 100 mm of rain per month is normally sufficient to ensure the growth of rice in the tropics, so with an average annual rainfall of 2400 mm the Philippines seem decidedly fertile.The majority of the rain falls in the mountainous areas, so naturally this is where the hydroelectric power stations have been built, which are the country's principal source of energy. Of economic importance, too, are the 59 inland lakes

which, as well as the sea, yield the fish that form the second most important element of the Filipino diet. The largest lake is Laguna de Bay southeast of Manila, which has an area of 922 square kilometers.

The islands are watered by 132 rivers, of which the longest are to be found in Luzon and Mindanao. They carry down large quantities of fertile alluvium to their deltas, and for this reason these areas are densely populated. But at least one-tenth of Philippine rivers are said to be biologically dead, having been abused for decades with industrial effluent and untreated sewage.

A land of wealth and poverty

Lost in one's dreams on a tropical island, it is easy to forget the increasing environmental problems which face the Philippines. But the government which came to power in 1998 under President Joseph Estrada can no longer avoid devoting much greater attention to nature

conservation. Already, 90 percent of the forest which, as recently as 1986 still covered about a half of Philippine land, has been cut down. The most recent research has revealed that only six percent of the coral reefs in the seas around the islands are still completely intact. The coastal waters have been overfished. Efforts to slow down the annual population increase of 2.3 percent (in 1999), on a long-term basis, have so far failed, largely due to the opposition of the Catholic church. Over 40 percent of Filipinos flock to the already overcrowded towns and cities to seek employment, and more than two-thirds of the rural population live on or below the poverty line.

Yet at the same time this land of many islands has been richly endowed by the moods of nature. More than half the working population is employed in the primary sector, particularly in the agricultural and fishing industries. Vegetables, fruits, nuts and root crops like sweet potatoes, cassava and yams are cultivated in all regions. Coconut palms

19

grow on more than 10 percent of the land and their by-products have placed the Philippines in the front rank of exporters in this field. The country also exports bananas, sugar, coffee, rubber and abaca, the famous "Manila hemp" for rope-making. Tropical hardwoods from the Philippines were also much in demand (and are still being exported despite the fact that this is now illegal.)

Rice, the population's staple food, has to be imported periodically. Large hopes are being placed in the intensified mining of copper, gold, silver, iron ore, lead, manganese, lead, cadmium, platinum, chrome and mercury.

Today, since unemployment rates (over 20 percent) and the foreign debt of 48 billion US$ (1999) are continuing to increase, the government is trying to attract as many foreign investors to the country as possible.

Above: Surviving in misery and filth – slum-dwellers in Tondo, Manila. Right: Pre-Hispanic mummy in Kabayan, North Luzon.

THE LIVING PAST

The history of the Philippines reaches directly into the present, more so than in many other countries; it is above all a history of colonial occupation, which began very early and continued for too long – in fact, for about 400 years. Not until the American forces relinquished their last bases at the end of the 20th century did this colonial presence come, at least temporarily, to an end. The foreign powers who ruled these islands for such a large part of their history have left a strange legacy, in which English, along with Pilipino, is still an official language; the majority of the population bear Spanish names although scarcely anyone speaks Spanish, and the indigenous Malay culture is overlayed by a colonial mentality.

This island republic is distinguished from the outset by its very name. It is the only Asian country to be named after a European ruler – King Philip II of Spain. The Filipinos live in the most Christian country in Asia, where the Catholic reli-

gion is practiced with more devotion than in most western countries. However, the Spanish and the Americans were not the only colonial rulers on the Southeast Asian archipelago. The seafaring Malay invaders supplanted the negroid aboriginal peoples who, isolated and drastically reduced in numbers, scarcely figure in the life of the nation.

The Early Islanders

Archeological clues about the prehistory of the Philippines are sparse. Finds made during excavations in Cagayan Province (North Luzon) indicate that about 250,000 years ago hominids, the earliest people, inhabited parts of what are today the Philippines. These relatives of Peking and Java Man may have come over from the Asiatic mainland by way of the land bridge which existed then, together with the animals which they hunted, such as the stegodon (an ancestor of the elephant) and the woolly rhinoceros. The remains of skeletons and

tools of *homo sapiens*, which are at least 30,000 years old, have been found in the Tabon Caves in Palawan island. They are very similar to some discovered in the Niah Cave in Sarawak, Borneo, which are believed to be 10,000 years older. At that time the Sunda Shelf between Borneo and Sumatra was still above sea level and linked present-day eastern Malaysia with Palawan. The aboriginal inhabitants of the Philippines, hunters and gatherers, who must have migrated here from the Asian continent during the Paleolithic age, more than 15,000 years ago, were called *Negritos* by the Spanish, because of their very dark skin, curly hair, and short stature.

From about 4000 B.C. the seafaring proto-Malays began to invade the islands, probably sailing over in large boats from Borneo after the submerging of the land-bridge. They drove the Negritos into the hinterland, where they wandered as nomads through the primeval forests which then covered most of the archipelago. A second wave of proto-Malay mi-

21

gration took place around 1000 B.C. The proto-Malays, the ancient Malay people of Mongolian-Caucasian origin, were culturally far superior to the *Aëta* or *Ati*, as the Negritos are also called. They brought the achievements and advances of the Neolithic period to the Philippines: a settled way of life and cultivation. Ethnographers consider the proto-Malays to be among the oldest racial groups of the Austronesian peoples, who by A.D. 1000 had spread over the whole of the Indian Ocean and most of the Pacific, west to Madagascar and east to Hawaii.

Similarly, from about 300 B.C., the so-called deutero-Malays, or neo-Malays, reached the Philippines in their seaworthy outriggers (*balanghai* or barangay) and they in turn drove out the proto-Malay settlers. Their arrival once again

Above: Weapons that have hardly changed in thousands of years – bamboo quiver with arrows fired from a blow-pipe, Palawan. Right: Mosque and stilt-houses near Zamboanga, Mindanao.

heralded the beginning of a new age on the islands, since the technical superiority of the newcomers pointed the way ahead: apart from their skill as sailors, they were also adept at metalwork and weaving, they introduced the cultivation of rice as a crop and they had an alphabet related to Indian Sanskrit. Their social structure, which consisted of small political units, was to be retained in the Philippines for centuries: a *barangay*, so named from the boats in which the migrants arrived, comprised anything from 30 to 100 families, all of the same tribe. The Barangays were themselves organized into a feudal form of class system. There were nobles, freemen, peasants, captives and bondmen. The top of the social pyramid was occupied by the *Datu*, or chieftain. Yet this social structure was not a rigid one – it was not simply a matter of being born into a particular class. The Barangays did not, however, seek close contact with one another. Only in the geographically and climatically inhospitable regions of the north, did the descendants of the early

Malay settlers combine to form large alliances. But when they did, it not only led to splendid cultural achievements, such as the famous rice terraces of the Ifugao and Bontoc, but created a very effective resistance to attempts by foreign powers to colonize the islands.

The people who inhabited the plains and coastal regions at that time enjoyed a relatively simple lifestyle, untouched by external influences. Occasionally, in the first few centuries A.D., they traded with seafarers from China and from the Buddhist empire of Sri-Vijaya, which was founded in Sumatra around the beginning of the millennium. The name "Visayas," which is given to the central islands today, derives from this Sanskrit word and serves as a reminder of these early connections. As a result of this trade, the Philippines, even in those days, became known as a supplier of commodities such as timber, spices, cotton, resin, honey, pearls and slaves, in return for which they imported silk, metal goods and porcelain. Although the great religions of Asia, Buddhism and Hinduism, advanced as far as Indonesia, their teachings did not reach the Philippines. Until the arrival of Islam in the 14th century and of Christianity in the 16th, the islanders worshipped the spirits of nature and of their ancestors, and in certain regions this animism is still practiced today. This would suggest a certain cultural independence, yet when colonizers arrived from the west, the Philippines was the only country in Southeast Asia which possessed neither a central government nor a reasonably homogeneous culture – a fact which made conquest by the Spanish, and later the Americans, relatively easy.

Imams and Sultanates

Even before the spread of Islam through Southeast Asia – the religion gained a foothold in Sumatra and eastern Malaysia from the 14th century onwards

– Arab merchants had already landed on the Philippine islands and in the 12th century had established one of their most important trading posts at the mouth of the Pasig river, later to be the site of Manila. However, the sons of the Prophet did not display any missionary zeal until 1380, when the Koranic teacher Karim al-Makdum ordered the building of the first mosque in the Philippines, on the Sulu island of Simunul. He was followed by the Raja Baginda from Sumatra, whose daughter married the Islamic missionary Abu Bakr. He was from the Malayan sultanate of Johore, and in 1450 established the first Philippine sultanate on the island of Jolo. In 1475 Sharif Muhammad Kabungsuan, a direct descendent of the Prophet Mohammed, advanced as far as Mindanao. Through his marriage with a native princess he was able to convert several tribes to Islam and establish the sultanate of Maguindanao.

The influence of the Muslim missionaries and merchants encouraged, for the first time, the spread of a single culture and a comprehensive system of political organization, at least in the southern Philippines. The inhabitants were thus able to offer correspondingly stronger resistance to the Spanish, who never really succeeded in their attempts to gain complete control of the Sulu Islands and Mindanao, which were now committed to Islam. At the beginning of the 16th century this large island in the south was governed by various sultanates, united by the teachings of Mohammed. Meanwhile, the western Visayas had also come under Muslim influence, and the town of *May-nilad*, later to become Manila, had developed from being an Arab trading-post into a small independent sultanate. Contemporary historians have put forward the hypothetical, but interesting notion that, if the Spanish had arrived in the Philippines just a century later, the nation would today be entirely Muslim.

Las Islas Filipinas

The Spanish were not really interested in the Philippines, but they were attracted to them because of their rivalry with the Portuguese, whom they envied for their lucrative spice trade in the Indonesian islands. In 1519 Hernán Cortéz conquered the Aztec empire in Mexico and in the same year the Spanish king, Charles V, yielded to the persuasion of the seafarer Fernão de Magalhães (who ironically was Portuguese)himself) and gave him the task of exploring the west-to-east sea route to the Moluccas. In order to break the Portuguese monopoly, this old seadog, better known to us as Ferdinand Magellan, sailed with his small fleet around the southern tip of South America and crossed the previously unknown ocean which he named "El Pacifico" ("The Peaceful One"). The Europeans, exhausted by the long sea voyage, landed in 1521 near what is today called Samar – in the east of the archipelago. Magellan named his discovery "the Saint Lazarus Islands," after the saint on whose nameday he had landed there. He then sailed confidently further, since the islanders had greeted him in a friendly way, without suspicion.

The expedition reached *Zubu*, today the island of Cebu, on March 16, and here Magellan succeeded with the help of gifts and barter-goods, in converting the Rajah Humabon and his 800 subjects to Catholicism: that is to say, the astonished islanders allowed themselves to be showered with gifts and baptized from morning till night,.

The neighboring princes were no less impressed by the new religion, with the exception of a certain Lapu-Lapu, a warrior and a newcomer from the Sulu Archipelago, who as chief of Mactan, the island which lies off the modern Cebu City, opposed the orders of Magellan and his men. Magellan made an attempt to intimidate Lapu-Lapu but was killed in the battle of Mactan, on April 27, 1521.

Magellan's men returned to Cebu where Humabon gave them a further surprise. The Europeans learned here for the first time, among other things, that the hospitality of the Malays has its limits, and they were given a violent demonstration of the natives' desire to keep things on an equal footing. The white men's leader was dead, their magic gone, several of the sailors had overstepped limits with the native women, and the new strong-man was flexing his muscles on the next-door island. Humabon decided to throw in his lot with Lapu-Lapu, and had some of the Spaniards massacred – during a feast to celebrate the conclusion of further barter trading.

On September 6, 1522, Magellan's expedition ended after an odyssey through the Indonesian islands and around the southern tip of Africa, back to Seville –

Right: Historical opponents – Lapu-Lapu and his "descendants". Ferdinand Magellan, in an engraving from 1673.

FERDINAND MAGELLANUS.

but of the original five ships and 256 crew, only one ship and 18 men had survived this circumnavigation of the globe. The Spanish king, determined not to be beaten, dispatched three further expeditions to Southeast Asia, all of which ended in failure. In 1543 Ruy Lopez de Villalobos returned empty-handed, but at least with the satisfaction of having rechristened the islands, which from now on were to be called "Las Islas Filipinas" in honor of the future king of Spain. Eight years later Philip II, who had come to the throne in 1556, decided to send another fleet of ships to "his" islands, under express orders to employ careful diplomacy. Miguel Lopez de Legazpi landed on the island of Bohol in 1556 with four ships and 400 men, and (to impress the natives) concluded a pact in blood with Rajah Sikatuna. Using a combination of diplomacy and force, Legazpi quickly succeeded in subjugating Cebu and the other Visayas islands, and thus began the 333-year long colonial domination of the Philippines by Spain.

In 1571 Legazpi conquered the strategically important *May-nilad*, modern-day Manila, at that time a Muslim stronghold at the mouth of the river Pasig, under the command of Rajah Sulayman. One year later all the Philippines were under Spanish control, with three important exceptions: Mindanao and the Sulu Islands in the south, and the mountainous region of North Luzon. In the subjugated areas the Spanish built upon the tactic they had already used successfully in Latin America, that of playing the native rulers off against each other. And everywhere the cross followed the sword. If there were no spices and little in the way of mineral resources to be found, nevertheless there were at least souls to be won for Church and Crown.

In many respects the Philippine people seem to have been predestined for this abrupt conversion to Catholicism. They believed in *anitos*, in nature spirits, but also in a powerful deity by the name of *Bathala*. They identified their spirits with the Christian saints, and Bathala became

25

merged with the Christian God. The Filipinos' patience and capacity to endure suffering, still legendary today, found a parallel in the Gospel, their fatalistic philosophy was confirmed by the new teaching about a God, whose will was all-powerful, in good as well as in evil.

The Spanish called the Malay natives *Indios*, in recollection of the people of Latin America. However, the Muslim inhabitants of Mindanao they dubbed *Moros*, as they had called the Moors, who had conquered half of Spain a few centuries earlier. The European masters had sought for three centuries to extend their sovereignty to the Moros, but in vain. Not until 1851 did the Spanish succeed, for a short time, in establishing themselves on the Sulu Islands.

Madre España

Initially, this new crown colony was governed by Spain's viceroy in Mexico. There were a number of reasons for this, firstly the direct route to Spain in a westerly direction round Africa was too dangerous – these were Portuguese waters. Secondly, in order to protect Spanish home produce, it was decreed that the Philippines were only permitted to export to Mexico. Manila was primarily an entrepot for Chinese goods – porcelain, silk, perfume and spices – which were shipped to Acapulco; payments came from mexico in the form of silver. Between 1565 and 1815 the legendary galleons shuttled across the Pacific. Tempted there by the extremely lucrative trade, Chinese merchants in increasing numbers settled in the Philippines. The Spanish mistrusted them and tried to suppress them, but in fact they were dependent on them.

Right: A memorable event – the erecting of a cross and mass-baptism conducted by Magellan on Mactan in 1521.

The great disadvantage of this external trade was that the country's own economy was neglected. If the Spanish were the beneficiaries of colonization and the Chinese its opportunists, then the Filipinos were, from the outset, most certainly its victims. The Spanish ruled the islands by a system of government already tried and tested in America, that of *encomiendas*, which is to say provinces alloted to favored indivduals. In the country seats granted by the crown the natives had to pay *bandala*, a fixed contribution of rice, cotton, or sugar, and in addition had to provide labor, often unpaid, for the building of churches, fortresses and roads.

Priests and monks came in great numbers to continue the task of converting the people, but also to support the colonial government. The centuries of Spanish rule in the Philippines were characterized by this ecclesiastical colonialism. While the governors had their residences in the towns, the Church was master in the countryside. There the priests came into direct contact with the *Indios*, learnt their languages, and often enough fathered children by the Indio women. In the provinces they enjoyed a position of absolute power, which was bound sooner or later to lead to feelings of resentment on the part of the natives. However, the Spanish kept the indigenous people in an – apparently – subservient position. For a long time the majority of Filipinos could not attend Spanish schools nor aspire to the priesthood. Clerical excesses led to the temporary expulsion of the Jesuits in 1768, but rebellions against the greed of the church continued unabated. In Spain itself there was continuing doubt about the economic potential of the distant Philippine islands, and for a time the abandoning of the colony was considered, but external political factors and Spain's position as an influential, if by now somewhat ramshackle, world power decided against this step. Las Islas

Filipinas were, however, increasingly neglected and soon became more or less the property of the priests and monks. It was they who controlled the local communities, who gave their blessing to occasional elections, and were responsible for admissions to the schools. Only the *mestizos*, those of mixed Spanish and native blood, were alowed to learn Spanish; education for the rest of the people was limited to instruction in the Catechism.

Despite the widespread presence of the clergy, the Spanish administration did rely to some extent on the help of the indigenous population. From Manila, the Governor-General ruled through *alcades mayores*, based in the provincial capitals. Filipinos were employed at a lower level, mostly *datus*, whom the Spanish called *cabezas de barangay* (clan-chiefs). Those placed in charge of village communities were called *gobernadorcillos* (petty governors). Initially the Filipino officials were no more than the lackeys and helpmates of their colonial masters. They collected the *bandala* or land-tax,

and organized the *polo*, forced labor. This was not an easy task but it had its advantages: they themselves were exempt from paying taxes, they had the opportunity for embezzlement and bribery of every sort, while enjoying military protection. Before the Spanish arrived in the islands, there had been no concept of individual ownership of land. But now the *datus,* formerly the socially respected village chieftains, seized the land for themselves in imitation of their colonial masters, and forced their countrymen into abject serfdom. One can see in this the embryonic Filipino oligarchy, which even today holds a large part of the national economy in a stranglehold. In the Philippines, as in other Third World countries, there is a continuing debate about whether social evils such as corruption, prostitution, nepotism and favoritism have their roots in colonization, or whether they are born of the nature of the people themselves. The Filipinos incline to the former theory, while many resident foreigners would support the latter.

The development of a bourgeoisie in the Philippines coincided with radical changes in international trade. The Manila-Acapulco monopoly was broken in 1811, and the last of the galleons, the *Magellanes*, sailed across the Pacific in 1815. An increasing volume of agricultural produce made its way to Europe, a change which gave a boost to the island economy. In the towns, the middle-men soon began playing a key role in the economic growth, and some of these brokers and merchants were Filipinos.

But now the colony was being attacked from outside again. Since 1571 the Spanish had been obliged to ward off attacks by foreign powers. The Chinese pirate chief, Lee Mah Ong, threatened Manila in 1574-75, and Japan also posed a threat. Portuguese attacks only ceased when Philip II annexed Portugal in 1580. The Dutch, who had already replaced the Por-

Above: Colonial ruins make an adventure playground. Right: A watch-tower from the Spanish period in Maribojoc, Bohol.

tuguese as the colonial power in Indonesia, threatened Manila several times between 1600 and 1646, and two years later, under the treaty known as the Peace of Westphalia, the city was finally ceded to Spain. Only the English succeeded in temporarily capturing the capital and plundering it in 1762, during the Seven Years' War, but they left again in 1764 following the Peace of Paris. The Spanish domination of the Philippines, which had almost united the fragmented country for the first time in its history, was once again secure.

The Struggle Against Church and Crown

Compared to other colonies, the Philippines were largely spared the vagaries and reversals of fortune that marked European history. It is often said that Italy was shaped by the Renaissance, France by the Enlightenment and Germany by the Romantic movement. If this is so, then the Spanish psyche, and that of their Asian colony, was definitively formed in the Middle Ages. It was not until the advent of the French Revolution, with its worldwide repercussions, that any real changes took place in the Philippines. At last the Filipinos were now able to enter the priesthood. An intellectual stratum began to develop alongside the native bourgeoisie. For there were no state-run schools in the country before 1863, and even after this date education was supervised by the church. Higher education was entirely in the hands of the religious orders, and even today the most respected universities in the Philippines still are: these include the Jesuit Ateneo in Manila, the University of Santo Tomas, founded by the Dominicans, and the De La Salle University of the La Salle order.

Nevertheless, at that time less than 20 percent of the native population could read or write. Wealthy Filipinos, particularly the *Mestizos*, preferred to send their

children to Spain to be educated in order to avoid discrimination by the Church. The opening of the Suez Canal in 1869 accelerated this development. In 1861 Spain had once again permitted the Jesuits to open up their missions in the Philippines. Naturally the monks came up against the resistance of the native priests, who had now taken over the spiritual leadership of the people. At first this resistance merely took the form of a passive rejection of the administration and of the Spanish clergy.

But after two years of relatively liberal colonial politics – Queen Isabella II of Spain was toppled from the throne in the Spanish revolution of 1868 – the restoration of the monarchy brought new restrictions imposed by the government and the church, both at home and in the Philippines. Filipino mercenaries mutinied at Cavite in 1872 and the reaction of the Spanish was swift and cruel. All the ringleaders, and three Filipino priests accused of rebellion, José Burgos, Mariano Gomez and Jacinto Zamora, were ex-

ecuted by garotting – the strangling-irons still used in Spain up to Franco's time. The Spanish had unintentionally provided the Filipinos with their first martyrs in the struggle for freedom. The death of these men unleashed a wave of sympathy throughout the islands for the idea of a freedom movement. But they still needed a leader, someone with charisma, a theorist, who could rouse the nation's self-confidence from the apathy into which it had sunk.

Revolution and Spanish Blood-money

José Rizal was born in Calamba on June 19th, 1861, a Mestizo of mixed Spanish, Filipino and Chinese blood. As a member of the class known as the *ilustrados* – descendants of the educated upper class which included *hacienderos*, officials, Chinese merchants and the illegitimate offspring of the Spanish – he began his studies in medecine, philosophy and literature at the respected University of Santo Tomas. At the age of

twenty, he traveled abroad, to Europe, the United States and Japan.

While he was in Spain, Rizal met the Filipino journalist, Marcelo H. del Pilar, who denounced the power of the monks in his native land. Del Pilar had founded the revolutionary newspaper, *La Solidaridad*, and now Rizal too began to write for the paper. The *ilustrados* in Spain used the paper as an organ to call for reforms: freedom of speech, restriction of that power of the monastic orders, and – something which seems rather odd to us today – they demanded that Philippines be made a province of metropolitan Spain, in order to give the islands a greater say in the decisions which affected them. At the outset, therefore, their aim was not to gain independence, but rather to bring about the reform of an archaic system and a redistribution of political power. Shortly before his death in Barcelona Pilar realized the hopelessness of his idea which foundered, as always, due to bitter resistance from the church.

Meanwhile, Rizal had gained his doctorate and had become an ophthalmologist. He had been to Heidelberg and while there had translated Schiller's *William Tell* into Tagalog. He completed his most important work, *Noli Me Tangere* (Latin: "Touch Me Not") in Berlin in 1887. In it he denounced the unhappy state of affairs in his homeland. Although his novel, as well as *El Filibusterismo* ("Subversion") which had been smuggled into the Philippines, influenced the independence movement, Rizal remained an ambiguous figure. He wrote almost exclusively in Spanish, his ideas swung between intellectual revolt and gradual political evolution. He owed his moderate position to the influence of his friend Ferdinand Blumentritt, whom he had met in Austria. Blumentritt was a teacher and a senior civil servant in the imperial Austrian government, who was extremely knowledgeable about the Philippines, although he had never been there. Against the advice of his friends, Rizal returned to his native country in 1892 and established the *Liga Filipina*. This was a moderate organization, concerned with reform; its aims were compatible with loyalty to Spain, and not dedicated to gaining rapid independence. Rizal turned against the Church, but not against the wide-ranging powers of the colonial adminstration.

The Spanish, however, feared Rizal's influence and in the same year he was exiled to Dapitan on Mindanao. His writings were banned, but they continued nonetheless to circulate secretly, and fanned into flames the smouldering fire of nationalism. On the evening before Rizal left to go into exile, his friend Andres Bonifacio founded the KKK – *Kataastaasang Kagalangalangang Katipunan ng mga Anak ng Bayan* ("Highly respected and most honorable assembly of

Above: Today the national hero, José Rizal stands in every square (here in Guimbal, Panay). Right: His execution, portrayed by a Philippine artist in Fort Santiago, Manila.

the country's sons"), a secret organization whose aims were definitely separatist. Bonifacio had never been abroad, but precisely for that reason he was much closer to the people than Rizal. A self-educated, working man, he soon gained a large following. Besides independence from Spain, the Katipunan also demanded land reform.

At the same time there was a revolt against the Spanish overlords in Cuba. From exile, Rizal volunteered his services to the Spanish as a military doctor. Was this a touch of historical irony, a clever tactical move, or further proof of his political loyalty? At all events, his request was granted. Rizal had already embarked for Spain, when the Katipunan rebellion broke out in August 1896 in Manila and the surrounding provinces. On his arrival in Barcelona Rizal was arrested and returned to Manila, where he spent several weeks as a prisoner in Fort Santiago. Finally, he was condemned to death, allegedly for treason, although he had personally taken no part in the actual

uprising, but ultimately because the Spanish wanted to make an example of him. José Rizal was executed by a Spanish firing-squad on December 30th, 1896 at the Camp de Bagumbayan, where the three priests had earlier met their deaths.

Today this place is called Rizal Park, and Fort Santiago is a museum. The ambivalence of the Filipinos' struggle for independence is particularly well expressed in the poem Rizal composed in his cell on the eve of his execution:
Mi Ultimo Adios – "My last farewell":
> *Farewell, beloved homeland,*
> *dearest land of the sun,*
> *pearl of the eastern seas,*
> *our paradise lost!*
> *I shall happily give to you*
> *my sad and withered life;*
> *and had it been more brilliant,*
> *fresher and more blooming,*
> *I would still have given it for you,*
> *given it for your good.*

Most of the lines, like almost everything that flowed from Rizal's pen, were

written in Spanish, the language of his executioners. It is a hymn without a melody which every schoolchild still learns by heart today, though scarcely anyone speaks Spanish any longer.

The Katipunan rebellion failed, as Rizal had predicted it would. Bonifacio's aims, in particular those relating to social reform, did not suit the interests of the Filipino middle class. Bonifacio was betrayed. His declaration of a Philippine republic was premature; he might even have counted on support from part of the army, but it was all too soon. The Katipunan had addressed itself in ringing tones for the first time to the "Filipino people," so as to do away with the colonial concept of the *Indio*. However after months of fighting, the KKK rebels had to take refuge in the mountains. Bonifacio was double-crossed by the officer command-

Above: The Spanish-American War sealed the fate of Spanish colonial power in the Philippines; this battle was fought in Cuba, at San Juan Hill, on July 1, 1898.

ing his troops, General Emilio Aguinaldo, and was executed with his brothers, by members of his own movement, on May 10, 1897.

Aguinaldo, the son of a mayor of Cavite, belonged in fact to that rather obscure section of society who were less interested in liberating the people, than in getting a chance to step into the shoes of the Spanish. It is therefore no surprise that, on the arrival of the new Spanish commander in 1897, a compromise was reached in the Treaty of Biak-na-Bato. Aguinaldo received a substantial pay-off and willingly left for exile in Hong Kong. The Spanish promised genuine reforms: the expulsion of the monastic orders, representation of the Philippines in the *Cortes*, the parliament in Madrid, equal status for Filipinos and Spanish, and respect for basic human rights.

It is often claimed that neither side really intended to abide by the agreement: that the Spanish only wanted to consolidate their power, and that Aguinaldo only accepted the money in order to finance further revolutionary activity. On the other hand, the treaty represented exactly the kind of compromise that Philippine leaders were to enter into time and again in the course of history. Looking back over a turbulent century, we can see that this was not a turning point in the Philippine liberation movement. For only a year later the archipelago was once more swept up in world politics.

Changing of the Colonial Guard

As a result of the unrest in Cuba the United States had declared war on Spain in February 1898. The US Navy's Asia squadron, stationed in Hong Kong under the command of Commodore George Dewey, received orders to capture Manila. Warships from Britain, France, Japan, and Germany were already lying in the roadstead off Manila, ready to protect their citizens and advance their national interests. Hostilities between the American and German navies were only narrowly averted. On May 1, the Americans destroyed the outmoded Spanish fleet in a battle costing 380 Spanish lives and only one American. Dewey's signal to Washington summed up the confused situation: "Have captured Philippines. What shall I do with them?"

With Dewey's help, Aguinaldo and his followers returned to the Philippines. An alliance was formed which certainly suited the pragmatism of the moment, but which can also be seen as one of history's great misunderstandings. Dewey is said to have promised Aguinaldo that he would support independence, if they joined forces to defeat the Spanish. Aguinaldo in fact succeeded in taking several towns south of Manila. On June 12, 1898 he declared independence for the Philippines, and this date is still celebrated as a national holiday. However, the Americans did not force the Spanish to capitulate until August 13, after engaging them in a mock battle, so that they might make an "honorable" withdrawal without too much loss of face. The Americans occupied Manila, but Aguinaldo's troops were forcibly denied access to the capital, to the fury of the Filipinos who saw themselves cheated of victory.

Struggle Against the "Liberators"

On December 10, 1898 the Peace Treaty of Paris formally ended the Spanish-American War and ceded the Philippines, Puerto Rico and Guam to the USA – against compensation of US $ 20 million. Aguinaldo countered this by setting a government consisting entirely of Filipinos, in order to continue the struggle against the "liberators." What the American president, McKinley, described as a policy of "benevolent assimilation" and a "lenient regime of justice and the law" was condemned by Aguinaldo as "brutal occupation." The revolt against America's military government escalated into Asia's first guerilla war. No less than 120,000 US troops hunted down the soldiers of the Philippine republic, who put up a determined resistance for more than two years. Not until 1901 did the Americans, who had acted with extreme brutality, manage to take Aguinaldo prisoner. He then ordered his compatriots to lay down their arms.

Yet isolated groups of the Katipunan fought on until 1911. By the end the new colonial masters had lost 4,200 men dead, while on the other side some 16,000 guerillas had been killed. Far worse, the civilian population lost around 200,000 dead – 10,000 in the single town of Balangiga on Samar Island, where, as a reprisal in 1901, the Americans massacred all the inhabitants over the age of ten! The Filipino struggle for freedom ended once again in compromise and defeat, with Aguinaldo swearing allegiance to the Stars and Stripes.

Had the republic which was declared in 1898 been able to survive, the Philip-

pines would have been the first colony in Asia to shake off the yoke of foreign occupation. As it was, the Filipinos now had to wait a further 50 years before the United States finally granted them independence, and even then American influence made itself felt in the political life of the nation. It is evident even today that this delay has seriously impaired the Philippine people's national identity.

Big Brother

The territory they had gained in Southeast Asia was a mixed blessing for the Americans as the colony posed a certain moral problem. Only a century earlier the Americans had themselves won their independence from the British crown, and since then had considered themselves,

Above: The "American Way" brought urban development to the Philpppines. These old photographs of Cebu City show telephone poles in Colon Street (1906) and (right) the train station (1909).

with the world's first democratic constitution, to be a model for the ideals of freedom, justice and equality. But by the turn of the century the claims of democracy had come hard up against the reality of capitalism. Like all imperialism, the American variety was chiefly driven by economic ambition: to dominate markets, to trade on favorable terms and to exploit their interests more effectively with the help of military garrisons. But American rule in the Philippines justified itself from the start as a democratic mission, to nurse a politically immature colony through to independence. Until then the USA intended to be content with the economic fruit of this policy.

After their experience of Spanish rule, the Filipinos at first welcomed this attitude. William H. Taft, who later became president of the USA, was nominated Civil Governor of the country and a legislative council was established to assist him. However, the administration of the towns and local districts was put in the hands of Filipinos.

The Americans applied themselves with great zeal to reorganizing the educational system, and hundreds of teachers were sent to the islands from the United States, so that the Filipinos soon spoke English better than their native dialects. The decision of the colonial government to acquire the estates belonging to the Church and to sell these to the Filipinos, made a particularly good impression. The goodwill which the new rulers earned with these measures has not entirely vanished even today. Indeed, many Filipinos saw the United States as a "Promised Land," and many aspects of the "American Way of Life" have taken firm root in Filipino culture.

From 1907 the Americans speeded up the process of political emancipation. They set up a Filipino Assembly which was to be responsible for legislation in all regional matters.

The right to vote was initially limited to men who could read and write – women did not get the franchise until 1936 – but democracy caught on very quickly. In 1916 the Jones Act was passed, promising independence for the Philippines, as soon as a stable government was establishd in office.

Meanwhile, the continuing dependence of the country irritated the Filipinos. The Nationalist Party was formed under the leadership of Manuel Quezon and Sergio Osmeña and a delegation was soon sent to Washington. This was a successful move, since it resulted in the Philippines being allowed to set up a senate on the American model, with Quezon as its first elected chairman. In addition, Filipinos were soon filling the top posts in the judiciary and the executive. Economic reforms did not fare so well, however. A free trade agreement in 1909 had allowed the Philippines to export agricultural produce to the United States, free of tariffs, while the USA sent back chiefly manufactured goods. Local Philippine industries could hardly develop under these conditions, and the only people to profit were the big *hacienderos*, and the owners of sugar factories and rice mills. The con-

35

centration of landed estates in the hands of a powerful elite continued apace, since the official Philippine delegations to Washington consisted almost entirely of members of rich clans.

In 1933 the American Congress finally managed to decide on a date for Philippine Independence. Domestic problems, the Depression, and pressure from American farmers who had had enough of competing with the Filipinos, were what motivated this offer. Following independence customs duties were to be levied on a range of agricultural products from the Philippines. After a violent quarrel between Osmeña and Quezon over the "treacherous" gift from the Americans, the Philippines Assembly approved the Tydings-McDuffie Act in the following year. The Philippines were

Above: A glimpse of the bloody past on the island of Corregidor. Right: Immortalized in bronze, General MacArthur wades ashore at Palo, Leyte, to drive out the occupying Japanese forces.

now to hold the status of Commonwealth for a period of ten years. Shortly afterwards a constitutional assembly for the Philippines was elected, which drew up a constitution very close to the American model. The Commonwealth of the Philippines came into being on November 15th, 1935, with Manuel L. Quezon as its first president, and Osmeña as his vice-president.

Quezon was adroit in securing legislation for a number of social reforms. But this administration was hampered by the traditional corruption. The Philippines approached formal independence like a ship approaching a harbor entrance that is too narrow, and it was inevitable that the hopes of a nation which had suffered under colonial repression for so many years, would be dashed to pieces. Freedom would only have been possible in conditions of complete economic, political and intellectual independence. But a radical break with "Big Brother" would have been tantamount to a cultural revolution – something which no politician

was willing to provoke. A period of colonization lasting almost 400 years had left behind traces which distorted the face of freedom. From now on the Philippines were to be regarded as the "country between East and West" – though not before a last attempt to "Asianize" them had failed.

The Japanese Yoke

On December 8th, 1941, a day after the attack on Pearl Harbor, Japanese landed in the Philippines, and despite strong resistance by the combined Philippine and American forces, they soon captured Manila. The allied troops under General Douglas MacArthur withdrew to the Bataan peninsula and to the fortified island of Corregidor off Manila. The Japanese launched massive attacks on the remaining American strongholds before the US army surrendered on May 6th, 1942. General MacArthur had earlier left Corregidor with the famous words: "I shall return" – a promise he was to fulfil two

years later. President Quezon had already fled to the United States, leaving instructions with his government to mediate between the Japanese and the Philippine people. Many members of the Filipino elite who had remained in the country collaborated with the occupiers to protect their own interests. Quezon himself died in exile in 1944, without having seen his homeland again. Meanwhile the Japanese were anxious to win the people of the Philippines over to their side. Under the banner of "Asia for the Asians" they prescribed some reforms in the guise of nationalism, such as the replacement of English by Tagalog in the schools and the civil service. However, the majority of politicians and of the Philippine population remained pro-American, and underground resistance movements were formed. Even before the war most of the garrisons in the Philippines had been made up of Filipino rather than American troops. These now carried on a guerilla war and during the period of the Japanese terror, their numbers grew to over a quarter of a million. In 1943 the Japanese went as far as setting up a "Philippine Republic," and installing a puppet government with the judge, José Laurel, as president. At the same time Congress in Washington fulfilled its promise made ten years earlier to grant independence to the Philippines. Thus a grotesque scramble was acted out on the stage of history between two colonial powers, each trying to outdo the other with offers of independence to the country they had both been trying to grab.

At all events, in October 1944 General MacArthur made good his promise. He landed on the island of Leyte with four divisions. From here the Allies fought their way through to Manila, and in a terrible battle the capital was recaptured and the Japanese fled to the north of Luzon. The war raged on for many months, at the cost of over a million Filipino lives, before the Japanese commander, General Tomoyuki Yamashita, surrendered.

Following the death of Quezon, the exiled Osmeña took over as president of the Commonwealth in 1944. The liberating army under MacArthur, however, supported Manuel A. Roxas who, while appearing to be collaborating with the Japanese, had secretly been working for the Americans. In 1946 Roxas won the election and became president of the Philippine Commonwealth.

The Republic of the Philippines was called into being on July 4 of that year, on the same day that the Americans celebrate their own independence. With Roxas as its first president, the island state was now formally independent.

Republika Ng Pilipinas

The birth of freedom in the islands could scarcely have been less propitious.

Right: President Ferdinand Marcos, seen here in the province of Iloilo, sought to gain the trust of local politicans (c. 1965-67).

Politics were influenced by guerillas and collaborators, and social conditions had become almost intolerable, especially in the countryside. Roxas granted an amnesty to all collaborators, but continued to rely heavily on economic assistance from the USA. Not surprisingly, watching this double game, the people felt they would once again come off worst. The collaborators came mainly from the Filipino elite, and assistance was only offered by the United States under stipulations which assured them a privileged position in the Philippines. An amendment to the Philippines' constitution granted the Americans equal rights in the exploitation of mineral resources. The free trade agreement was extended, but it was now to exclude Philippine agricultural products. The United States negotiated a 99-year lease for their military bases which were to assume an important role during the Vietnam War.

Roxas died in 1948. He was succeeded by Elpidio Quirino, who came to power on the back of election results which had obviously been rigged. The remains of a guerilla army which had been formed in Luzon during the Japanese occupation once more stirred into life. The *Hukbalahap* ("people's fighters against Japan"), *HUK* for short, were the only resistance fighters who had striven not just for freedom but also for social reforms. After trying to make progress through parliament within a Communist-Socialist coalition, they returned to an armed struggle, prompted by Quirino's election. As early as 1950 their support from the people had reached such a level that an uprising looked likely. In 1953 Ramon Magsaysay was elected president, and a year later, with American help and the brutal use of military force, he succeeded in putting down the rebellion.

Magsaysay's subsequent attempts at reform failed due to the resistance of the big landowners, and he was killed in a mysterious air-crash in 1957. His succes-

sor, Carlos Garcia, was the first Philippine leader concerned to distance his country, politically and economically, from the United States. Both the Americans and his political opponents accused him of communism and corruption.

The pro-American Diosdato Macapagal came to power, with help from the USA, in 1961, and an era of economic stability dawned. Investment flowed into the country and large estates were converted into industrial-scale agricultural businesses. The Americans assured their monopoly of the fruit and rubber plantations on the island of Mindanao, where they also became involved in the timber industry. The rain-forest, which had already been heavily plundered by the Spanish, suffered further felling. This economic upturn meant that social unrest could be held in check for a while.

The Dictator

The post-war period saw the beginning of the career of a man whose shadow still lies darkly over the Philippines even after his death. Ferdinand Edralin Marcos was born in 1917 in Sarrat, in the province of Ilocos Norte. 18 years later in the village of Batac, where he spent part of his youth, a political opponent of his father was murdered. Ferdinand was at that time an outstanding law-student at the University of the Philippines (UP), but had a reputation for being crazy about firearms; he was accused of the murder but later acquitted.

He gained top marks in his law examinations – and once again there were rumors that perhaps a grateful hand had played a part in this. During the war Marcos was active in the resistance, he was taken prisoner and tortured. Later in life he adorned his chest with a row of medals awarded for bravery, few of which he had actually earned, or so his political opponents maintained.

Marcos was not only audacious, he was also extremely shrewd. They were proud of him in Ilocos Norte and promptly elected him to the senate.

39

Marcos wanted more. He married Imelda Romualdez, a beauty queen from Leyte and a girl of good family. In a country fragmented both geographically and politically this marriage represented a tactical alliance between the cool north and the rather more frivolous, fun-loving Visayas. Marcos was elected president in 1965.

The old land-owning oligarchy, and those who had benefitted from American subsidies, had driven the islands' economy into the ground. Smuggling, tax-evasion and bribery were part of daily life. Through clever tactics Marcos managed to win over the majority of the 200 most important families. He could not eliminate corruption – it simply became more tolerable. Marcos also got on well with the Americans, thanks to his nationalism and staunch anti-Communist stance. The United States, which at that

Above: Filipinos never cease to enthuse about status-symbols made in the USA.
Right: Parade of military units in Manila.

time was just becoming embroiled in the the Vietnam War, saw in him a reliable ally and made concessions to him, such as shortening the lease on their miltary bases to just 25 more years.

The nation rewarded Marcos with re-election in 1969. This made him the first president of the Philippines to serve for a second term of office, and according to the constitution it should have been his last. However, Marcos announced elections for a new constitutional assembly. After a remarkably honest ballot the public expected significant changes.

The manipulator Marcos, however, had only one intention: to prolong his period of office. The people, and especially the students, mistrusted him and violent rioting increased. Terror was spread by private armies, which had been formed by politicians and *hacienderos*. The prevailing climate was extremely tense; violence and lawlessness stalked the land and rumors spread rapidly that agitators, supported by the president, were behind it all.

On September 23, 1972, tanks rolled through the streets of Manila. Marcos had imposed martial law. He justified his actions by maintaining that this was the only way to restore order out of chaos. One of the men arrested was Benigno Aquino Jr., a senator from Tarlac, who was eventually to be the downfall of the man who was now a dictator. At first the hard line which Marcos adopted seemed to be successful. The crime-rate fell and unrest in the provinces came to an end. Marcos made concessions to appease foreign investors. The trade unions' right to strike was abolished. In January 1973 Marcos announced the new constitution, which assured him the post of prime minister as well as president. In spite of all this the public accepted his "New Order." The only resistance was in the south, where the Muslims were striving for autonomy.

Little notice was at first taken of what was ultimately to prove a very significant development. A number of students founded the Maoist New People's Army

(*NPA*) which was to support the people in their struggle against oppression. The rebels, who saw themselves as successors to the *HUK*, attacked military installations, executed corrupt mayors and members of the much loathed police force. They forced the rural population to support their struggle by supplying them with food. At first, the guerillas hid in the mountains, but by the mid-eighties these much-feared *Sparrow Units*, as they were called, were assassinating specifically targeted individuals in the cities. Marcos built up his armed forces from 55,000 in 1972 to over 250,000 men. Alongside the defense-minister, Juan Ponce Enrile, Marcos appointed as his chief-of-staff and trusted right-hand man, one Fabian Ver, who had formerly been his chauffeur and bodyguard. Thanks to the USA, who made only the occasional formal complaint about the lack of democracy in the Philippines, Marcos was for the time being given a free hand. He promoted his wife to several positions – she became Governor of the Metropolis of Manila

41

and Minister for "Human Settlements," a department which supervised virtually all welfare matters. Sinecures were found to be particularly fertile ground for bribery and embezzlement. The notorious lifestyle of Imelda Marcos, nicknamed the "Iron Butterfly," soon became plain for all to see, and it was obvious that the presidential couple complemented each other in more than just politics. He, the ambitious *Ilocano*, "earned" the money which she spent liberally.

Marcos wanted a place in history and from now on adopted the title of "Architect of the Nation." He set about forming a new party, the *Kulisang Bagong Lipunan (KBL)* or "Movement for a New Society." With every advantage, politically and culturally, the Marcos' three children also took part in the national advertising

Above: Students at the Ati-Atihan festival on Panay wearing likenesses of "Ninoy" Aquino. Right: This memorial in Makati, Manila recalls the murder of "Ninoy" Aquino in 1983.

campaign. The media were strictly controlled by the government, although officially there was no censorship.

The people were more impressed than convinced. The regime lacked a broad political base, particularly when the economic situation worsened in the late 1970s. Inflation followed the euphoric investment of earlier years and by 1984 it had reached an annual rate of 60 percent. Problems in the agricultural sector piled up, but loopholes in the law stood in the way of long overdue land reforms. Thousands of dissidents were thrown into prison where they were tortured and killed. The left-wing guerilla movement actually received some moral support from the Catholic church and one or two priests became actively involved. The regime began to totter and sought help from the United States.

When, in 1978, Marcos eventually allowed elections to the National Assembly, the opposition put up a strong showing but won few votes. Marcos' political opponents now accused him of electoral fraud, and the public became restless. To avoid a crisis, Marcos allowed Senator Aquino, who was ill and under sentence of death, to leave for the United States. As a huge publicity stunt, even the Pope was invited to visit the Philippines. Shortly before his arrival in January 1981, Marcos lifted martial law to pre-empt criticism from the Vatican. The ship of state was listing badly. The constitution was again amended and, despite a boycott by the opposition, presidential elections were held in June 1981. Marcos won 88 percent of the entire vote, and the US Vice-President, George Bush, traveled to Manila to congratulate him on "the preservation of democratic principles."

But appearances were deceptive. Washington feared that the Philippines would drift into the Communist camp, though at first they held off and waited, knowing that Marcos was seriously ill. Meanwhile, however, "Ninoy" Aquino had recovered and announced his intention of returning to the Philippines. A historical reckoning was in the offing. Aquino landed in Manila on August 23, 1983, despite all warnings, and before setting foot on the soil of his homeland he was shot in the back of the head. Despite hasty attempts to blame the murder on the Communists, the Marcos faction had forfeited all credit with the people. Millions mourned for Ninoy, who had been their great hope, and were convinced that the president, or at least his wife and trusted friend, had his murder on their conscience. The parliamentary elections of 1984 were a farce, rioting increased. The economy suffered from inflation and the flight of capital. Bowing to pressure from the USA, Marcos held new elections. The senator's widow, Corazon (Cory) Aquino, stood for the presidency against Marcos. According to Cardinal Sin, head of the Catholic church in the Philippines, a "struggle between Good and Evil" had begun.

People's Power

Now a drama unfolded, which was to keep the world in suspense. The last elections to take place under Marcos were on February 7, 1986. The crafty politician was facing a woman who held one moral trump card: she was the widow of his murdered opponent. But she was successful where no other adversary of Marcos had been: she was able to unite a turbulent nation. She had the support of the Church, while the leader of the opposition Nationalist Party, Salvador Laurel was her running-mate. The elections were marred by violence and Marcos delayed announcing the results for a week. He then declared that he had won narrowly, with 53 percent of the vote. There was a sensational outburst. Hundreds of thousands of people took to the streets while international observers confirmed that there had been a massive fraud and that about two-thirds of the votes had been for Cory. Defense Minister Enrile, deputy army chief-of-staff General Fidel

Ramos, and section of the armed forces went over to the opposition. General Ver urged military intervention but Marcos did not want a bloodbath. He called upon the deserters to give themselves up, but the masses offered flowers and prayers to the renegades and brought the government troops to a standstill on the EDSA (Epifanio de los Santos Avenue) with shouts of "We are the people" and "People's Power."

Cory Aquino allowed herself to be sworn in as president. Marcos called on the Americans for help, but all they did was send a plane to take the fallen leader, with his family and associates, to Hawaii.

Once there, Marcos maintained that he had been "kidnapped" and insisted on returning to the Philippines, but the Americans refused him an exit visa.

The former presidential residence in Manila, the Malacañang Palace, is now a museum where the public can see the astonishingly extravagant lifestyle which the Marcos family enjoyed. The 1,060 pairs of shoes belonging to Imelda Marcos have become an international joke. Marcos himself was accused of having amassed a secret fortune of obscene proportions. It was calculated that the total value of overseas assets hoarded by the Marcoses could pay off the entire foreign debt of the Philippines, which stood at US$ 25 billion in 1986. Not until 1998 did Swiss banks repay 500 million US$ to the Philippines, on the orders of the Swiss Federal Court in Berne.

Running the country turned out to be far more difficult than Cory Aquino had expected. Her style and charisma were totally unlike Marcos, still less Imelda. Her chances of survival in the political jungle were judged to be slight. Modest and tolerant, she was at least convincing in her observance of the democratic rules

Right: Short-lived attempt at national reconciliation – New People's Army rebels in the church of Jaro/Iloilo.

of the game. Freedom of the press and free speech were restored. The trade unions regained their right to strike. A new constitution was to replace the legacy of the Marcos years and the presidency was limited to a single 6-year period. The initial unity of the political partnership crumbled as factional interests came into play. In early 1987 soldiers fired on a crowd of farmers who were demonstrating on Mendiola Bridge in Manila, leaving 18 dead and 100 injured. As a result, the New Democratic Forum (NDF), a left-wing party, broke off negotiations with Aquino. The president was also under pressure from the military who felt their interests were being neglected.

Disaffected troops organized their first coup just one year after the "People's Power Revolution" and six further attempts to overthrow the government followed. With support from the army, Marcos loyalists barricaded themselves in the Manila Hotel and put forward Artur Tolentino, a friend of Marcos, as their presidential contender; the rebellion collapsed when the Aquino government cut off their electricity supply. Ramos ordered the soldiers who had taken part in the revolt to do 100 press-ups each. It was a typical episode. What appeared to be an attitude of tolerance concealed the government's increasing loss of authority. Corruption was rife again, but it was now the turn of Aquino's relatives to reap its benefits. Inflation and debt were running out of control. The New People's Army (*NPA*) and the Moro National Liberation Front (*MNLF*), active in Mindanao, had rearmed. There were increasing violations of basic human rights by police and army. Poverty was rife among the rural population, and thieves and brigands flourished. Moreover, the country was afflicted by typhoons, tidal waves and earthquakes. In 1991 Mount Pinatubo erupted and covered vast areas of land with ash and mud.

The government was repeatedly accused of incompetence, and it seemed that only the protecting hand of the United States was keeping Aquino in power.

When Ferdinand Marcos died in Hawaii in October 1989, Cory Aquino refused to allow his body to be returned to the Philippines. In December the most serious attempt to overthrow the government took place, leading to the deaths of 100 people in Manila. The situation was only brought under control by American jets thundering over the camps of the rebel soldiers. Enrile was arrested as the instigator of the revolt, but later released.

The final months of Aquino's term of office were marked by two events which symbolized much of the Philippines' postwar history. One of these was the expiry of the military treaty with the United States. While the Americans were playing for an extension, the eruption of Mount Pinatubo destroyed the American air-force base and forced them to evacuate it immediately. A proposal to extend the lease on the bases beyond 1992 was rejected by the Philippine senate. The second significant event was the election of a successor to Cory Aquino. Imelda Marcos was now able to return to the Philippines after six years in exile – the mortal remains of her husband followed a year later. Although more than 80 criminal charges were hanging over her, she took part in the elections, to the amazement of the world, and was even voted into Congress in 1996. Aquino supported Fidel Ramos, who was her loyal and trustworthy defense minister up to the end. For six years, he made a successful effort to improve the nation's economy. His program, named "Philippines 2000," involving concerted political, economic, and technological action aimed at inner political stability and social peace, was continued by his successor, former actor Joseph "Erap" Estrada. A peace agreement, signed in September 1996 between the government and the Muslim freedom movement MNLF, aroused great hopes, but some areas of the southern island, Mindanao, remain unstable.

GATEWAY TO THE PHILIPPINES

MANILA

A resonant name, an exotic place – Manila is the principal gateway to the Philippines, an island realm full of anomalies and contradictions. The visitor usually expects to find an oriental metropolis, but instead enters a concrete giant of a city, seemingly western in character. Yet, in spite of this, a visit to Manila reveals the true Asian temperament, with all its casualness and chaos.

Approximately 12 million people live here, and the results of the city's growth are literally overwhelming: everywhere there are milling crowds, noise and traffic-jams, filth in the gutters, pollution in the air. In fact the term "environmental pollution" is hardly appropriate, since one has to travel for hours before seeing any environment at all. Manila is one of the most spread-out cities in the world – 636 square kilometers in area!

Sometimes, especially in the splendor of a sunset over Manila Bay, it is possible to imagine what the original Manila was like, before it became the urban monster it is today – a small tropical settlement on the South China Sea, a Malay village in the 5th century A.D., lying on the almost perfect arc of the bay, which forms one of

Previous pages: Climbing the Mayon volcano. Roxas Boulevard, Manila. Left: Rizal Park in Manila.

the finest natural harbors in the world, and an unchanged and a panorama never changing in its fascination.

Its name is romantic too: *May-nilad* – meaning "where white water-flowers grow" – was the name of the village which the Spanish found here. Sadly, the *nilad* flowers no longer grow on the banks of the sluggish river Pasig. It is an open sewer today, carrying Manila's untreated waste down to the sea.

The recorded history of the town on the Pasig began in 1570. The advance guard of Miguel Legazpi came upon the wooden fortress of Raja Sulayman at the mouth of the Pasig river. At first the Spanish were satisfied with plundering the settlement, but returned a year later, again led by Legazpi, to lay siege to this strategically situated port. Sulayman was killed, and on June 24, 1571 Legazpi declared the "most honorable and ever loyal town" the property of the Spanish crown. His new fortress, named *Intramuros*, still stands today in the center of Manila. At first, only the Spanish, and perhaps the *Mestizos*, were allowed to live "within the walls" and a little above sea level. The *Indios* lived in the swampy areas on the edge of the town, while the Chinese merchants had to settle on the river bank, within range of the cannon. In 1584 Governor Santiago de Vera had further forti-

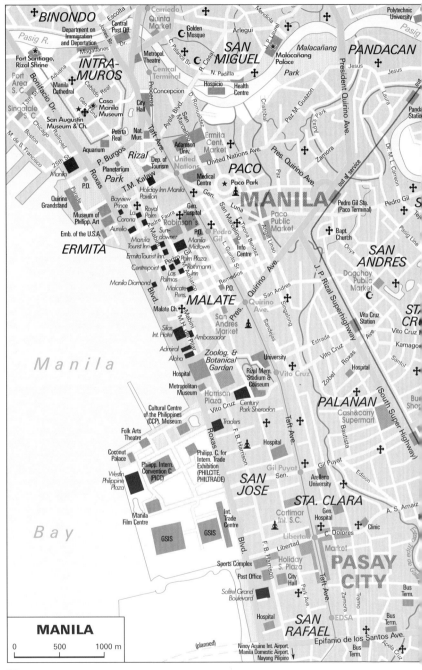

fications constructed, including Fort Santiago, which bears his name. This was made necessary by the attacks, which the Chinese pirate, Lee Mah Ong, and local chieftains, launched against the Spanish possession.

Manila, now an archbishopric and the capital of the colony, expanded rapidly, but at the same time became the scene of ethnic tension. At the beginning of the 17th century the Chinese ransacked the Quiapo and Tondo districts of the town, and even dared to launch an assault on Intramuros. The Spanish were only able to put down the revolt with the help of Filipino mercenaries. Further attacks from outside followed.

The advent of the galleon trade with Mexico further increased the population, which grew from 42,000 in 1650 to 86,000 in 1780, and thousands of Chinese flooded into the metropolis. Several new districts such as Ermita and Santa Ana grew up outside the walls. But once again civil strife broke out among the populace. Boatloads of priests and monks were dispatched from Spain with a mission to lead the Filipinos, who had first rebelled in 1660, "back to the path of righteousness." Naturally the clerics soon erected monuments to their faith, in Manila. The building of the church of San Augustin had already been started in 1599; the Santo Tomas University, the oldest college in Asia, was founded by the Dominicans in 1611.

The English occupied the town from 1762 until 1774, an event known as the *Sack of Manila*. In the years that followed there were repeated cholera epidemics. The end of the monopoly enjoyed by the galleon trade compelled Manila to open up to international commerce. At first ships from Asia, and then from all over the world, were allowed to drop anchor here. The opening of the Suez Canal in 1869 brought only advantages for trade, but the colonial rulers were much less keen on importing European ideas of freedom and independence. The revolutionary, Andres Bonifacio, who founded the revolutionary secret league, called Katipunan, in 1892, grew up in Tondo, near the harbor, a place that is still a byword for working-class poverty.

The promise of democracy and education arrived with the Americans. Manila, the population of which had increased from 220,000 in 1903 to 620,000 in 1938, played a central role in this. The University of the Philippines (UP), which was founded in Quezon City in 1908, has ever since then been the country's leading secular university.

The capital suffered grievously during World War II. After the retreat of General MacArthur it was declared an open city in 1942 and was occupied by the Japanese. Two years later bitter fighting resulted in the destruction of most of the centuries-old Spanish architecture.

In the 1950s Manila became industrialized and experienced a revival of its role as a trade center. The newly independent country wished to make a fresh start: in 1948 Quezon City was declared the official seat of the Philippines government. Massive buildings and apartment-blocks soared skywards to mark a new progressive attitude, and to house the thousands who were streaming into the capital from the countryside. A multinational business center, a would-be Manhattan, was built on land belonging to the influential Ayala family in Makati.

The Marcoses deliberately fostered the image of a Mecca beckoning to poor provincials. As Governor of Manila, Imelda Marcos pursued the idea of developing a "City of Man" where everyone might find a place. The bus system was improved and building-land reclaimed from the sea. Slums had to be cleared along prestige streets or, as in the case of Tondo, were camouflaged with attractive

Right: Manila's banking and business center, Makati.

façades. In 1976, by order of the president, dozens of outlying boroughs were combined to form Metropolitan Manila, Metro Manila for short. The capital now consists of the old districts of Intramuros, Tondo, Binondo, Santa Cruz, Quiapo, San Miguel, Santa Ana, Ermita, Malate; also Calaocan in the north, Quezon City in the north-east and Pasay in the south.

The city also includes 13 other districts: Makati, Mandaluyong, San Juan, Malabon, Navotas, Parañaque, Las Piñas, Muninglupa, Taguig, Valenzuela, Marikina, Pasig and Pateros. The aim was to make the layout of the city more convenient and to improve public services. But to the visitor today, Manila, barring wealthy quarters and some peaceful suburbs, will seem as chaotic as ever. The introduction of the LRT (*Light Rail Transit*), or Metrorail, has improved things. Opened in 1984, it provides a fast north-south link between Calaocan and Badaran. Work started in 1992 on flyovers to ease traffic.

For this reason from 1999 a highway will connect Pasig with Makati. Traffic is still a problem owing to lack of public road works, an obsolete sewage system, and power failures that are particularly frequent during the rainy season. At these times whole areas of the city are flooded, garbage blocks the drains, and fires are started by short-circuits.

Air pollution and transport problems are probably the worst things the tourist will encounter in Manila. The thousands of "jeepneys" which shuttle across the city offer cheap but uncomfortable transport and are generally jam-packed. The beat-up old taxis without air-conditioning, which had a certain charm in spite of their lack of comfort, have for the most part been secretly ushered out of the city.

Rizal Park and Intramuros

Rizal Park lies at the northern end of **Roxas Boulevard**, the five kilometer

long thoroughfare that runs along by the sea. It was here that the national hero, José Rizal, was executed and buried. Luneta Park, as the place is more commonly called, is the favorite place for a Sunday stroll, or *pasyal*. Lovers, families and students mingle with ice-cream vendors, photographers and beggars. Chess-players indulge their passion in the shade of the trees, orchestras play in the open air, and entertainments are staged even on weekdays. There is a small lake with a miniature replica of the archipelago, and you can circumnavigate a huge model of the globe on roller-skates. There is a Chinese and a Japanese garden, full of greenery and a planetarium nearby takes visitors on cosmic journeys

The **Rizal Monument** at the western edge of the park is a reminder of the sad fate of this political idealist. The monument bears his poem *Mi Ultimo Adios* ("My Last Farewell") in several languages. The nearby fountain, at which Rizal is said to have drunk during his years in Germany, was presented to the

city by the village of Wilhelmsfeld, near Heidelberg.

On the opposite side of the Roxas Boulevard the atmosphere is lively. The **Quirino Grandstand** was the scene of many political rallies: here both Marcos and Cory Aquino mobilized their supporters, and military march-pasts with gleaming weapons and stern-faced soldiers have taken place. Facing it is the tall, luxurious **Manila Hotel.** Built in 1912, it has hosted to such illustrious guests as Ernest Hemingway, General MacArthur and the Duke of Windsor, and is famous for its colonial charm.

Memories of a still earlier period are evoked by **Intramuros.** For three centuries this "town within the walls" was the heart and mind of the ecclesiastical colony. The mighty stone walls and tunnel-like gateways bear sombre witness to the power of the Spanish empire. The visitor who wants to journey back in time from modern Manila to a corner of the past, can hire a *kalesa* outside the walls. This is a colorful, two-wheel horse-

drawn carriage. The clattering hooves and swaying motion transport you to another age.

Not far from **Puerta Real** to the north of Rizal Park lies one of the few preserved masterpieces of old Spanish architecture in Manila – the **Church of San Augustin**, which is considered the oldest Christian church in town. Legazpi, who is buried here, is said to have chosen the site, on the corner of General Luna Street and Calle Real, shortly before his death in 1572. The church was first just a wooden building erected by the Augustinian monks but this was destroyed in 1574 during one of the attacks by the pirate Lee Mah Ong. The present building, begun in 1599, has survived earthquakes and American bombing in World War II. Despite its Spanish-Mexican baroque style, the church does have a Philippine character of its own, chiefly in its interior

Above: Manila Cathedral and the Palacio del Gobernador. Right: Life in the suburban streets is quite provincial.

detail. The 68 choir seats are hand-carved from dark molave wood, as is the pultpit, which is decorated with a relief of a tropical landscape. The monastery next door, the **Convento de San Augustin**, houses a library, sadly depleted during the English and Japanese occupations – as well as the **San Augustin Museum**, with an extremely important collection of Philippine religious art.

The **Casa Manila** opposite is a vivid presentation of the Spanish colonial way of life. This faithful reproduction of a 19th century residence is a good example of the less old-fashioned way in which history is now recreated within the walls of Intramuros.

The Intramuros Administration has already reconstructed more than 70 percent of the ramparts and near the Casa Manila, on the **San Luiz Plaza**, a number of cafés, restaurants and antique shops have been built into the old walls. Concerts, exhibitions, flea-markets and book-fairs are held in Intramuros. Nowadays, in contrast to earlier times, it is Filipino life

that should take place within these massive stone walls.

The **Plaza Roma** (on the corner of General Luna Street and Cabildo Street) is dominated by the **Manila Cathedral**, the modern counterpart of the church of San Augustin. A huge modern office block now rises up beside it on the site where once the Spanish *Ayuntamiento* (town hall) and the *Palacio Real* (governor's palace) stood. The *Basilica de la Immaculata Concepcíon* (Basilica of the Immaculate Conception) is the sixth church to have been built on this site, the earlier ones having been destroyed by war or natural disasters. The present neo-Romanesque building was completed in 1958. The organ which has 4500 pipes comes from Holland and is said to be the largest in Asia.

Northwest of Intramuros lie the renovated remains of **Fort Santiago,** once the headquarters of the colonial administration. The main attraction of the fortress is the two-storey-high **Rizal Shrine**, a former barracks and now a national monument. Rizal spent the last six weeks of his life here and composed his farewell poem in his death cell. Dungeons of a far more spine-chilling kind can be seen in the powder-magazine beneath the outer walls, at sea level. Prisoners died a slow death by drowning as the tide came in, a form of execution last practiced by the Japanese. Happily, today, the **Raja Sulayman Open Air Theater** in Fort Santiago serves more peaceful purposes. The Philippine Educational Theater Association (PETA) puts on its critical productions before big audiences here. Nearby is a somewhat neglected **collection of old state coaches**.

Chinatown

Chinatown lies north of the Pasig river, and comprises the districts of **Binondo** and **Santa Cruz**. On the other side of Jones Bridge, at the northeast corner of Intramuros, the first of three Chinese-Philippine friendship gates marks the entrance to a different Manila – the two

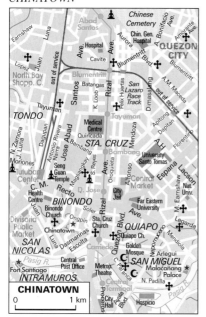

CHINATOWN

0   1 km

other gates are at either end of the long Ongpin Street. Many Chinese came to the country as traders before the arrival of the Spanish, and lived mainly in what was then the village of *Binundok*. Later, for commercial reasons, they found it necessary to adopt the Christian faith, since the Catholic government used religion as an excuse for discrimination. The Spanish needed the Chinese to help run their economy, but at the same time they were constantly in fear of the threat from the "Yellow Peril." This fear was so strong indeed that they kept the Chinese in a state of subjection, and when they revolted in 1603, 1639 and 1762, the Spanish took revenge with massacres and expulsions – then allowed them to return again. Later, wealthy Filipino-Spanish *mestizos* and foreigners also moved into Binondo, which the industrious Chinese had made the business center of Manila. Only the remains of what was once a

Right: Magnificent interior of a mausoleum in the Chinese cemetery.

magnificent mixture of colonial and Chinese architecture now serve as a reminder of this uncomfortable symbiosis: Chinese signs on run-down businesshouses, with arcaded shops underneath, and concrete blocks now frame the stupa of the **Seng Guan Temple** ("temple of ten thousand Buddhas") in Narra Street, close to the Tutuban shopping center.

Chinatown's main attraction these days consists of more worldly pleasures. Hand-painted film posters advertising the biggest cinemas in Manila adorn Rizal Avenue, which runs from north to south. The films they show cater to popular taste – regulated by the official censors – for violence and soft porn. Innumerable Chinese restaurants, food-stalls and street markets provide a distraction from the roar of the traffic.

Chinatown's main shopping streets are **Escolta Street** (parallel to the Pasig river) and **Ongpin Street**, which sweeps in a wide arc westward from the **Plaza Santa Cruz**, east of Rizal Avenue. After it was destroyed in 1945 the **Church of Santa Cruz** was faithfully restored in the style of the original Jesuit church, which dated from 1608.

Not far from here, on **Plaza Miranda** to the east of Rizal Avenue, stands an important place of pilgrimage, **Quiapo Church**, also known as the "Church of the Black Nazarene." Every Friday, and with particular devotion during Holy Week, thousands of penitents shuffle along on their knees to pray to a black statue of Christ. The figure is said to have been carved in Mexico by an Aztec and then brought to Manila in the 17th century. It heads a procession every year on January 9. The church was built in 1899 and restored in 1935.

From here you can make a little detour to the **Malacañang Palace** in San Miguel, on the north bank of the Pasig river. The Marcos family were the last people to occupy the palace, which was originally built in 1802 for the Spanish aristo-

crat Luis Rocha, and was subsequently the official residence of the colonial governors and presidents of the Philippines. The name may come from the Tagalog *may lakan diyan* ("Here lives a noble lord"), or from the Spanish *mala caña* ("bad reeds"), referring to an earlier time when the land here was a swamp. Unfortunately only a small remnant of the Marcos glory can still be seen in the Museo ng Malcañang. The famous collection of Imelda's shoes has been removed.

A stroll along busy **Ongpin Street** brings you to the western end of **Plaza Calderon de la Barca** and **Binondo Church** (the church of Santissimo Rosario). The present building, which was reconstructed after the war, is a replica of the church founded by the Dominicans in 1595 and destroyed in 1945.

The district of **Tondo** lies northwest of Binondo, beneath a permanent cloud of grime and hopelessness. This is the capital's most notorious slum, and one of the largest in Asia, with a population of over 300,000. During the day children play in the fetid streets beside the *esteros,* or open sewers, while by night the same streets are gangster territory. The people of Tondo have a fierce pride which ironically gives them an edge over "normal" citizens with their colonial mentality. **Smokey Mountain** is the name given to a symbol of this misery – a vast, smouldering refuse dump where the more ambitious used to sort through Manila's garbage in the hope of finding something valuable or useful. After years of unfulfilled promises, the public authorities actually doused the stinking, smouldering mountain in 1996 and re-settled the people living in its vicinity.

The **Chinese Cemetery** offers a peaceful and orderly respite from all this. It can be found in the north of Santa Cruz, at the end of José Abad Santos Avenue, and is an impressive monument to Chinese ancestor-worship. It is actually a city within a city, a city consisting of mausoleums and streets lined with graves. Rich families – the name "Millionaires' Row"

speaks for itself – have created memorials in their own lifetime on a site covering more than 40 hectares: complete with telephone, toilets, air-conditioning, security-guards and gardners. When they finally come to rest in these palaces, their descendants pay them due honor and respect, meeting for exuberant graveside celebrations, especially on All Saints day. But the hierarchy of the living persists in death: tens of thousands of the poorer Chinese, Christians and Buddhists alike, have to make do with a drawer in the cemetery wall for a grave.

Ermita, Malate and Makati

The districts of Ermita and Malate lie to the south of Rizal Park. Separated from the sea by Roxas Boulevard, **Ermita** was once a respectable residential quarter, but since the 1970s it has made itself a name as a "tourist belt." Until re-

Above: Manila's construction boom continues unabated.

cently the two main streets, named after the 19th century patriots, Marcelo H. del Pilar and Apolinario Mabini, were pulsing with life. Since coming to office in 1992, Mayor Alfredo Lim has made a serious effort to "clean up" Ermita. His mission to remove prostitution, which, however, quickly becomes established in other districts, from the tourist area, known as "sin city," has above all benefitted wealthy Chinese businessmen, who want to open restaurants, hotels, and establishments for "decent" entertainment (music bars, cafés) in this former bastion of the horizontal trade. The two streets running parallel to Roxas Boulevard still look very run-down in part. The sunset over Manila Bay does help somewhat, reconciling the dirt and the glory, by bathing both in a romantic light.

Religious power beams forth from **Malate Church**, on the corner of M.H. del Pilar and Remedios Streets, at the beginning of the once high-class district of **Malate**. The church, which is one of the oldest of the countless places of worship in the city, was built in the 18th century out of the ruins of a 200-year-old chapel, combining Spanish and Moorish architecture with Mexican influences. Malate Plaza, which lies in front of the church, is adorned with statutes of the church's patron, *Nuestra Señora de los Remedios* ("Our Lady of Mercies") and of Raja Sulayman.

A little way south of the intersection of Vito Cruz and Roxas Boulevards, the **Cultural Center of the Philippines** (CCP) is the incorporation of modern architecture. Built at great expense in 1969, this concrete block houses the national opera, a ballet company and a symphony orchestra. There is a library and the **Museo ng Kalinangang Pilipino** (Philippine Cultural Museum), both devoted to the art and way of life of the various ethnic groups. Exhibitions and concerts here are always well attended.

Behind it are the **Philippine International Convention Center** (PICC), designed, like the CCP, by Leandro Locsin, for the UNCTAD conference in 1976; and the **Folk Arts Theater** (an open air theater.)

The site also includes the **Philippine Center for International Trade Exhibitions** (PHILCITE) and **PHIL-TRADE**. Until 1986 the Manila Film Festival was held annually in the notorious **Picture Palace**, hastily erected by Imelda Marcos in 1981.

Nearby stand the resplendent **Westin Philippine Plaza Hotel** and the **Coconut Palace**, which was built for the visit of Pope John Paul II in 1981 wholly from native woods and decorated inside and out with materials all of which are derived from the coconut tree. The palace is used today as a museum.

Makati can be reached quite quickly from south of Roxas Boulevard by way of Sen. Gil Puyat Ave. or the EDSA (Epifanio de los Santos Ave.). Anyone who comes here on business, or to shop, will find it very much like the financial districts of Frankfurt or New York. Makati consists of high-rise buildings, streets like canyons and people apparently in a permanent hurry.

The shops imitate western values even more than banks and offices. **Landmark** and **SM Mega Mall** are the flagships of major chains, in whose glittering interiors crowds come just to stop and stare.

On the cultural side, the **Ayala Museum** on Makati Avenue offers much of interest in history and ethnography. Its aviary is a refuge in this jungle of high-rise blocks. A **bronze statue** at the intersection of Ayala Avenue and Paseo de Roxas recalls the murder of Ninoy Aquino on the steps of his aircraft when returning from his American exile on August 23, 1983.

The **Manila American Cemetery**, close to the army HQ at Fort Bonifacio, also serves as a national memorial – 17,000 US soldiers who died in World War II are buried here. The Fort Bonifacio zone is at present being prepared for its future, predominantly civilian use. By the year 2000 the largest construction projects should be finished: this will create the Bonifacio Global City, a suburb with 215 hectares of shopping centers, residential areas, luxury hotels and leisure facilities. The planning and finances have come from the Ayala family, who have been the leading members of the Philippine elite since Spanish colonial days, and who have already created a monument to their name by shaping the modern district of Makati.

Forbes Park is the most exclusive of a number of elegant residential enclaves in Makati, which can often only be visited with permission of or accompanied by a resident.

Nayong Pilipino (Filipino Village) displays all the charm of the archipelago in a pleasant setting. At Pasay, on a 35-hectare site near the **Ninoy Aquino International Airport** it shows housing styles and ways of life of various ethnic groups.

MANILA

Accommodation

LUXURY: **Century Park Hotel**, Vito Cruz, Malate, Tel: 5221011. **Holiday Inn Manila Pavillon**, United Nations Ave., Ermita, Tel: 5261212. **Sofitel Grand Boulevard**, Roxas Blvd., Pasay, Tel: 5268588. **Mandarin Oriental**, Paseo de Roxas / Makati Ave., Makati, Tel: 8163601. **Manila Hotel**, Rizal Park, Tel: 5270011. **Manila Midtown Hotel**, Pedro Gil St. / Adriatico St., Ermita, Tel: 5267001. **New World Hotel**, Esperanza St. / Makatai Ave., Makati, Tel: 8116888. **The Peninsula Manila**, Ayala Ave. / Makati Ave., Makati, Tel: 8123456. **Shangri-La's Edsa Plaza Hotel**, Garden Way, Ortigas Center, Mandaluyong, Tel: 6338888. **Manila Diamond Hotel**, Roxas Blvd., Malate, Tel: 5362211. **Westin Philippine Plaza**, CCP Complex, Roxas Blvd., Malate, Tel: 5515555.
MEDIUM: **Aloha Hotel**, 2150 Roxas Blvd., Tel: 5268088. **Palm Plaza Hotel**, Pedro Gil/Adriatico St., Tel: 5213502. **Hotel La Corona**, 1166 M. H. del Pilar St., Tel: 5242631. **Hotel Las Palmas**, 1616 A. Mabini St., Tel: 5245602. **Roma Hotel**, 1407 Sta. Monica St. / M. H. del Pilar St., Tel: 5219431. **True Home**, 2139 Adriatico St., Malate, Tel: 5260351. **Rothmann Inn Hotel**, 1633 Adriatico St., Tel: 5219251. **Royal Palm Hotel**, 1227 A. Mabini / P. Faura St., Tel: 5221515. **Centrepoint Hotel**, 1430 A. Mabini St., Tel: 5212751. *BUDGET:* Mostly in the "Tourist Belt," e.g.: **Pension Natividad**, 1690, M. H. del Pilar St., Tel: 5210524. **Mabini Pension**, 1337 A. Mabini St., Tel: 5245404. **Malate Pensionne**, 1771 Adriatico St., Tel: 5238304. **The Townhouse**, 201 Roxas Blvd. Unit 31, Parañaque, Tel: 8331939.

Restaurants

PHILIPPINE: **Aristocrat**, Roxas Blvd./San Andres St., Malate. **Barrio Fiesta**, J. Bocobo St., Ermita und Makati Ave./Valdez St., auch 977 Aurora Blvd., Quezon City. **Calle 5**, Mabini St., Ermita. **Harbour View**, South Boulevard, Manila Bay. **Ilustrado** (also Spanish dishes), 744 Calle Real del Palacio, Intramuros. **Kamayan**, 523 Padre Faura St., Ermita. **Palais Daan**, 1718 Adratico St. **Seafood Market**, 1190 J. Bocobo St., Ermita. **Zamboanga**, 1619 Adriatico St., Malate, (evenings folklore). **The Islands Fisherman**, Arquiza St., Ermita.
CHINESE: **Mrs. Wong Tea House,** Padre Faura, Ermita. **Maxim's Tea House**, Roxas Blvd./Kalaw St., Ermita. **Green Lake**, 778 Ongpin St., Santa Cruz. **Hong Kong Tea House**, M.H. del Pilar St., Ermita. **Kim Wan Garden** (also vegetarian), General Malvar St., Malate. **Shin Shin Garden**, 2126 Mabini St., Malate. **Pink Patio**, Quintin Paredes St., Chinatown.

WESTERN: **L'Orangerie**, Zodiac St., Makati, French. **Café Adriatico**, Adriatico St./Remedios Circle, Malate. **Tia Maria's**, Remedios/Carolina St., Malate u. Makati Ave., **Greenbelt**, Makati, Mexican. **Prince of Wales**, New Plaza Bldg., Greenbelt, Makati. **Old Heidelberg**, J. Nakpil/J.Bokobo St., Malate. **Rooftop Restaurant** (Australian, on roof of the Iseya Hotel), Padre Faura/M.H. del Pilar St., Ermita. **Schwarzwälder**, Greenbelt Park, Makati Ave. **Treffpunkt Jedermann**, Jupiter St., Makati (German/Swiss/Austrian cuisine). **El Comedor**, Paseo de Roxas, Pasay Road, Makati, Spanish. **Muralla**, Gen. Luna St., Intramuros, Spanish.
In Ermita, Malate (Adriatico St.) and Makati there are Indian, Arab, Korean, Japanese und Thai restaurants.

Shopping

CLOTHING: **Greenhills Shopping Center**, Ortigas Ave., San Juan, **Harrison Plaza**, Harrison St., Malate. **Makati Commercial Center**, Ayala Ave./Makati Ave. **Robinson's**, Adriatico St., Ermita. **SM Megamall**, Edsa, Mandaluyong.
MARKETS: **Divisoria Market**, Santo Cristo St., San Nicolas. **Paco Market**, Gen. Luna St./Pedro Gil St. **San Andres Market**, San Andres St., Malate.
SOUVENIRS: **Ilalim ng Tulay Market**, Quiapo Market (underneath Quezon Bridge). Several shops in United Nations Ave. and A. Mabini St., Ermita. Rustan's, Makati Comm. Center, Makati.
ART: Several shops in: A. Mabini St., United Nations Ave., Ermita. Good selection in: El Almanecer, 744 Gen. Luna St., Intramuros. Cortada St., Ermita (Muslim.); Arlegui St., Quiapo (Muslim.) T'Boli Arts and Crafts, 1362 A. Mabini St., Ermita.

Museums / Galleries / Zoo

Ayala Museum (History), Makati Ave., Makati. Tue-Sun 9 am-5 pm. **Casa Manila** (Spanish Residence, 19th century), Gen. Luna St., Intramuros. Tue - Sun 9 am -12 noon, 1 - 6 pm. **Cultural Center Museum** (Muslim and contemporary Philippine art), Roxas Blvd., Malate. Tue - Sun 9 am - 6 pm. **Lopez Memorial Museum** (private collection, library, historical travel literature, classical Philippine paintings), Chronicle Bldg., Neralco Ave., Pasig. Mon - Fri 8:30 am - 12 noon, 1 - 4:30 pm. **Metropolitan Museum of Manila** (collection of coins, art exhibitions), Central Bank Compound, Roxas Blvd., Malate. Tue - Sat 9 am - 6 pm. **Museo ng Buhay Pilipino** (furniture, 19th century art and crafts), Central Bank Mint Bldg., East Ave., Quezon City. **Museo ng Malacañang** (Marcos Residence), J.P. Laurel St., San Miguel. Mon, Tue, Thu, Fri 9 am - 12 noon, 1 - 3 pm. Sat 9 am - 3 pm.

Museum of Arts and Sciences (history, natural history, archeology, library of the oldest Philippine university), University of Santo Tomas, Espaa St., Sampaloc. Tue - Sat 9 am - 12 noon, 2 - 4:30 pm. **National Museum** (Philippine history, prehistoric finds, e.g. from the Tabon caves), Burgos St., Rizal Park. Tue - Sat 9 am - 12 noon, 1 - 5 pm. **Philipp. Museum of Ethnology** (cultural minorities), Nayong Pilipino Complex, Pasay City. Tue - Sun 9 am - 6 pm. **Rizal Shrine** (memorial to national hero), Ft. Santiago, Tue - Sun 9 am - 12 noon, 1 - 6 pm. **San Agustin Museum** (paintings, liturgical requisites), San Agustin Church, Gen. Luna St., Intramuros. Daily 9 am - 12 noon, 1 - 5 pm. **Ateneo de Manila Gallery** (post-war Philippine art, paintings, sculptures), Ateneo de Manila University, Quezon City, Mon - Fri 8 am - 12 noon, 1 - 5 pm. **The Luz Gallery** (sculpture, paintings), Locsin Bldg., Makati Ave./Ayala Ave., Makati., Tue - Sat 9 am - 5 pm, Sun 9 am - 1 pm. **Manila Zoo** (e.g. dwarf buffalo and eagles, conditions for animals rather shocking), A. Mabini St./Harrison St. Daily 7 am - 6 pm.

Cultural Events

Cultural Center of the Philippines (CCP) (concerts, dance, theater), CCP Complex, Roxas Blvd., Tel. Auskunft: 8321125, 8323704. **Folk Arts Theater** (ballet, concerts, theater), CCP Complex, Roxas Blvd., Tel: 8321120. **Philippine Educational Theater Assoc.** (PETA) (Filipino-Theater), Ft. Santiago, Intramuros. **William Shaw Theater** (English musicals, classics, comedy), Shangri-La Shopping Center, Edsa, Mandaluyong, Tel: 6334821. **Wilfrido Ma. Guerrero Theatre** (Avantgarde), University of the Philippines, Quezon City. **Nayong Pilipino** (Muslim folk dances), Airport Rd., Parañaque, Sat 2:30 - 4 pm. **Pistahan sa Plaza** (Dinner and Cultural Show) Philippine Plaza Hotel, CCP Complex, Roxas Blvd. Daily from 7 pm. **Maynila Restaurant**, Manila Hotel (Bayanihan Philippine Dance Company), Mon - Sat 9:30 - 10:30 pm. Information on events in the magazine *What's on in Manila* (available in the large hotels) and from the Department of Tourism.

Tourist Information

Department of Tourism Bldg., Agrifina Circle, Rizal Park, Ermita, Tel: 5238411. Mon - Sat 8 am - 5 pm. 24 hours telephone info.: 5241728, 5241660.
Tourist Police: 24 hour telephone no.: 5241660.
Polizei: Tel: 166

Post

General Post Office, Liwasang Bonifacio, Intramuros. Mon - Sat 8 am - 5 pm, Sun until 12 noon.

Rizal Post Office, Rizal Park (opposite Manila Hotel), Ermita, Mon - Fri 8 am - 6 pm, Sat 8 am - 12 noon. **Makati Central Post Office** (CPO), Gil Puyat Ave. (same hours).
There are also post offices at both airports.

Hospitals

Makati Medical Center, 2 Amorsolo St./De la Rosa St., Makati. Tel: 8159911.
Manila Doctors Hospital, 667 United Nations Ave., Ermita. Tel: 503011.

Immigration Authority

Commission on Immigration and Deportation, Magellanes Dr., Intramuros. Tel: 5273265.

Arrival / Means of Transport

BY AIR: Ninoy Aquino International Airport (NAIA), Parañaque, 8 km southeast of city center, taxi service. Domestic Airport, Parañaque, Taxi service to city about 500 m away (Harrison St.); with jeepney and bus, from South Terminal, Baclaran (inconvenient).
AIRLINES: **Philippine Airlines**, PAL Bldg., Legazpi St., Makati, Tel: 8171479. S & L Bldg., Roxas Blvd., Ermita, Tel: 5218821. **Grand Air**, Tel: 8939767. **Air Philippines**, Tel: 5264741. **Cebu Pacific**, Tel: 8939667. **Pacific Air**, Domestic Rd., Pasay City, Tel: 8322731. **Air Ads**, Tel: 8333264. **Soriano Aviation**, Tel: 8040408.
SHIP: Almost all ferries to the island provinces leave and arrive at: North Harbour, Tondo. Between pier 2 and pier 14 are the harbor offices of the shipping lines, e.g. **WG & A Company** (William, Gothong & Aboitiz Lines), Tel: 202726, **Asuncion Shipping Lines**, Tel: 204024. **Negros Navigation**, Tel: 2511103, 8183804.
RAIL: Manila - South Luzon from Tayuman Station.
BUS: There is no central bus terminal. The bus companies have their own terminals, spread over the whole city.
Most important bus companies in the **North**: Aparri, Bulacan, Baliwag - Baliwag Transit, Tel: 9123343 (Cubao). Laoag, La Union, Vigan - Philippine Rabbit, Tel: 7115819 (Sta. Cruz). Alaminos, Olongapo - Victory Liner, Tel: 8335019 (Pasay City). Angeles, Baguio, Laoag, San Fernando - Philippine Rabbit, Tel: 7115819, Santa Cruz.
Most important bus companies in the **South**: Batangas, Calamba, Lucena, Naga, Sorsogon, Davao - BLTB, Tel: 8335501, Philtranco, Tel: 8335061, both in Edsa, Pasay City, Superlines, Tel: 9123447, Edsa, Quezon.
LOCAL TRANSPORT: Local transport consists of jeepneys, busses and taxis.

LUZON
THE MAIN ISLAND

CENTRAL LUZON
CENTRAL PLAINS
ZAMBALES REGION
ILOCANDIA
CAGAYAN VALLEY
CORDILLERA CENTRAL
SOUTHERN LUZON

With Manila as its political and economic center, Luzon is the most important of the 7,017 islands, and the largest. With an area of 105,708 square kilometers, it makes up around 35 percent of the total land area of the country.

From north to south the island is 830 kilometers long; at its widest point it is 240 kilometers from the South China Sea to the Pacific Ocean. The landscape of Luzon offers a variety rivalled only by Mindanao. Topographically, the island can be divided roughly into two large regions. South and southeast of Manila we find a coastline indented by a large number of bays and offshore islands, giving a rather ragged effect on the map. The north, on the other hand – with the exception of the Gulf of Lingayen and the north coast – is very regular in shape. Through it, from north to south, run two great mountain chains: the Cordillera Central and the Sierra Madre. Between them, the river Cagayan – at 354 kilometers, the longest river of the Philippines – flows in a wide valley, from the southern Sierra Madre to the Babuyan Channel. North of Manila and east of the Zambales Mountains lies the densely populated central

Previous pages: A cordillera village in the Chico River valley, Mountain Province. Left: The bamboo organ of Las Piñas.

plain, which stretches as far as the Lingayen Gulf. The economic prosperity of the plain has suffered long-term damage as a result of the eruption of the Mount Pinatubo volcano in May 1991. Near the southern tip of Luzon towers the mighty volcano, Mayon: its last eruption, in Februrary 1993, cost 70 lives. Luzon possesses one other active, though small, volcano – Mount Taal in Batangas province. The area surrounding this fire-spewing mountain is spectacular.

About half of the population of the Philippines live in the 32 provinces of Luzon – excluding Manila itself; and the nature of the inhabitants is as varied as the geography of the island: there are city-dwellers, farmers, fishermen, aboriginal islanders and traditional mountain people, like the Ifugao, whose ancestors created magnificent rice-terraces. The Spaniards established their first base on Luzon, but even so were unable to penetrate into large areas of the island. Later it was here that the anti-Spanish rebellions started, and even today the NPA guerillas and local autonomy movements make trouble for the government. Meanwhile, natural upheavals are caused by typhoons that rage across the island toward to the mainland of Asia. Nevertheless, Luzon has so much to offer that visitors could almost forget the rest of the archipelago.

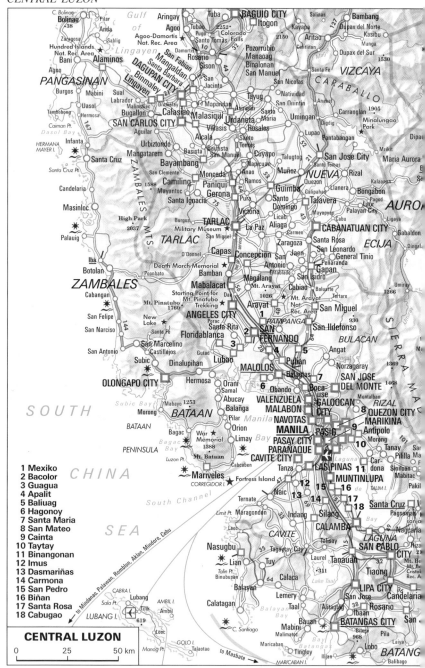

1 Mexiko
2 Bacolor
3 Guagua
4 Apalit
5 Baliuag
6 Hagonoy
7 Santa Maria
8 San Mateo
9 Cainta
10 Taytay
11 Binangonan
12 Imus
13 Dasmariñas
14 Carmona
15 San Pedro
16 Biñan
17 Santa Rosa
18 Cabugao

CENTRAL LUZON

0   25   50 km

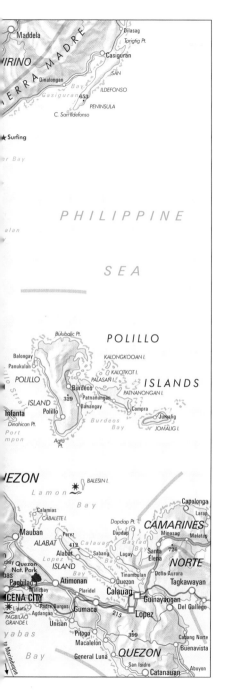

CENTRAL LUZON

The small town of **Las Piñas**, which takes its name from the pineapple plant, and has slowly been absorbed by the metropolis, is of course administratively now a district of Manila city. We begin our description of central Luzon here because Las Piñas acts as a "southern gateway" through which one can escape into the countryside from the teeming city. The place is above all known for its world-famous **bamboo organ** in the **Church of San José**. By jeepney from Ermita via Baclaran or on the bus which goes to Cavite City, it takes about an hour to get to this extraordinary curiosity of musical history. The church, built at the end of the 18th century, stands at the roadside on the highway, leading into the adjoining **Cavite Province**.

Necessity was the mother of invention when the Spaniard, Father Diego Cera, began the construction of the organ in 1816. For want of better materials, and no doubt also to save money, he spent eight years building the five-meter-high instrument, using 832 bamboo pipes and 122 metal ones. Earthquakes, storms and the insatiable termites have taken their toll on this work of art and a long overdue renovation was undertaken in 1973. The organ was sent all the way to the German town of Bad Godesberg, where the work lasted two years. Since then a competition is held every February in Las Piñas, in which musicians of international renown coax the sound of Bach fugues and chorales from the bamboo pipes.

A very different noise alerts one to the presence of the second attraction of Las Piñas. The **Sarao Jeepney Factory**, in which these popular and amusingly decorated vehicles are still produced by hand, is situated on the highway less than three kilometers south of San José church. Management is happy to allow visitors into the assembly shops; you just ask the man at the gate. Here the Filipino

69

descendants of World War Two jeeps are manufactured entirely by hand.

The road runs on into **Cavite Province**, a region steeped in history, which flanks the southern part of Manila Bay. It was here that Filipino soldiers rose up against the Spanish in 1872. This mutiny sparked the independence movement, which was not to be extinguished again until the country achieved full nationhood in 1946. In the town of **Kawit** Emilio Aguinaldo, president of the first Philippine republic, was born in 1869. The house where he was born, the **Aguinaldo Shrine**, is a museum and the old revolutionary lies buried in its garden. To this day the Caviteños are considered to be hot-blooded and pugnacious – and not always with the best democratic motives.

Manila, being so close, has promoted the development of the Cavite region as a center of the manufacturing and processing industries, but the accompanying building-boom has brought the usual problems in its wake. In former times the province was very important to its Spanish colonial masters, because in the heyday of trade between Manila and Acapulco in Mexico, galleons were built at the port of **Cavite City**. The close connection with seafaring and the influence of distant lands have bequeathed to the province its own linguistic heritage: *Chabacano*, meaning "clumsy" or "without style" is the name of a Spanish-sounding dialect. It is also spoken, with local variations, in Zamboanga on Mindanao.

Cavite City and **Sangley Point**, the site of the former American and now of the Philippines naval base, lie on a narrow peninsula which juts out into the bay of Manila in the shape of half of an anchor. The name Cavite derives from this, *kawit* meaning "hook." Do not expect to find clean beaches here; the place to go for these is along the coast near **Ternate**,

Right: In the midst of a fertile landscape – the volcano Taal, in the crater lake.

about 40 kilometers southwest of Cavite City. **Puerto Azul Beach Resort** is only one of several exclusive resorts, which were built to cater for the leisure activities of wealthy Manileños.

A short distance inland lies **Maragondon**, a town which was laid out by the Jesuits, whose richly decorated **rococo church** is proof once again of the power of the clergy. Here is another reminder of the revolutionary past: Andres Bonifacio, the warehouse-worker from Tondo who founded the Katipunan, is buried in Maragondon.

The cratered landscape around the **Mount Taal volcano**, one of the outstanding natural sights of the country, can be reached from Manila and Cavite City by a choice of two routes. Both the road from Las Piñas via Kawit and Silang, and the road from the Ternate area via Naic and Indang, lead to **Tagaytay City.** One should allow about two hours for the journey, perhaps even more, because it is so tempting to stop at the roadside stalls that sell fruit of all kinds. Depending on the season, pineapples, mangoes, rambutans, lanzones and various other wonderful sources of vitamins, thrive on the lava-fields of **Batangas Province**. Thus refreshed, you can enjoy the magnificent view from Tagaytay, 700 meters above sea-level, or from **Taal Vista Lodge** nearby: before you lies **Lake Taal**, with an area of over 270 square kilometers. In its center is an island which rises 400 meters to the **volcanic peak of Taal**, in whose northwestern crater, now extinct, a second lake shimmers. This alternation of land and water looks like a snapshot from the very creation of the archipelago. And the story is still not finished. Taal is, despite its modest size, one of the most dangerous volcanoes in South East Asia. Since the arrival of the Spanish it has erupted some 30 times. In 1911 the death-toll was 1,300 and in 1965 a new crater opened up in the southwest of the island, killing 200 people in the process.

Each time the farmers and fishermen moved back to the volcano and the shores of the lake – drawn by the fertility of the soil – in spite of the volcano's destructive power. When, in February 1992, the water in the lake heated up to 60°C and the mountain rumbled, the surrounding villages had to be evacuated once again. There is speculation that Taal and Pinatubo may one day erupt simultaneously, but vulcanologists avoid raising fears of such an awesome prospect. At all events, before attempting to climb Taal, you should consult the experts at the Volcano Observatory in Buco, west of **Talisay**. Taal is reached by driving along a narrow road to Talisay or **Laurel** and then taking a boat across the lake.

Not far away from here are some excellent, reasonably priced beach resorts. The main road runs from the crater lake straight to **Lian** on the west coast of Batangas, where the South China Sea surges into a series of bays. Between **Nasugbu** and, further south, **Matabungkay** and **Calatagan** on the western tip of Balayan

Bay numerous holiday developments have appeared. These beaches, the best in the vicinity of Manila, offer the full range of facilities that the local tourist industry has to offer, from simple bamboo huts to luxurious clubhouses. The former provide an alternative income for local fishermen, while the latter are run as a hobby by people like the Zobel de Ayala clan, one of the richest families in Southeast Asia. They own the luxury resort of **Punta Baluarte** – and the whole Calatagan peninsula.

At **Anilao** on Balayan Bay and **Mabini** on Batangas Bay you can learn to scuba-dive and go on expeditions to coral reefs and islands such as Sombrero, Maricaban and Verde. Fortunately the authorities have restrained the use of dynamite and poison for fishing; for if the coral started dying, the stream of tourist income would very quickly dry up.

Anyone who hankers for more history as a change from the beach and snorkeling, may admire some of the colonial houses in Taal which are more than 200

the same way can still visit the 17th-century **church of San Sebastian** in **Lipa**, northeast of Batangas City.

Laguna de Bay

When making a trip round Laguna de Bay – the largest lake in the country with an area of 922 square kilometers – the first place to visit is **Calamba**, which is reached from Manila along the Southern Superhighway. The place is full of those reminders of Philippine history that every schoolchild in the country knows about. The national hero, José Rizal, was born in what is now known as the **Rizal Shrine,** a well-stocked museum.

The **International Rice Research Institute** at **Los Baños** brings us back to the present. Scientists from all over the world develop strains of rice that give ever greater yields and are increasingly resistant to disease, though at the cost of a reduction in their nutritional value. At least, that is the argument put forward by critics of genetic engineering. However, everyone agrees that *Los Baños* –"the baths" – are good for one's health. On the road from Calamba that leads to this popular spa, hot sulphur springs bubble out at the foot of the dormant Makiling volcano, and spa buildings, hotels and restaurants make a good living from those afflicted with gout and arthritis who come for the healing waters.

Between Batangas and Laguna provinces the great mountain of **Makiling** soars to 1144 meters. For hikers and bird-watchers it makes a good destination that is not too far away from Manila. It can be climbed in two days. Its virgin jungle conjures up images of the mythical figure of Maria Makiling: she was a fairy who watched over the forest and is said to have given shelter to young men, whom the Spanish wanted to force into military service. However, the story goes that she never let them go again. In 1976, President Marcos' daughter Imee founded the

years old. Remarkably, archeologists have found evidence of human settlement around Balayan Bay dating to about 250,000 years ago. Much later, in the 13th century A.D., seafarers from Borneo occupied this fertile region as a convenient place from which to ply their trade with Arabia, China and India.

The provincial capital, **Batangas City**, is a lively port. It is the most important industrial center in southwestern Luzon, and has a population of 200,000, with further growth planned. Its power stations, oil refineries and shipyards, slum districts and dirt, do not make it an inviting place for a lengthy stay. But there is a quick way out into more rural places: ferry-boats and outriggers depart from here bound for Puerto Galera on Mindoro. Those who want to stay on Luzon but do not want to drive back to Manila

Above: Colorfully decorated buses run between Manila and villages in Central Luzon. Right: Tempting, juicy fruit in Batangas Province.

Makiling Arts Institute and Academy (MARIA) at the foot of the mountain, as part of the **National Art Center** (NAC), where gifted artists seek inspiration from the fascinating surroundings.

South of Laguna the town of **San Pablo** has many attractions for the visitor: seven lakes, from which fish are caught and served in the local restaurants, and the **Hidden Valley Springs Resort**, a private, very well maintained vacation resort, located in the middle of a 92-meter-deep extinct crater, west of San Pablo. Here, in the "hidden valley," close to **Alaminos**, one can bathe in warm and cold springs or swim beneath a waterfall. All this can be enjoyed under the dense, humid, primeval jungle foliage.

The combination of nature and tourism has also been translated into profit by the *haciendero*, or landowner, Conrad Escudero. His **Villa Escudero** is at **Tiaong,** south of San Pablo, just over the border in Quezon province. This ambitious farmer has converted part of his 900 hectare coconut and rice plantation into a tourist attraction. Visitors, the majority of whom are Filipinos, come here for the feeling of really being in the country. They are driven through the idyllic landscape in water-buffalo carts or jeepneys, they can sit beneath jungle trees in the open-air waterfall restaurant, or go to a small auditorium to see a pageant of the nation's history presented as a colorful dance-drama, and performed by the employees of the *padron*. His museum is also worth seeing. This houses the antiquities and strange mementos collected by the much-traveled Don Escudero himself. For those guests , who wish to stay overnight there are elegant bamboo bungalows set in peaceful scenery, near the banks of a river.

The second great mountain in this area is **Mount Banahaw**, a 2177-meter-high volcano, east of San Pablo, which has only been "asleep" since 1743. It is known by local tradition as the male partner of Maria Makiling. The courageous are supposed to climb it, so that their strength and wisdom do not diminish.

On the northeastern side of the mountain, on the border with Quezon province, is **Lucban**. The best time to visit it is in mid-May, when the festival of *Pahiyas* in honor of San Isidro is celebrated. Then this agricultural town is festooned with colorful decorations using fruit, vegetables and flowers, with Chinese lanterns and *kiping*, which are imitation leaves made from rice-starch. Huge papier-mâché figures sway amidst the procession to the festival mass held in front of the old colonial church. The Franciscans were very active in the neat and tidy, tradition-conscious town of Lucban, as well as in **Nagcarlan,** and in neighboring **Majayjay**. The churches in these towns, which were built using slave labor, are worth visiting.

Pagsanjan, near **Santa Cruz**, the provincial capital of Laguna, is a great tourist honeypot. The very wet but excit-

Above: A boat trip on the river near Pagsanjan. Right: Coconut shoots and offspring of the nation.

ing attraction of the place is "shooting the rapids", for which whole busloads of visitors come to Pagsanjan every day. Before the exceedingly fast boat-trip downstream, through a deep jungle ravine, comes a laborious journey upstream over the rapids. Two *banqueros* (boatmen) paddle and push the narrow boat over rocks and treacherous whirlpools up to the 30-meter-high Magdapio falls at the the end of the gorge. The scenery is fantastic – especially early in the morning before the buses have arrived with their hordes. Incidentally, Francis Ford Coppola shot part of his Vietnam film, *Apocalypse Now* on this location.

There was drama of a more mundane kind, when an army of banqueros, waiters, fruit-sellers and photographers had taken over this tourist-spot to the extent that the authorities felt obliged to close it completely for a while, because of the shameless rip-offs and absurd prices being charged. Then, in the 1980s, the image of the idyllic rapids was further tarnished when paedophiles made use of

the location. Now everything is very civilized again, though some of the tips demanded can still make you bristle.

It is a good idea to get a little relaxation among the foothills of the **Sierra Madre,** before continuing the journey along the eastern shore of the Laguna de Bay and through Rizal province – which incidentally is the most densely populated region in the Philippines. In the recreational developments on the **Caliraya reservoir** in Quezon province there are facilities for water-sports and riding.

The little villages on the eastern shore of the Laguna are strung out like the beads of a rosary. **Lumban**, on the waterfront, is a tailoring center, famous for for making the *Barong Tagalog*, the special shirt that Filipinos wear on official occasions. Woven from fibers of pineapple and abaca (*jusi*) and richly embroidered, the shirt is worn, over the trousers, and is the pride of every well-dressed man. It takes the place of a suit and is considered the national costume. The Spanish are said to have ordered the Filipinos to wear

their shirts with a fitted waist and outside their belts, so that any weapons worn on the body could be more quickly discovered.

Further north, **Paete** and **Pakil** have also specialized in traditional crafts. Wood-carving and modelling in papier-mâché have a religious as well as a secular tradition, for here too the *padres* held sway for hundreds of years. However, the *Paeteños* are proud that the name of their village is dedicated not to a saint but to the tool that they have made famous: *paet* means "chisel." Their works of art in wood have won international prizes. A cross from Paete hangs in the Vatican, sermons are preached in San Francisco from a pulpit carved here, and even the yo-yo, the toy popular the world over, was, they say, invented in Paete in 1890.

Near **Siniloan** lies the **National Botanical Garden** where you can admire a dazzling display of several hundred types of orchids. Unfortunately in many parts of the country nature can no longer be seen as it is here.

The churches are the things to look at in **Mabitac** and **Morong**, and in **Tanay**, where the **Daranak Waterfalls** offer another refreshing diversion. The village of **Cardona**, situated on a peninsula, was built by the waterside for good reason. The people here live mainly from the chief product of Lake Laguna, a fish called the *bangus*. They are bred in large, arrow-shaped bamboo cages in the lake, grow to about the size of a herring, and then processed in factories, sometimes for export. There is a small island called **Cielito Lindo**, a little way out from the shore, where the swimming is particularly tempting.

Still in Rizal province, **Antipolo** lies in the hilly country east of Manila. The great attraction of this well-known place of pilgrimage is the black statue of "Our Lady of Peace and Safe Journeys" in **Antipolo Church**. It is said to have been

Above: North of Manila salt-pans on the coast mark the change from million-city Manila to rural provinces.

carved by a Mexican Indian and brought across the Pacific Ocean in a galleon. Each year in May, since 1632, it has attracted streams of the devout who come to kiss and touch it. Often believers, who are about to make a journey abroad, pray for protection at the feet of Our Lady of Antipolo. The saint however, was not able to protect the area from unscrupulous developers, who have been blamed for a landslide, which in the summer of 1999, following heavy typhoon rains, destroyed a whole residental district, and caused numerous deaths.

When traveling through **Rizal Province** one must remember that the region is a product of American colonization. The successors to the Spanish chose a name that meant business when they created this province from the old Manila province and the district of Morong: José Rizal was the national hero executed by the Spanish. The new province was then faithfully introduced to the American way of life. This area to the west of the sparsely populated Sierra Madre is now an urban sprawl, made up of Manila's dormitory suburbs and industrial towns. After leaving Antipolo one is soon caught up in the smoggy purlieus of the sprawling metropolis: for example in **Pasig,** where the river of the same name, practically an open sewer, runs into the river Marikina; and **Pateros,** where vast duck-farms supply the Manileños' appetite for the delicacy called *balut* – eggs that have been partially incubated and are eaten in the evenings as a pick-me-up. Further north, in **Marikina**, there are factories turning out shoes by the million, while near **Montalban,** on the slopes of the Sierra Madre, a dam and reservoir provide Manila with drinking-water.

CENTRAL PLAINS

Driving north out of Manila it takes a long time to shake off the dust of the city. You take the Northern Expressway, the main route to Angeles City, which runs parallel to the old MacArthur Highway, through the Central Plains, a highly fertile lowland region. This alluvial plain, which has always provided about one-third of the nation's rice supply, extends from Manila Bay as far as the Gulf of Lingayen, and from the Sierra Madre to the Zambales Mountains. The area encompasses the provinces of Bulacan, Pampanga, Tarlac and Nueva Ecija.

Bulacan Province, which borders on Manila's metropolitan region, has always been fertile ground for liberation movements as well as rice. In **Balintawak**, the northern district of Caloocan City, you are treading in the footsteps of heroes. It was Andres Bonifacio who in 1896 unleashed the uprising against the Spanish with the "Battle-cry of Balintawak." In the provincial capital of **Malolos**, 30 kilometers away, the revolutionaries then rose up *en masse*, and two years later Aguinaldo's followers drew up their declaration of independence here. Marcelo H. del Pilar, a friend of Rizal, was just

one of the many intellectuals who have come from this province. He in turn modelled himself on the poet Balagtas, from Bigaa – a town south of Malolos, which has now been renamed **Balagtas** in honor of its famous son. Born at the end of the 18th century and educated by the monks, who gave him the Spanish name Francisco Balthazar, Balagtas developed into a perceptive poet of protest. By reverting to his Tagalog name, and above all through his best-known poetic work, *Florante at Laura*, he struck a blow at colonial rule.

The many festivals in this region testify to the fact that even today the *Bulakeños* cast longing glances back to pre-Spanish times. In **Obando**, only a few miles north of Manila, "fertility rites" take place every year in mid-May; and although these are ostensibly dedicated to Christian saints, the invocation of divine assistance against infertility and crop failure has its roots deep in the Malay culture. Similarly, the adoration of the Holy Cross is a thin disguise for belief in the nature-spirits, in the *Pagoda-sa-Wawa* festival held in nearby **Bocaue** at the beginning of July. According to legend, ancestors fished this cross out of the river Bocaue some 200 years ago. Nowadays the event is celebrated with an exuberant river procession. And in **Pulilan,** north of Malolos, there is even a festival in honor of "the farmer's best friend," the stolid water-buffalo (*carabao*). In mid-May hundreds of decorated carabaos receive a solemn blessing outside the church of the patron saint of farmers, San Isidro Labrador.

A rather bizarre kind of homage is paid to Christianity in **San Fernando**. Every Good Friday the capital of **Pampanga Province**, which adjoins Bulacan, is inundated with tourists and curious spectators. They are here to watch emulators of Jesus Christ gather in a rice-field outside the town to have their hands pierced by real nails, so that they can be crucified voluntarily for about half-a-minute each.

Astonishingly little blood is shed in the process. On the same day, in this area and elsewhere in the country, *flagellantes* enthusiastically flay their own backs with a "cat o' nine tails" and razor-blades.

San Fernando's second great event, the splendid Lantern Festival, takes place on December 23 and 24. Then the town is ablaze with light from Chinese lanterns, one meter high, made from beautifully decorated rice-paper and cellophane rigged up with state-of-the-art electronics and innumerable light-bulbs. A large number of Chinese Filipinos live in San Fernando. Their forefathers fled from Manila to escape Spanish persecution and helped to build the town's wealth.

Another center of attraction in Pampanga province is **Angeles City**. It was first a boom town, thanks to American patronage, and then a wasteland buried

Above: Wet but happy – a river procession in Bocaue. Right: Pinatubo's masses of mud and ash have drastically transformed the the the landscape.

under Pinatubo's ash. Now it is a lively center with growing industries and busy nightlife. It is all too clear how severely the eruption of the volcano **Pinatubo** (which had been dormant since 1380) not only transformed the landscape but the entire socio-political structure of the region.

Angeles City had for decades depended for its livelihood on the US Air Force's nearby Clark Air Base – until June 1991 when a rain of ash and devastating *lahar* – avalanches of hot, liquid lava from the mountain, just 20 kilometers away – enveloped the town, laying waste to streets, bars, and fighter aircraft, tearing down bridges and damming rivers.

Pinatubo made nearly a million people homeless and an area of over 800 square kilometers under rice cultivation has been rendered useless for generations to come. The Americans, for whom a decision was due in any case, since the lease on their base was soon to expire, found themselves forced to abandon overnight a

facility of 530 square kilometers, employing some 8000 US service personnel and over 800 Filipinos. Some of the local inhabitants were able to find jobs in the factories and businesses of the *Clark Field Special Economic & Free Port Zone*. Even the recreational district of **Balibago** has reopened its doors to the crowds. Tourists form the bulk of the visitors. A new generation of workers for the bars was virtually produced when the nightlife of the Ermita district in Manila was restricted.

The pervasive layer of gray ash which covers Angeles and its environs became even thicker when the 1760-meter-high volcano started rumbling and erupting again. Whether the routes and sights described in the guidebooks will be there for much longer is a matter for doubt, given the danger of further eruptions and floods of *lahar*. Meanwhile the tourist authorities are busy: while tens of thousands still have no roof over their head, adventure tours in the Pinatubo area are being advertised! You are better advised

to head for **Mount Arayat**, the nearby dormant volcano, which rises to 1026 meters above the plains, east of Angeles City. Its protected forests are a nature lover's paradise. And in the village of **Magalang** you can see the old church and colonial houses dating from the Spanish period.

Two memorials in the immediate neighborhood waken painful memories of the Second World War: in **Mabalacat** Japanese *kamikaze* pilots are commemorated; while near **Capas** in the neighboring province of Tarlac, the **Death March Monument** recalls the grim trek of allied troops into captivity after the long and bloody battle of Bataan. Thousands of Filipinos and Americans died on the march and in the Japanese camps.

Tarlac Province with its capital, Tarlac, is the sugar country of Luzon. Wealthy landowners are the dominant force in local politics and economy, like the Cojuangcos, whose most famous member is Cory Aquino, the former president. Her **Hacienda Luisita** (12,000

hectares) was, ironically, never seriously affected by her farcical attempts at land reform.

Between Tarlac and the southern foothills of the Sierra Madre stretches the rice bowl of the Philippines: **Nueva Ecija**, the largest province in the region. Thanks to the fertile sediments of the Pampanga and three other rivers, to irrigation and copious rainfall, the farmers can harvest three crops per year. Apart from the big **Pantabangan Dam** and the neighboring **Minalungao National Park** (northeast of San José City), as well as a few springs and some cool mountain scenery, there is scarcely anything in the province to interest the tourist. However, **Central Luzon State University** near the capital, **Cabanatuan City** is important for the study of agriculture and animal husbandry.

From here the rough road through Bongabon gives you a chance to cross the

Above: A practical use of an asphalt road – drying rice. Right: In Hundred Islands National Park.

Sierra Madre to the Pacific coast. There is an attractive spot on the coast called **Baler** in **Aurora Province**.While the countryside inland is wonderful for walking, Baler Bay is irresistible for surfers, especially in December, when the breakers are large and numerous. This is the time of the year when **Cape Encanto** ("Cape of Delight") truly lives up to its name. Scuba-diving enthusiasts will find many places to enjoy along Quezon's coast, such as the area near Baler or **Casiguran Bay** farther north, between the mainland and the peninsula of San Ildefonso.

ZAMBALES REGION

West and southwest of the great plain and the Zambales Mountains lie the coastal provinces of Bataan, Zambales and Pangasinan. The **Bataan Peninsula** has an important place in the history of the Second World War, when it was bitterly fought over by the Japanese and the Allies. The "Fall of Bataan"on April 9, 1942 is remembered with respect and the day has been designated a national holiday. Several memorials and monuments, such as the the 92-meter-high high cross on **Mount Samat**, near the provincial capital, **Balanga** are reminders of the terrible loss of life. Near **Mariveles** and **Bagac** in the south of the peninsula was the starting point for the "death march" of 76,000 allied prisoners-of-war into Japanese captivity. Almost one third of them did not survive.

Although the northern part of Bataan's west coast is reserved for use by the Philippines navy, the character of the province today is predominantly peaceful. In 1970 a free trade area was created around Mariveles for the export industry. Nearby is the rotting nuclear power-station at **Napot Point** near Bagac, which was built in Marcos' time, with staggering lack of foresight close to the exclusive **Montemar Beach Club**. It was shut down in

1986. Buses from Manila and San Ferdinando run to **Morong** in the northwest. At **Sibul** on the east coast there are sulphur springs, in which one can bathe or you can visit the rushing Pasukylan waterfalls near **Abucay**.

Corregidor Island, the scene of another great World War II battle, lies off the south coast of Bataan. It can also be reached from Manila, 50 kilometers away, by hydrofoil. "The Rock," as it was called, was made famous by the dogged allies' defense against Japanese bombardment in spring 1942. Apart from military installations, the island offers delightful scenery, though even here one keeps finding traces of war. These are now being exploited for tourism. There are guided day-long tours, a light-and-sound show in the tunnels; also several kinds of accommodation, some quite luxurious, have been constructed.

"The most American town in the Philippines," **Olongapo City**, in the south of Zambales province, underwent noticeable changes following the final withdrawal of the US navy. Since 1947 the Subic Naval Base of the US 7th Fleet, in the sheltered **Subic Bay**, had been the engine of the town's economy and infrastructure. Now international companies shape life in Subic Bay Freeport, a flourishing duty-free zone for industry and commerce on the former military site of Olongapo – a town which even more than Angeles city catered to the needs of the raw recruits. And just as happened there, the eruption of Pinatubo has contributed much to recent changes.

There is no little pride in this development, which also offers some tourist attractions (diving to wrecked ships, golf, riding, jungle treks). Although the damage caused by the the the Pinatubo cataclysm has brought some compensation, the majority of the Aëta tribespeople, who lost their homes on the wooded slopes of the volcano face a less promising future.

As you continue up the coast at the foot of the Zambales Mountains, beautiful beaches open up in front of you; the further north you go from Olongapo, the

81

cleaner are the sand and water. The coastal road, though very pot-holed, leads past many bays and offshore islands – wonderful places for diving – and on to **Iba**, the capital of Zambales, and **Santa Cruz** in **Pangasinan Province**.

The scenic and historic focus of this stronghold of fishing, rice-growing and salt production – *pang-asin-an* means "where sea-salt is found" – is the **Gulf of Lingayen**. In the mid-16th century the Chinese pirate, Lee Mah Ong, with 3000 men, tried unsuccessfully to set up a base here after failing to capture Manila. You can still see the ruins of the tunnel, through which the Chinese fled to their ships.

The chief tourist attraction is the **Hundred Islands National Park** near the small town of **Alaminos**. There are indeed almost one hundered of these little coral islets, covered with shrubs and flowers and with beaches in tiny bays, ideal for round trips or Robinson-Crusoe-style adventures, with self-catering. Sadly, fishermen with dynamite have long ago ruined things for scuba-divers.

Those interested in history and nature will enjoy visiting the **Church of St James** (built in 1609), in the northwestern town of **Bolinao**. There is also a **Regional Museum,** which gives an insight into the life and culture of the Philippines from the 7th to the 15th centuries. Further treasures await discovery in sunken ships off Cape Bolinao and between the islands of Santiago, Dewey and Silaqui.

At the provincial capital **Lingayen** and at **Dagupan**, both founded by Augustinian monks in the 16th century, there are wide beaches with grey-colored sand, a popular destination for the air-pollution-weary Manileños, who prefer to take the direct route through the plains of Luzon to spend the wekend here.

Where the coast of the gulf swings northward near **San Fabian**, the foothills of the Cordillera meet the sea, forming the southern border of North Luzon.

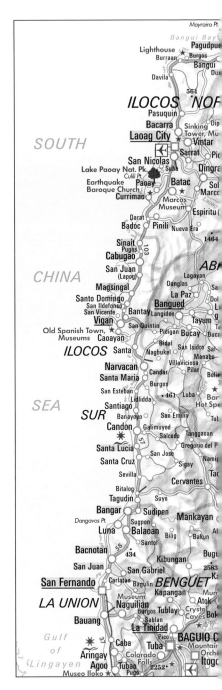

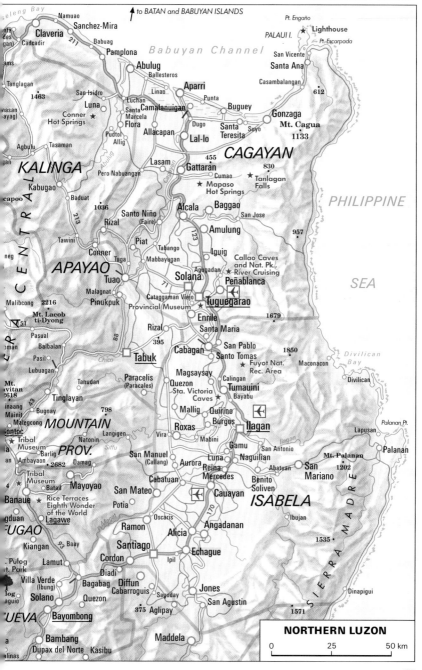

to BATAN and BABUYAN ISLANDS

seleng Bay
Namuao
Sanchez-Mira
Claveria
Cadcadir
Babuag
211
Pamplona
Pt. Engaño
Lighthouse
PALAUI I.
Pt. Escarpada
San Vicente
Santa Ana
Casambalangan

Babuyan Channel

Abulug
Ballesteros
Aparri
Punta
Buguey
612
Gonzaga
Mt. Cagua
1133

Tanglagan
1463
San Isidro
Luna
Luchan
Camalanuigan
Santa
Marcela
Flora
Allacapan
Linao
Dugo
Santa
Teresita
Suyo
Conner
Hot Springs
Pudtol
Allig
Lal-lo

Agbulu
Tasaman
Lasam
Gattaran
455
Cumao
Mapaso
Hot Springs
Tanlagan
Falls
830

KALINGA
Kabugao
Baduat
capoo
1036
Pero Nabuangan

Santo Niño
(Faire)
Rizal
Alcala
Baggao
San Jose
Amulung
957

Tawini
Piat
Tabango
Iguig
Callao Caves
and Nat. Pk.,
River Cruising

PHILIPPINE

Conner
Tuga
Mabbayugan
Agugadan
Solana
Peñablanca

APAYAO
Tuao
Malagnat
Cataggaman Viejo
Tuguegarao

Malibcong
2216
Pinukpuk
Provincial/Museum
Enrile
Santa Maria
1679

Mt. Lacob
ti-Dyong
51
Rizal
395
San Pablo
Santo Tomas
1850

SEA

Pasual
Balbalan
Cabagan
Fuyot Nat.
Rec. Area
Maconacon

Pasil
Tabuk
Magsaysay
Calingan
Tumauini

Lubuagan
Chico
Paracelis
(Paracales)
Quezon
Sta. Victoria
Caves
Bayabu
Divilican
Bay

Mt.
avitan
2618
Tanudan
Mallig
Quirino
Burgos

Divilican

inaang
Mainit
Tinglayan
798
Roxas
Vira
Mabini
Ilagan

Malegcong
ontoc
Bugnay
Natonin
Langigen
Siffu
Gamu
San Antonio
Mt. Palanan

Tribal
Museum
Barlig
Ambayaon
2682
Damag
San Manuel
(Callang)
Aurora
Reina
Luna
Naguilian
Abatuan
San
Mariano
1202

Palanan

Tribal
Museum
Batad
Mayoyao
Cabatuan
Reina
Mercedes
San
Benito
Soliven

Banaue
Rice Terraces
Eighth Wonder
of the World
San Mateo
Potia
Cauayan

ISABELA

gduan
UGAO
Lagawe

Kiangan
Baay
Ramon
Oscaris
Angadanan
1535

Pulog
t. Park
Lamut
Santiago
Alicia
Echague
Ibujan

Villa Verde
(Ibung)
Cordon
Ipil

log
aguio
Solano
Diadi
Bagabag
Diffun
Cabarroguis
Jones

UEVA
Quezon
375
Sayoduy
San Agustin
1571

Bayombong

Dinapigui

Bambang
Maddela

Dupax del Norte
Kasibu

CAGAYAN

CENTRAL

MOUNTAIN

PROV.

SIERRA MADRE

NORTHERN LUZON

0   25   50 km

ILOCANDIA

Between the Cordillera Central and the coast of the South China Sea lies the region of Ilocandia, which comprises the provinces of La Union, Ilocos Sur and Ilocos Norte in the west of North Luzon. Between the two Ilocos provinces, the mountainous Abra Province reaches almost to the coast.

An "unfair climate" determines much of the life of the people here. Between November and May it is moderately hot but very dry, allowing the cultivation of maize, onions, sugar cane and tobacco, as well as rice. But after that, and especially between July and September, typhoons often rage across the area and destroy the results of all their hard work.

Over the years, many *Ilocanos* – the word has been Hispanicized and means "lowlanders " – have moved away from

their harsh homeland to try their luck in the south or overseas. The Ilocanos, or Samtoy, as they prefer to call themselves, are said, with some justification, to be hard-working, determined and tight-fisted. In fact, they are supposed to be almost as mean as the Scots and, similarly, they are the subject of endless jokes. However, nature can certainly not be accused of miserliness in Ilocandia, nor can the cultural heritage of the region.

La Union Province, which was created in 1854 out of the southern part of Ilocos Sur and the north of Pangasinan, is renowned for its beaches. Along the coast is a string of impressive reminders of the Spanish colonial period, which began here in 1572 with Juan de Salcedo's conquest: massive churches and watchtowers, built like fortresses to withstand earthquakes and pirate attacks. Museums such as the **Museo Iloko** in the small town of **Agoo** in southern La Union record the turbulent history. In the basilica there the "Madonna of Charity" is honored; while in Marcos Park near **Pugo**,

Above: In La Union the pigs like nothing better than a good scrub in the morning... Right: A "kalesa" in Vigan.

on the road to Baguio City, you see the enormous bust of the ex-dictator, which he himself commissioned in his own lifetime, and had cemented to the rock face.

Beach resorts are the attraction of **Bauang**, a coastal town; the name simply means "garlic," as this grows here in vast quantities. Between here and the provincial capital **San Fernando**, 10 kilometers away, there are wide beaches as far as the eye can see. Grapes grow on the hills, although the local wine, the reddish *basi*, is made from fermented sugar cane sap.

San Fernando is the regional center, founded in 1768 in honor of the Spanish king Ferdinand. Here the **Museo de la Union** provides a good introduction to local cultural history; while the **Chinese pagoda** and the Taoist **Ma-cho Temple** remind one of the Chinese contribution to the development of the town. The Spanish watchtowers a little further north, near **Carlatan**, **San Juan** and **Bacnotan** also testify to attacks on the town from outside. La Union has a long tradition of craftsmanship. For example, decorative

earthenware is made in **San Juan** and handwoven blankets in **Bangar,** a town on the border to **Ilocos Sur Province**. The village churches of **Santa Lucia**, **Santa Maria** and **Candon** are all worth visiting.

Another watchtower near **Narvacan,** stands, where the road into **Abra Province** turns off to the northeast. This impoverished mountain province lives mainly from tobacco and timber from its dwindling forests. It has gold and iron-ore deposits, but these are as yet scarcely exploited. The unequal distribution of property has turned parts of Abra into a war-zone between the New People's Army and the regular army. The military situation will dictate whether a visit to such attractions as the **Bani Hot Springs**, set in wild mountainous scenery near **Boliney**, or **Lake Kimkimay** near **Pilar** south of the provincial capital **Bangued**, or a journey into Mountain Province (see p. 93) will be possible.

If Olongapo is "the most American town" in the Philippines, then Ilocos Sur is definitely the most Spanish. And the coastal town of **Vigan**, founded in 1574 by Salcedo as *Ciudad Fernandina*, does indeed have a Spanish ambience unmatched anywhere else in the country. Despite this, tourism has more or less passed it by. In Vigan's old nooks and crannies and its streets, such as Mena Crisologo Street, in the *mestizo* quarter, which is to be restored, using UNESCO funding, the dusty world of *Madre España* continues to live – especially in the early morning as the first rays of sun wake the sleepy houses and department - stores, and before the smelly "tricycles," or motorized rickshaws, have started rattling around. This "piece of Castile in Southeast Asia" is history that one can feel, touch and even live in. A *kalesa* trip is certainly worth making, even more so here than in Intramuros. But not all memories of Vigan are so pleasant: one of its 18th-century sons was Diego Silang, the leader of a tragic rebellion against the colonial power. After a five-month struggle, he died in 1762, felled by a *mestizo*'s bullet. His courageous widow Gabriela continued to lead the uprising, until she was hanged in Vigan in 1763.

One is reminded of yet another martyr of the freedom movement in the birthplace of the priest José Burgos, who was executed in Manila in 1872. Today the building is the **Ayala Museum**, with its interesting display of details of Ilocano culture. The centers of power are grouped round the **Plaza Salcedo**: the Archbishop's Palace, the provincial parliament and the **Cathedral of St Paul** with its impressive altar of hammered silver. On the corner of Gomez Street and Liberation Boulevard is the **Pagburnayan pottery**, which makes the glazed earthenware jugs so typical of Ilocandia.

There are more churches worth visiting north of Vigan at **San Vicente** and

Right: Ilocandia's most famous church is here in Paoay.

Magsingal, where the portrait of St William is supported by two mermaids. **Magsingal Museum**, once a monastery, is devoted to the Tingguian, former headhunters whose descendants live in the mountains east of Vigan.

Three kilometers beyond **Cabugao** it is worth stopping at the beach at **Pugos** before continuing into **Ilocos Norte Province**, which starts north of Sinait.

The famous 19th-century painter, Juan Luna, was born in **Badoc**. **Luna's house**, which has been restored, has reproductions of some of his work on display. **Currimao** has beautiful beaches. Like the rest of Ilocandia, this area is tobacco country; and Ilocos Norte has always been Marcos territory as well. Even before one reaches the capital, Laoag, traces of "the great Ilocano" are unmistakable.

The **Lake Paoay National Park** lies some way north of **Paoay**, where one of the most interesting early-18th-century Baroque churches, built to withstand earthquakes, combines a massive exterior with a delicate Javanese decor inside. It is now included in the UNESCO World Cultural Heritage. Legend has it that a sunken pre-Hispanic town lies at the bottom of the 70-meter-deep lake. Marcos' former residence, the **Malacañan ti Amianan,** now a museum, stands proudly on the northern side of the lake.

In **Batac**, on the main road to Laoag, another Marcos house, **Balay ti Ili**, is open to the public. In nearby **Sarrat**, the dictator's birthplace, the personality cult is taken further: you are invited to admire, among other things, the bed where little Ferdinand came into the world.

For the wedding of Marcos's daughter Irene, in 1983, the airport of the provincial capital, **Laoag City,** was extended and the exclusive **Fort Ilocandia Resort Hotel** was specially built beside the sand-dunes of **Suba** beach. In Laoag City the **bell tower** of **St William's Cathedral**, standing 85 meters away is more interesting than the actual church. It has been

"shrinking" since the early 17th century. Both church and "Sinking Tower" are also solid examples of what could properly be named "earthquake baroque." The **Town Hall** (19th century) and **Ilocandia Museum** are also worth visiting. In 1882 a monument was erected in front of the provincial parliament building in gratitude to the Spanish King Alfonso XII, who ended the unfair tobacco monopoly by introducing mixed farming.

Bacarra has a fine 18th century "catastrophe church" with a **bell-tower** that you can climb for a good view of the area. Nature here has its impact, however: until the earthquake of 1930 this tower was substantially higher; and the tremor of 1984 brought it lower still.

Near **Burgos** on the north coast stands the **Cape Bojeador Lighthouse** – which has been flashing its warning light to mariners since 1892. Near **Pagudpud** there are wide, enticing beaches, promoted as "the Riviera of North Luzon." But happily the parallel ends there: there are no crowds and no infrastructure.

Forgotten Islands of the Rugged North

Where the foothills of the Cordillera Central come right down to the sea, along the curve of **Paseleng Bay**, **Cagayan Province** begins. This covers the northeastern corner of Luzon and the Babuyan Islands. Yet even this is not the northernmost part of the country. Considerably further out, and not even marked on some maps, is the smallest and most sparsely populated province of the Philippines: **Batanes Islands**. Spanish monks landed on them more than 100 years after the colony was first founded, and they now have a population of about 20,000. There are three main islands and a few other fragments of land lying about 160 kilometers north of Luzon, in subtropical latitudes. In some ways they do not seem part of the Philippines at all. For one thing, the language spoken here, Ivatan, is hardly related to any of the other national languages. For another, the inhabitants, also called the Ivatan, build their houses of stone, with thick walls and

87

grass roofs, a style found nowhere else in the archipelago. The extreme climate, with its monsoons and typhoons, has shaped the islands and their people.

On **Batan**, the most important of the green islands, lush jungle surrounds the dormant volcano **Iriya**, 1008 meters high. **Basco**, the little provincial capital, has Mediterranean flair, narrow streets and alleyways, an 18th-century church and houses adorned with white balconies. Several bumpy roads cross the island, on which only a few jeepneys and motorbikes travel between isolated villages.

Time has stood still to an even greater degree on **Sabtang** and **Itbayat**, the two other populated islands. One curiosity is the typical Ivatan headgear: the *suot,* a kind of hat made from natural fibres reaching down over the wearer's back, giving protection against both sun and rain. The unassuming and friendly islan-

Above: Grandma and granddaughter on the Batanes Islands. Right: Car repair-shops are badly needed in North Luzon.

ders live from fishing and raising cattle. Visitors must be prepared for severe weather. When heavy rain reduces visibility so that the landing strip at Basco is unusable, the aircraft turns round and flies back. But anyone who happens to be marooned on Batanes because of the weather is in no bad location for a Robinson-Crusoe-style adventure.

CAGAYAN VALLEY
The Large Valley

Mountains on three sides – the Cordillera Central in the west, the Sierra Madre in the east and the Caraballo mountains in the south – and between them a long lowland area, open to the north; this is, roughly defined, the **Cagayan Valley**. The valley of the Rio Grande de Cagayan is shared by three adjoining provinces, **Cagayan**, **Isabella** and **Nueva Vizcaya**. Although the region is very fertile, thanks to the river and its tributaries, and is sheltered from typhoons, it is also developing as a center of industry and tourism.

Claveria, the northernmost town on the "mainland," lies where the Cordillera pulls back from the sea, leaving a narrow coastal strip. Taking a leaf out of Hawaii's book, Claviera has its own **Waikiki beach**, but a boat-trip to the **Babuyan Islands** is more rewarding. Three active volcanoes loom over Babuyan and Camiguin, while further east Didicas rises directly out of the sea. The privately owned **Fuga Island** is a great place for diving; in Claveria they will tell you how to get permission.

A bumpy section of National Highway 3 leads along the coast and over the river Abulug to **Aparri** at the mouth of the Cagayan. Salcedo landed here in 1567, though it was not until 1581 that the Spanish built a fort in **Lal-lo**. This diocesan town, later called *Nueva Segovia* for a while, is a typical relic of the conqueror's many violent but unsuccessful ventures into the interior. The inland tribes, the Ibanag people, bitterly resisted the foreign invader for centuries, and their trading partners from Japan and Borneo helped them in this.

Aparri has always been the commercial center for this coast, where fish are plentiful. Big-game fishing is organized from here, mainly to the northeast tip of Luzon and to **Palaui Island**. Particularly at Point Escarpada, near San Vicente is is the shoals of marlin that attract would-be Hemingways; but the currents here are treacherous. In the north of Palaui, on **Cape Engaño**, two of life's great treasures can be found: nature and solitude. Even the local Dumagat Negritos can enthuse over the view of the sea from an old **lighthouse** on the peninsula.

From Aparri, continue south on National Highway 5, stopping at **Gattaran,** 35 kilometers away, which is a good base from which to make trips to the **sulphur springs of Mapaso** and the **Tanlagan Falls**. Though it is a tough 40-kilometer drive to the falls, the dramatic 100 meter drop makes them worth the journey.

Cagayan's capital, **Tuguegarao,** is merely a boring town to be hurried through. The **Cagayan Museum and Historical Research Center** is, however, worth seeing; pride of the collection are the paleolithic finds. Amateur speleologists can go down into the **Callao Caves** in the **Peñablanca Limestone Formation,** 24 kilometers east of the capital. With a total area of 192 hectares, they are the largest of their kind in the country and still have many unexplored corners. Their name comes from *kalaw*, a bird that used to nest here.

To the south one crosses into **Isabela Province**, named after Queen Isabella II of Spain (1830-1904). This large tobacco-growing region is also the "rice-bowl" of North Luzon. The once dense forest has largely been cleared. The main areas of settlement – which include many Ilocano people – lie in the middle of the Cagayan valley, while the inaccessible Sierra Madre rises to the east.

There is a fine old **church** in **Tumauini**, but more interesting is the natu-

ral architecture of the **Santa Victoria caves** in the country nearby. In the **Fuyot National Park** one can see the flora and fauna from what remains of Isabella's jungle. Lovers of old churches will also want to stop in **Cauayan** and **Echague**, even though, if regarded superficially, these are just badly weathered brick constructions.

Nueva Vizcaya, the southernmost province of the Great Valley, is land-locked in the middle of North Luzon. Fairly undeveloped, it consists largely of the lower ranges of the Cordillera and the Caraballo. Even the outer fringes of the province are well populated, with towns like Ilongot, Igorot and Dumagat. More than half the inhabitants live in the countryside, growing vegetables and rice and weaving baskets.

Many travelers merely pass through Nueva Vizcaya, because at **Bagabag** in

Above: A street-market in Benguet Province. Right: On the road to Bontoc, after a landslide.

the north is the turning for the road to the famous rice-terraces of Banaue (see p. 94). The most important towns of the province – **Solana**, **Bambang** and the capital **Bayombong** – are all on Highway 5. A few kilometers west of Bambang you see what looks like white hills shining in the sun. These are deposits from the salt springs of **Salinas**. Further south, the long-distance buses regularly stop at the top of the **Dalton Pass,** near **Santa Fé**. With an altitude of 940 meters, the view from the pass on a good day is superb. However, the real purpose in stopping is to remember some heroes of the Second World War: it was here that a division of American and Philippine troops,under General Dalton drove back the Japanese.

CORDILLERA CENTRAL

Some of the most magnificent landscape in the Philippines is to be found in the four central highland provinces of Benguet, Ifugao, Mountain Province and

Kalinga-Apayao. The inhospitable yet fascinating world of the Cordillera Central is far from most people's idea of a tropical island. Similarly, its inhabitants are very different from the lowland Filipinos; they are descended from the proto-Malays who migrated to the island from the mainland of Asia around 3000 years ago. In the protection of the mountains, the Ibaloi, Kankanay, Bontoc, Ifugao and Kalinga were able for many long years to defend themselves against the white race who came, with their enigmatic religion, to seek gold. Until 1850 the Spanish were unable to gain a foothold among the warlike *Igorot*, as the tribes of the Cordillera are still collectively known today.

The Americans were quicker to strike lucky, equally driven by a missionary zeal to convert the "heathen headhunters." Still, after these efforts, with the help of some eager religious sects they not only built hospitals and roads, but improved education, something which was long overdue nation-wide.

However, these mountain people still feel threatened. Authorities and resistance movements confront each other today in a struggle that has lasted for decades. Traditional distrust of Manila is not lessened by the plundering of resources, the diluting of native culture and the depopulation of the countryside through migration to the cities. These people have lived with privation for a long time. Now they face complete impoverishment.

For the lowland Filipinos a trip to **Baguio City** in **Benguet Province** is one to the wilds of the north. The region seems exotic to them partly because it is "very cold" there. And that is precisely the attraction of this summer resort, which lies at an altitude of about 1500 meters. In the months of April and May, tens of thousands of Manileños flee the city heat and seek the cool of the pine-forests in the southern Cordillera, where temperatures average a pleasant 20°C). It was the Americans who, at the beginning of the 20th century, established a health resort

here, on the site of the ancient Ibaloi settlement of Kafagway, later used by the
Spanish as a base for expeditions. At first
it was used exclusively by colonial staff
who drove here to recuperate, along the
Kennon road from Manila, which took
three years to build. Then gold and cop-
per-mines brought rapid growth to the
town; a military academy was established, as well as the St Louis University
with its school of silversmithing, a center
for Philippine faith-healers and of course
a great deal of tourism – until the earthquake of 1990 reduced much of the town
to rubble and took 1000 lives. Baguio has
largely recoverd and is working hard to
regain its title of "town of pines, flowers
and lovers."

Still as cheerful as ever is the **City
Market** in the town center, which offers
basketwork, silvercraft and wood carvings, as well as mouthwatering straw-
berry products. Just a few streets further
south is **Burnham Park,** named after the
American planner who laid out Baguio. It
withstood the earthquake fairly well. The
Orchidarium there is probably of
greater interest to Europeans than boat-
trips on the artificial lake. **Camp John
Hay**, the large recreational area for the
US army on the southeast edge of Baguio, is where General Yamashita signed
the surrender. It is now a recreational
park open to the public. The valuable exhibits from the damaged **Museum of the
Mountain Provinces** can also be seen.

North of Camp John Hay is Imelda
Park, which has now reverted to its old
name of **Botanical Garden** and shows
houses in the style typical of the region.
From there it is very pleasant to go on to
Mansion House, either on foot or on hor-
seback; horses can be hired in neighboring **Wright Park**. Mansion House was
formerly the official residence of the US
Governor, and then until 1986 of the

*Right: The Ifugao have been cultivating their
rice-terraces for over 2000 years.*

presidents of the Philippines. All around
are villas belonging to families of the
Philippine elite, which, unlike the poorer
houses, have remained undamaged. The
"weekend cottages" of the Marcos family
are also among them. Igorot tribespeople
pose for the camera in threadbare traditional costumes. Poverty and cultural
change have forced them to sell themselves as photo souvenirs for a handful of
rice.

The crowds on the Sunday pilgrimage
to the **Lourdes Grotto** on **Mirador Hill**
at the western edge of town also hope for
better times. The blessing of the Virgin
Mary and a wonderful view over the
town, built on seven hills, are their reward for climbing 220 steps. Heading
southwest, one soon reaches the **Asin
Hot Springs**, where swimming-pools are
fed by naturally warm water.

A trip northward takes one into the
"salad-bowl of the Philippines," the valley of Trinidad, which is famous for the
European vegetables grown there. In **La
Trinidad**, the provincial capital, the
Benguet Museum provides a good preparation for your expedition into the
mountains. A side-road turns off to the
Ambuklao Reservoir. If you take the
breathtaking bus journey into the east of
the highland province, you will never
forget the hairpin bends and magnificent
ravines.

Ambuklao Reservoir is fed by the river
Agno and is one source of Manila's water
supply. A track follows its deep valley
upwards; to the right rises **Mount Pulog**,
at 2930 meters the second highest peak in
the Philippines. Beyond **Bokod** one
reaches **Kabayan**, which was a holy
place some 500 years ago. Evidence of
this are the numerous mummies dating to
that period that were found in the area,
mainly around **Mount Timbac.** The
ancient Ibaloi, who laid their dead naked
and bent double in wooden coffins, could
not foresee that 20th-century looters
would rob their ancestors of their final

dignity. For this reason some of the cata-combs are now closed. With the help of local guides it is possible to go hiking in the mountains, on the high **Pulog**, to see lakes and visit gold-mines.

Pine Forests and Rice Terraces

The journey of 150 kilometers along the Halsema Highway from Baguio to **Bontoc**, the capital of **Mountain Province**, is quite an experience. The road twists and turns for about eight hours through rough country with exciting, panoramic views, in some places at heights of over 2000 meters above sea-level. Travelers who have been jolted about all day can spend the night in the **Mount Data Hotel** and relax in front of an open fire. Bontoc, a small town nearly 900 meters high is mainly built of corru-gated iron, but is a good base for expedi-tions. Before starting, however, **Bontoc Museum** is a must.

A three-hour hike north leads to the fascinating stone rice terraces of **Maleg-cong**, whose superb architecture could scarcely be improved on. **Mainit** ("hot") is notable for its steaming sulphur springs and for the gold strikes that have been made there. The village of **Guinaang**, on the way back to Bontoc, still has a tradi-tional look.

Although very remote, **Sagada**, west of Bontoc, has become a rather popular destination for globetrotters. Its charm lies in the cool tranquillity of its setting, among pine woods and rice terraces, its plentiful supply of simple accommoda-tions, and the fine treks in the area, which could fill up days and even weeks. Sa-gada was the home of the photographer, the late Eduardo Masferré, whose pic-tures from recent decades portray his compatriots of Kalinga and Bontoc with a gentle understanding. There are also some mysterious catacombs, the so-called "Hanging Coffins," dug into the limestone mountain. But here, too, skele-tons have been stolen and the sacred place desecrated – as so often happens in the Philippines.

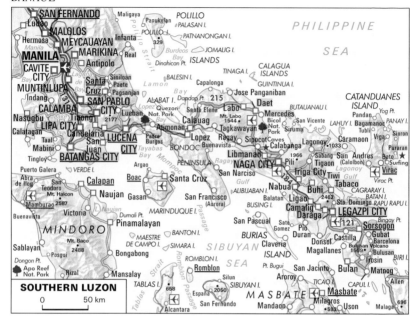

Until the early 1980s, **Bugnay**, a village on the river Chico in Mountain Province, was still untouched by the outside world. But too much tourism has destroyed the innocence of the villagers. They now charge you for taking photos and for compulsory guided tours, and muggings are not unknown. This kind of irritation can occasionally disrupt travel in Mountain Province and the Kalinga area. The controversial project to dam the Chico river has admittedly been halted, but the Kalinga have no delusions about their safety. There are too many valuable minerals beneath their feet, too many of their trees and rivers are a temptation to foreign companies looking for easy profits, and even a sympathetic tourist is, after all, an intruder in the land of their ancestors.

Still on sacred soil, the famous **rice-terraces of Banaue** in **Ifugao province** rise steeply upward. Around 2000 years ago the Ifugao, who had fled into the mountains, built these terraces at a height of 1200 meters. They considered the ter-

races a "staircase to the heavens;" tourists now see them as the eighth wonder of the world. The 50-kilometer bus ride from Bontoc to Banaue Valley takes three hours; from Manila it can be reached in a day. The nearby rice terraces, supported by clay walls are even more impressive.

The village of **Batad** nestles in an amphitheater of rice fields, its small, tin-roofed church contrasting oddly with the sublime backdrop. Rice-growing is still protected by two good spirits of the Ifugao, *Bu-lul* and *Lumauig*. Long may they preserve the terraces, which in 1995 were at last declared part of the UNESCO World Cultural Heritage.

SOUTHERN LUZON

Seen from space, the area known as Bicol, or **Southern Luzon**, might look like the gnarled branches of a tree. Jagged peninsulas alternate with deep inlets dotted with islands. The landscape is mountainous with a chain of volcanoes, crowned by Mount Mayon, north of Legaspi City. **Bicolandia**, this chaotic jumble of peninsulas is joined to Luzon by no more than a narrow bridge of land and comprises the four provinces of Camarines Norte, Camarines Sur, Albay and Sorsogon. Geographically, the adjacent southern part of Quezon province and **Catanduanes Island** also belong to it, and, politically, so does Masbate Island. The climate of this region, washed by the Pacific, is characterized by frequent violent typhoons, like the rest of Luzon. Otherwise there are no distinct seasons; the rain falls in equal measure all year round. This favors agriculture, as do the fertile lava fields, and so the area has been settled since earliest times.

When the Spanish landed in Bicol in the 16th century, the people living there called themselves and their land *Ibalon*. It is possible that they had migrated from Borneo some 300 years earlier. According to a legend passed down by the Spanish, they were survivors of a battle fought by three heroes against terrible monsters. At first the Spanish were interested in the veins of gold in Camarines Norte, then the town of Legaspi on the Gulf of Albay became the center of the region thanks to the galleon trade. Nowadays, as well as its fishing industry and copra production, Bicolandia is an important supplier of *abaca*, better known as Manila hemp.

With its superb views and beaches, Bicol is a rewarding side trip when exploring the southern part of the archipelago. You will want to go on mountain tours and trips to lakes such as Lake Buhi, the home of what is allegedly the world's smallest fish. The people of Bicol are warm-hearted and friendly; and known for their love of hot, spicy food.

Driving from Manila to Legaspi City takes a full day along a 540-kilometer stretch of the Pan-Philippine Highway. For travellers weary of the roads, Bicol offers something special – a trip with the Bicol "Express," the last public railway-line in the Philippines.

The Southern Part of Quezon Province

Coming from Manila, you could postpone your arrival in Bicol and make a detour by leaving the main road, which runs from north of Laguna de Bay in a south-easterly direction. Near **Siniloan** there is a turning on to a minor road which crosses the Sierra Madre and ends at **Infanta** on the Pacific. From here, and from nearby **Real**, boats leave for the small archipelago of the **Polillo Islands,** which are scarcely known to tourists.

From **Santa Cruz** on the southern shore of Laguna de Bay, a bumpy road leads to **Lucena City**, the capital of **Quezon Province**. Lucena City itself is of no particular interest, but the buses from Manila usually make a fairly long stop here before continuing the journey south. From the small harbor at **Cotta** close by, you can be ferried over to the island of **Marinduque**. There is little pleasure to be had on the town's polluted Dalahican beach, but a plunge into the **Quezon National Park**, which is half an hour by jeepney, east of Lucena can be recommended. Although wood is cut here to fuel the limestone-grinding mills on the north side of the park, there is still a great deal of virgin jungle standing, which is a real delight to walk through. With a bit of luck you might spot a hornbill or meet a troop of mischievous monkeys.

The coastal village of **Padre Burgos,** southeast of Lucena, faces a pair of islands, **Pagbilao Grande** and **Pagbilao Chico**, in Tayabas Bay. Wind and water have hollowed out many small caves in these coral islands. There is a legend which says they were born of a Romeo-and-Juliet love-affair between the wind-god and a beautiful mortal. On the other hand, an all-too-real suicide was committed on Pagbilao Chico by hundreds of stranded Japanese in World War II. To escape the shame of captivity they leapt to their death from **Estamper Point.**

Camarines Norte and Camarines Sur

The National Highway leads quickly to **Atimonan** on the north coast. The peaceful small-town atmosphere makes it a pleasant place for an overnight stay, and there is an old **church** to visit. You can take a boat from to the unspoilt **Alabat Island**, a little way offshore.

The journey further east follows. a coast lined with mangroves; the villages along here seem sleepy and forlorn. **Daet**, the capital of **Camarines Norte Province**, has more charm and one of the loveliest beaches in the region. **Bagasbas beach**, 3.5 kilometers outside Daet, is practically deserted except for a few fishermen. From Daet, it is a walk of an hour-and-a-half along the beach to the picturesque fishing-village of **Mercedes.**

Unless you want to laze around on the island of **Apuao Grande** you should go

Above: Farmworkers and water-buffalo return home from work in Camarines Norte.
Right: Coconut harvest near Mercedes.

inland from Daet for an object lesson in how *not* to manage the environment. **Bicol National Park** reveals what human folly has contrived to do with the once abundant local flora. A host of signs at the entrance invite you to come and experience nature, but the park in fact no longer exists. May it rest in peace! Hundreds of poor smallholders, some of them settled there by unscrupulous local politicians, have turned the area, which was once virgin jungle, into a black desert. Anything that still struggles to grow simply shrivels in the hot sun. Not even the fast-growing silver acacias on both sides of the road can hide the wasteland.

Naga, capital of **Camarines Sur Province**, has a dash of metropolitan style. It boasts good hotels and restaurants, and in ice-cream parlors and discos one encounters the poised natural manners that distinguish the Bicolanos. Founded 1575 as *Nueva Caceres* by Spaniards from Extremadura on the site of an Ibalon settlement called Naga, the town ranks as one of the oldest in the Philip-

pines. Nevertheless, though the Europeans established themselves here early, they also soon tired of it. Repeated uprisings by the *Indios* forced the Spanish to withdraw from Bicol even before it was taken over by the Americans. Barring one tower, the **Church of San Francisco**, built in 1578, was destroyed by an earthquake in 1915 and was replaced by a rather ugly new building.

The **Quinze Martires Monument** in the square opposite the church commemorates 15 patriots from Naga who were executed by the Spanish in 1896. A further building from the time when the Franciscans held sway in Bicol is **Naga Cathedral**. Built in 1595 and destroyed several times by fire, earthquakes and typhoons, it was last rebuilt in 1890.

A high old time is had in Naga during the third weekend in September each year, when the River Parade in honor of the Virgin of Peñafrancia, patron saint of all Bicolanos, keeps the town and its surrounding area jumping with excitement. The main attraction of the festival which is pious as well as jolly, is a miraculous portrait of the Virgin Mary that was brought over from Spain. The festivities last for seven days; the icon is devoutly worshipped in the Cathedral and then carried back in a splendid procession of river craft, to its traditional shrine on the bank of the river Naga. Other attractions include waterfalls and springs near **Panicuason** in the east, and the caves near **Libmanan** in the northwest of Naga.

From near Pili there is an excursion to be made to **Sabang** on the Gulf of Lagonoy, where swordfish are caught. If you want to look over an unusual sort of shipyard, stay on the same road and call in at the German firm of "Buddl-Bini" in **Tigaon**. It builds large numbers of dredgerboats for the export market.

The next town of any size on the way south is **Iriga City**, a regional center of commerce. It is dominated by **Iriga volcano**, also known as Mount Asog which is 1140 meters high. The Agta people, the "negritos" of Bicol, live on its upper slopes, on the land of their fathers, who

97

are thought to have been among the original inhabitants of these islands. Recent research has shown that even at the beginning of the 17th century, this now peaceful mountain was a volcano in the shape of a perfect cone, like its big brother Mayon in the southeast. Some time before 1650 a powerful explosion must have shattered the southwestern half of Iriga and, by depositing debris, created **Lake Buhi** nearby.

This picturesque stretch of water lies 15 kilometers east of Iriga and is inhabited by a Filipino superlative, "the smallest edible fish in the world." It is only due to the very strict control by the fishery authorities, that the *sinarapan*, less than one centimeter in length, has survived in these waters. They had previously been fished mercilessly with fine mesh nets. The lake and the pretty village of **Buhi** are definitely worth visiting. There are boat-trips and walks to the nearby waterfalls, and in Buhi's town hall a shoal of the tiny fish swim in an aquarium.

The Filipinos like to erect religious statues in places with particularly beautiful views. This is the case in Iriga City, where the shrine to the Virgin Mary, called the **Emerald Grotto**, has a panoramic view over the landscape and the mighty volcanoes. From the highest point of the grotto all the Bicol chain of volcanoes is visible on a clear day, except for Mount Bulusan in Sorsogon: Iriga, Masaraga, Mayon and Malinao on the right, and Isarog on the left – combine to make a truly majestic scene.

Albay and its Beautiful, Angry Volcano

Mayon, at 2462 meters, one of the highest peaks in the Philippines, is extolled as "the most nearly perfect conical vol-

cano." This may be rather an exaggeration, but it is certainly a beautiful mountain. And that is what the Bicolano word *magayon* in fact means: beautiful. However, the behavior of this elegant giant can sometimes be quite horrible. Towering right on the edge of the Philippine rift valley, at a point where, deep below ground, the Eurasian and Philippine tectonic plates grind against each other, the volcano is under constant pressure from the magma pushing up beneath it. Mayon is one of the most active volcanoes in the country and also one of the most destructive, because of the density of the surrounding population. It has erupted with devastating consequences several times since its first documented outburst in 1616. The violent explosion on February 1, 1814 represents the worst incident so far in its "career." Several villages were completely destroyed and over 1200 people died. All that remained visible of the little town of **Cagsawa** was the top of the church tower – everything else was buried under avalanches of mud. The survivors built a new church and the settlement of **Daraga** nearby. The most recent big eruptions took place in 1984 and 1993; no doubt there will be others. When it is at peace, the mountain is a fascinating place for climbing, although the ascent takes at least two days and is by no means easy. Near the crater the climbing is particularly difficult and in places even dangerous. But then the impact of the view from the summit makes up for all the effort.

Legaspi City, named after the first governor-general of the Philippines, Miguel Lopez de Legazpi, was not founded until 1639. As the present capital of **Albay Province**, at the foot of Mayon, it is worth a visit, especially for the delightful country surrounding it. The town itself does not have any real tourist sights, but the atmosphere is friendly. In the **market** you can buy a lot of handicrafts, mostly made from abaca, and of course

Right: The Mayon volcano rises majestically above Legaspi.

the speciality of Bicol, the elongated *pili* nut. In the **Church of St Raphael**, built in 1834, stands a massive altar carved from a lump of volcanic rock. The **"Headless Monument"** by the harbor recalls the town's terrible suffering under the Japanese and commemorates the patriots who were killed.

Some 25 kilometers northwest of Legaspi City, near **Camalig**, are the **Hoyop-Hoyopan Stalactite Caves**. As part of a huge labyrinth in the limestone rock, they are not only home to countless bats but also have an archeological interest: In 1972 bone and burial gifts were found here probably dating back as much as 4000 years. Some of these can be seen in the little **museum** near Camalig church. This village at the foot of Mayon still has some fine 19th-century houses.

A long beach of lava stretches north for 11 kilometers from Legaspi City along the west coast of the Gulf of Albay. At the other end lies **Santo Domingo**, a pleasant village where the beach has a few facilities. Better places for bathing

can be found at the northern tip of the gulf; they can be reached by boat. One can also swim from the beaches on the islands of **Cagraray**, **Batan** and **Rapu Rapu**, whose attractions are clean water, white sands, good places for diving and, from the northern shores, magnificent views of the mighty Mayon.

In **Tiwi**, near the important seaport of **Tabaco**, north of Legaspi City, a huge thermal power station has been built. Until the early 1980s Tiwi was a sleepy spa. The electricity company brought life to the village but took away the steam from the vacation resorts.The spa-owners protested, but today few of the hot springs are in use. There is more activity, especially at weekends, at the lava beaches of sogod and Putsan, which however are not particularly enchanting.

Island of the Howling Winds

The ferry from Tabaco to **Catanduanes** takes four hours. This island province has the reputation for being the

most peaceful place in the Philippines. People live here as one big family, and if there is trouble, then it is a family affair which does not concern the outside world. There is just one exception: two clans are sworn enemies, since each one claims to have rescued Ronald Reagan from the Pacific during World War II, after he was forced to ditch his aircraft in the sea. Several of the old people even swear they wiped the blood from the forehead of Ronnie the "war hero."

The truth is that Reagan was playing small roles in Hollywood movies at the time and never left the States throughout the war. This is how the Catanduanese have earned a name among the other Filipnos for being dumb. Maybe they amuse themselves with these stories when wild storms are raging through the night, for Catanduanes certainly gets its fair share of typhoons. The island, with an area of 151,148 hectares, stands like a

Above: A boy on Catanduanes Island. Right: A Negrito and his son return from fishing.

breakwater far out in the Pacific, and almost all of the 20 or more tropical storms each year thunder with their full force against this bulwark. Anything that has been newly built or planted is quite likely to be swept away the next day. Consequently, patience is the chief quality of the people who live on the "Island of the Howling Winds."

The visitor will not want to spend long in **Virac**, the capital of the province, but the east coast is very picturesque. Empty beaches, like the one near **Puraran**, 30 kilometers northeast of Virac, alternate with wild, jagged cliffs, where the heavy swell of the ocean breaks into seething surf. Swimmers, and surfers must beware of strong currents. The untamed climate and power of the ocean repeatedly destroy the simple beach accommodation. There is a quiet, better-built complex at Bosdok beach, 12 kilometers southwest of Virac, near Magnesia.

Treasure-hunters can try to locate three sunken galleons: the *Espíritu Santo*, which went down in 1576, is probably

off **Sioron**, the *Santo Tomás* is said to have been wrecked in 1601 near **Bagamanoc**, and the *San Gerónimo* has lain since 1600 off the **Horadaba Rock**.

The thickly-wooded interior of the island also promises adventure. If you only know the products of abaca, but not the plant itself, you can learn about it on Catanduanes. You will need plenty of time, since there are very few motorized vehicles on the island; and that is part of its austere charm.

At the Tip of Luzon

Sorsogon, the capital of Sorsogon Province, lies on a wide semicircular bay. There is not much of interest in the town apart from its colorful market. In **Gubat** on the Pacific coast, half an hour away by bus, there is more. South of Gubat stretches the five-kilometer **Rizal Beach**, so clean that it sparkles. The water is clear and the Pacific sends in a fine swell. Except for weekends and public holidays, the place is deserted, lonely in fact. A few

more or less plesant resorts provide accommodation. Along the rest of this stretch of coast there is a colossal offshore reef, 60 kilometers long. The diving is good – for those strong and experienced enough to hold their own against the current and the surf.

The next place south is called **Barcelona**, though the name is the only thing it has in common with the Catalan capital. But when one reaches **Bulusan** the country does begin to look "European." The district around the 1559-meter-high mountain of the same name, a sporadically active volcano, is called "Philippine Switzerland." This is not pure fancy: the countryside is not only lush and green, but astonishingly clean. The magnificent **Mount Bulusan,** with the idyllic **Lake Bulusan**, lying at a height of 600 meters, is a landmark for ships as it is visible for many miles.

From here it is not far to **Matnog** at the tip of Luzon. Across the dangerous **St Bernardino Strait** the island of Samar can just be seen.

CENTRAL LUZON

Accommodation

LUXURY: **TERNATE**: Novotel Resort Puerto Azul, Tel: 5259248. **Caylabne Bay Resort Resort**, Tel: 7321051. **TAGAYTAY: Club Estancia Resort Hotel,** Tel: 4131331. **Punta Baluarte Resort**, Calagtan (20 km south of Matabungkay), Tel: Manila 8924202. Near **ANILAO: Aqua Tropical Resort**, Tel: Manila 5216407. **Hidden Valley Springs Resort**, Tel: Manila 8144034.

MEDIUM-PRICED: **TAGAYTAY: Taal Vista Lodge**, Nat. Rd., Tel: 4131223. **Milos Paradise**, Balas (Taal Lake). **NASUGBU: Maya-Maya Reef Club**, diving, Manila 8108118. **White Sands Beach Resort**, Tel: Manila 8335608. **Anilao Seasport Centre**, Mabini, Tel: Manila 8011850. **LOS BAÑOS: City of Springs Resort**, Villegas St., Tel: 5360731. **SAN PABLO: Villa Escudero**, Tiaong (10 km to the south), Tel: Manila 5232944. **Pagsanjan Falls Lodge**, Tel: 6451251.

BUDGET: **SAN NICOLAS: Lake View Park & Resort**. **LOS BAÑOS: Los Baños Lodge** (near the City of Springs Resort). **BATANGAS CITY: Avenue Pension**, 30 Rizal Ave., Tel: 7253760. **Grethel Beach Resort**, Lobo (30 km southeast of Batangas). **PAGSAN-JAN: Camino Real Rizal St.,** Tel: 6452086**. River-side Bungalow**, Garcia St., Tel: 6452465.

Getting There
Means of Transportl

BUS: From Manila: BLTB Terminal Pasay City.

CENTRAL PLAINS

Unterkunft

MEDIUM: **ANGELES: Sunset Garden Hotel**, Malabanas Rd., Tel: 8882312. **Tropicana Resort Hotel**, Fields Ave. **Swagman Narra Hotel**, Orosa St. **CABA-NATUAN: Manrio Hotel**, Marhalika Rd.

BUDGET: **PULILAN: Calabao Lodge**, Doña Remedios Hwy. **SAN FERNANDO: Pampanga Lodge**. **ANGELES: New Liberty Inn**, MacArthur Hwy. **BALER** (Aurora): **Baler Guest House**, Sabang, **MIA Surf & Sports Resort** (Sabang).

Getting There
Means of Transport

BUS: Buses daily to and from Manila, on the expressway via Dau; there possiblility to change for continuation of journey to San Fernando or Angeles by jeepney.

Tourist Information

SAN FERNANDO: DOT, Paskuhan Village, Tel: 9612665.

ZAMBALES-REGION

Accommodation

LUXURY: **INSEL CORREGIDOR: Corregidor Hotel**, Tel: Manila 5247141. **BATAAN: Montemar Beach Club**, Mariveles, Tel: Manila 8153490. **OLONGAPO**: Subic International Hotel, Sta. Rita Rd., Tel: 8882288. **SAN FABIAN: Presidential Resthouse**, Bolasi.

MEDIUM-PRICED: **OLONGAPO: Subic Bay Garden Inn**, National Highway, Tel: 2224550. **IBA: Palmera Garden Beach Resort**, Bagantalinga, National Rd. **LINGAYEN: Lingayen Gulf Resort**, Prov. Capitol Ground (on the beach). **DAGUPAN: Victoria Hotel**, A.B. Fernandez Ave. **Snow White Inn**, Bonuan (Tondaligan Beach, 3 km out of town).

BUDGET: **OLONGAPO: Ram's Inn**, Rizal Ave. **IBA**: **Vicar Beach Resort** (outside town). **HUNDRED IS-LANDS NAT. PARK: Alaminos Hotel**, Alaminos, Quezon Ave. **LUCAP** (at the ocean, northeast of Alaminos): **Ocean View Lodge**. **BOLINAO: A&E Garden Inn**, near Five Star Bus Terminal. **Celeste Seabreeze Resort**, central, at the ocean. **LINGAYEN**: **Lion's Den Resort**, Lingayen Beach. **DAGUPAN**: **Vicar Hotel**, A.B. Fernandez Ave.

Museum

BOLINAO: Regional Museum, Mon - Fri 9 am - 12 noon, 1 - 5 pm.

Getting There / Means of Transport

BUS: Bataan, Mariveles: several times daily with Philippine Rabbit. Zambales: Victory Liner. Pangasinan: Victory Liner, Pangasinan Five Star, Dagupan Bus. *SHIP:* Insel Corregidor: Organized day trips (Sun Cruises) from Ferry Teminal, Manila, near CCP. Info: Tel: 8318140.

ILOCANDIA / CAGAYAN VALLEY

Accommodation

LUXURY: **BAUANG: Cresta del Mar**, Paringao, Tel: 413297. **LAOAG: Fort Ilocandia Resort Hotel**, Calayab, Tel: 7721167. *MEDIUM-PRICED:* **BAUANG**: **Cesmin Beach Cott.**, Pagdalagan Sur, Tel: 412884. **Villa Estrella Beach Resort**, Paringao, Tel: 413794. **Cabaña Beach Resort**, Paringao (diving courses), Tel: 412824. **SAN FERNANDO: Plaza**, Quezon Ave., Tel: 412996. **Blue Lagoon**, Canoay (Bay of Poro), Tel: 412531. **Sunset German Beach**, San Juan (9 km to the north). **VIGAN: Cordillera Inn**, M. Crisologo St. **Ancieto Mansion**, M. Crisologo St. **LAOAG: Hotel del Norte**, Pr. Lazaro St. **CURRIMAO: Villa na Pintas, Poblacion 1**, Tel: 7922917. **TUGUEGARAO**: **Callao Cave Resort**, Peñablanca, Tel: 8441801. *BUDGET:* **BAUANG: Hideaway Beach Resort**, Baccuit. **SAN FERNANDO: Ocean Deep Resort**, San Francisco(diving course). **Hacienda Beach Resort**, Urbiztondo (5 km to the north). **VIGAN**: **Vigan Hotel**, Burgos St. **BANGUED** (Abra): **Marysol Pension House**, Taft St. **LAOAG: Pichay Lodging**, M. Nolasco St. **PAGUDPUD** (60 km north of Laoag): **Villa del Mar**. **BATANES-INSELN**: In the town BASCO: **Mama Lily's Pension**. **CLAVERIA: Company House**, Taggat (west of town). **APARRI: Pipo Hotel**, Macanaya District (before Aparri). **Ryan Mall**, Rizal St., Tel: 22369. **TUGUEGARAO: Hotel Leonor**, Rizal St., Tel: 8441806. **Delfino**, Bonifacio St./Gonzaga St., Tel: 8441952. **CAUAYAN: Amity**, National Hwy. **SANTA FE: Golden Rose**.

Getting There / Means of Transport
BY AIR: PAL flies several times weekly Manila-San Fernando, Laoag City, Basco (Batanes Islands), Tuguegarao, Cauayan. *BUS:* several times daily from Manila via Angeles City (Dau), Baguio-San Fernando, Vigan, Laoag City: Phil. Rabbit, Times Transit. To Aparri, Tuguegarao: Baliwag Transit Co..

Museums
AGOO: Museo Iloko, daily 9 am - 12 noon, 1 - 5 pm. **SAN FERNANDO: Museo de La Union**, Mon - Fri 9 am - 12 noon, 1 - 5 pm. **VIGAN: Ayala Museum**, Burgos House, Tue - Sun 9 am - 12 noon, 2 - 5 pm. **LAOAG CITY: Ilocandia Museum of Traditional Customs**, Mon - Fri 8 am - 12 noon, 1 - 5 pm. **BATAC: Marcos Museum**, daily 8 am - 12 noon, 1 - 5 pm. **TUGUEGARAO: Provincial Museum**, Mon - Fri 9 am - 12 noon, 2 - 5 pm.

CORDILLERA CENTRAL

Accommodation
LUXURY: **Vacation Hotel Baguio**, Leonard Wood Rd., Tel: 4424545.
MEDIUM-PRICED: **BAGUIO: Burnham**, Calderon St., Tel: 4422331. **New Belfrant**, Gen. Luna St., Tel: 4425012. **Supreme**, Magsaysay Ave., Tel: 4432011. **Woods Place Inn**, Military Cut-off, Tel: 4424641. **Baguio Palace**, Legarda Rd., Tel: 4427734. **Mountain Lodge**, 27 Leonard Wood Rd., Tel: 4424544. **Mount Data Hotel**, Bauko, Tel: (Manila) 8121984. **BANAUE: Banaue Hotel**, Tel: 3864087.
BUDGET: **BAGUIO: Highland Lodge**, Gen. Luna Rd. **Benguet Pine Inn**, Chanum/Otek St. **Casa Vallejo**, Session Rd. Ext. **BONTOC: Pines Kitchenette & Inn** (central). **SAGADA: Sagada Guesthouse**. **St. Joseph Resthouse**. **Masferré Inn**. **Mapiyaaw Pensione**. **BANAUE: Fairview Inn**. **Halfway Lodge**. **Stairway Lodge**. **J&L Pension**. **Banaue Youth Hostel**. **BATAD: Batad Pension**. **Christina's Guesthouse**.

Getting There / Means of Transport
BY AIR: PAL several times per week Manila-Baguio. *BUS:* Phil. Rabbit, City Trans, Dagupan Bus Victory Liner. Baguio-Bontoc: Dangwa Tranco Co. Bontoc-Sagada: Jeepney. Baguio-Banaue: Dangwa Tranco Co. Bontoc-Banaue: Bus and jeepney. Manila-Banaue: Dangwa Tranco Co. (9 hours).

Tourist Information
S. FERNANDO, LA UNION: DOT, Mabanag Hall, Capitol Hill, Tel: 412411. **BAGUIO: DOT**, Tourism Complex, Gov. Pack Rd., Tel: 4426708 / 4427014.

Museums
BAGUIO: Mountain Province Museum, Camp John Hay, Tue - Sun 9 am - 12 noon, 1:30 - 5 pm. **BONTOC: Museum** (Ethnography), daily 8 am - 12 noon, 1 - 3 pm.

SOUTH LUZON

Accommodation
MEDIUM-PRICED: **LUCENA: Travel Lodge**, Isabang Distr., Tel: 714489. **Lucena Fresh Air**, Isabang Distr., Tel: 712424. **ATIMONAN: Victoria Beach Resort**, Maharlika Hwy. Bei **DAET/MERCEDES: T.S Resort**, Apuao Grande Island (Res.: Swagman Hotel, Manila). **NAGA: Crown**, Burgos St., Tel: 212585. **Moraville**, Dinaga St., Tel: 8111807. **IRIGA: Parkview**, S. Roque St., Tel: 92405. **Ibalon**, S. Francisco St., Tel: 92352. **LEGASPI: La Trinidad**, Rizal St., Tel: 22951-55. **Legaspi Plaza**, Lapu-Lapu St., Tel: 243085. **Victoria**, Rizal St., Tel: 243476. **SANTO DOMINGO: Reyes Beach Resort**. **VIRAC: Bosdok Resort**, Magnesia. **BULUSAN: Villa Luisa Celeste Resort**, Dancalan. *BUDGET:* **LUCENA: Tourist Hotel**, Iyam Distr., Tel: 714456. **DAET: Karilagan**, Moreno St., Tel: 7212314. **NAGA: Sampaguita Inn**, Panganiban Drive. **PILI: El-Alma**, Old S. Roque. **IRIGA: Lemar's**, S. Nicolas St. **LEGASPI: Catalina's Lodging House**, Penaranda St., Tel: 23593. **Tanchuling Internat.**, Tel: 22747. **Legaspi Tourist Inn**, Lapu-Lapu St., Tel: 23533. **SANTO DOMINGO: Sirangan Beach Resort**. **TABACO: VSP Hotel**, Riosa St. **TIWI: Youth Hostel & Mendoza's Resort**. **VIRAC: Catanduanes Hotel**, San José St., Tel: 8111280. **Sandy's Pension**, Piersite. **SORSOGON: Dalisay Lodge**, Peralta St. **BULUSAN: Villa Luisa Celeste**, Dancalan.

Getting There / Means of Transport
BY AIR: PAL and other airlines several times weekly Manila-Daet, Naga, Legaspi City-Virac. *RAIL:* Manila-Calamba, Lucena, Ragay. *BUS:* Manila-Lucena-Daet-Naga-Legaspi City: Philtranco, BLTB, Superlines, J.B. Bicol Express Line. Direct service to Matnog, further connections to Tacloban or Davao: Philtranco.

THE MIDDLE ISLANDS

MINDORO / MARINDUQUE
ROMBLON ARCHIPELAGO
MASBATE
VISAYAS:
SAMAR / LEYTE
PANAY / NEGROS
SIQUIJOR / CEBU / BOHOL

Once the traveler has left the vast northern island of Luzon, there is a confusingly large number of islands to choose from. However, the efficiency of transport varies widely, as many regions are still undeveloped; so "island hopping," simple as it may sound, demands considerable time and perseverance.

This island world is one of contrasts, both geographical and cultural. There are flat atolls and sandbanks, miniature islands which you can practically wade across to at low tide; some islands consist entirely of mountains which form steep coastlines, and are still covered with virgin forest. Some islands are known to the outside world, if at all, for a single beach resort, while others have made tourism the most important element of their economy. In some places, individual families have controlled the destiny of the islanders for generations, and still manage to maintain a certain independence from Manila. Bitter poverty and exploitation frequently drive people to migrate in large numbers to the population centers.

For some regions annual typhoons, flooding and drought are the rule, while others are more like the Promised Land, with plenty of rice to go round and everyone making a comfortable living. On some islands you will find people leading a way of life practically unchanged since the Stone Age, in complete harmony with nature – only a few kilometers from modern civilization with its noise, air-pollution and over-population.

Contrasts like these are typical of the middle of the archipelago which, as well as the islands belonging to Luzon's provinces, includes Mindoro and Marinduque, the Romblon group, the island of Masbate, administered from Bicol, and the many islands of the Visayas.

Linguistically, the region is a melting-pot. In the west the mother tongue is still Tagalog, but in some areas it has been hybridized with the dialects of migrants from the Visayas or Bicol; the people of the island of Panay have to make themselves understood in four main languages. A varied geographical and cultural heritage is reflected in the people today. Unlike those in much of Luzon, the jolly Filipinos of the central islands are more often directly descended from Malay migrants and Spanish conquerors. Even more than in the north, the indigenous peoples have been forced to retreat into the mountains and thus into a place of insignificance for society.

Previous pages: Sinulog Festival, third Sunday in January. Left: A masked dancer at the Ati-Atihan festival in Kalibo, Panay.

MINDORO

Arriving in Mindoro, one usually lands at Puerto Galera which was once a harbor for ocean-going galleons. The seventh largest of the Philippine Islands, it is divided into two provinces: Mindoro Occidental (west) and Mindoro Oriental (east). It is astonishing to find that this island, only five hours away from the vast city of Manila, is still one of the most unspoilt parts of the Philippines. In Puerto Galera, a tourist magnet with a highly dubious reputation, this is far from obvious. The northeast of Mindoro, with its regional center at Calapan, is also well developed, and is known as one of the "rice-bowls" of the Philippines. Similarly, San José in the south of the island is quite important and even has an airport, while smaller planes land at Mamburao in the northwest.

Yet apart from these three keystones of its infrastructure, the island is more like pioneer country. The major highway between Puerto Galera and Calapan has been rebuilt but parts of it are still knee-deep in mud after heavy rain. A western route was long supposed to be constructed for use all year round. But the rainy climate, difficult terrain and frequent earthquakes make the construction of a continuous coast road unrealistic.

This is particularly true of the west, where countless rivers from the mountainous interior run into the South China Sea. Here the rainy season in the middle of the year can assume the proportions of Noah's Flood, and not infrequently a whole section of road will simply disappear. Apart from the coastal ring road which has been worked on for years, there are no permanent highways on Mindoro.

The interior of the island, which has a surface area of about 10,000 square kilometers, is dominated by a chain of mountains running from northwest to southeast. And although the chain-saw

THE MIDDLE ISLANDS

0   50   100 km

has been hard at work, there are still sizeable tracts of jungle on the slopes.

The name Mindoro originated with the Spanish, who arrived here in 1570. Thenceforth the island was called *Minas de oro* ("goldmines"), and at that time its inhabitants were already exporting the precious metal to China in barter trade. Long before the Europeans arrived, migrants from Borneo had Mindoro under their control and were able for a while to defend the west of the island, in particular, against Spanish incursions. Gold is still extracted today, albeit in small quantities. The most productive deposits are in Baclayan near Puerto Galera, and around Santo Tomás on the northern slopes of Mount Calavite. Both places are worked almost exclusively by the Mangyan, the original inhabitants of Mindoro.

It is the Mangyan people who give the island its special charm. Six main groups,

Above: Riding a carabao (water-buffalo) is fine if you're not in a hurry. Right: A jeepney trip through Mindoro on very rural roads.

numbering around 80,000 in total, live on Mindoro. They have their own languages and even a syllabic writing system which may have come to the Philippines from India in the 13th century. The Mangyan are peaceful, reticent forest-dwellers who often reject the achievements of modernity in the surrounding area. So-called civilization has treated them badly. The "Tagalog," predominantly immigrants from the Ilocos and Visayas provinces, for example, gave them almost nothing in compensation for grabbing their land and stripping their forests bare. Thus, with a few exceptions, the Mangyan are anxious to preserve their own identity. They follow ancient traditions, and mostly reject any clothing other than their customary loincloth. Thanks to European missionaries, who have supported the Mangyan in their quest for self-assurance, these aboriginals have frequently succeeded in asserting their rights. Officially the Philippine government now supports them, as do some (occasionally) over-zealous international organizations.

A Journey Round the Island

In **Puerto Galera**, the tourist magnet of Mindoro, the church has prevailed upon some of the Mangyan to exchange their loincloths for jeans and T-shirts. You now see all the more naked flesh on the beaches in the region, and prostitution in not unknown. Manila and the bars of Ermita, from where the clients and the "working-girls" come, are not so far away, and many of the latter stay. The atmosphere in and around Puerto Galera has definitely changed for the worse. Drugs, theft and serious crime, even the murder of foreigners, shape its reputation. Since the mid-1990's the tourist authorities have been trying to improve the town's image, by developing exclusive hotel and club complexes.

At the same time, it is hard to deny the scenic charm of Puerto Galera. Anyone

arriving straight from the turbulence and crushing heat of Manila is bound to be smitten by the glowing panorama set amidst fresh green vegetation, the perfect natural harbor and the magnificent white beaches lapped by blue waters. Of the beaches around Puerto Galera, **Sabang** and **White Beach** will appeal to those who like company, while **Aniuan** and **Talipanan Beach** promise more peaceful pleasures. The **La Laguna beaches** are popular with divers and snorkelers.

Some foreigners have chosen to settle in Puerto Galera permanently – though the locals would prefer to see many of them depart again as soon as possible. Anyway, you do not have to stay here. Mindoro has so much more to offer. The jeepney ride from Puerto to Calapan in **Mindoro Oriental Province**, is a minor adventure in itself. The partially unsurfaced road runs in a series of crazy bends through the palm- and jungle-covered mountains along the coast and up to the impressive **Tamaraw Falls.** From here a wonderful view unfolds over the pic-turesque coastline with its intricate coastline of bays and creeks. A swimming pool and several restaurants tempt one to stay for a while. As one drives on, the mountains recede from the road, eventually giving way to paddy-fields. However, the colossal **Mount Halcon** massif, at 2587 meters, Mindoro's highest peak, continues to dominate the landscape.

Calapan, the island's most important port, is colorful and lively, as one would expect of a fast-growing capital. The ferries to Batangas, Manila and the Visayas are nearly always full to bursting. People, cattle, and goods of all descriptions share the transport.

Calapan is also the departure point for buses traveling round the east coast. They terminate at Bulalacao far to the south. This stretch of road leads first of all through flat rice-growing country. The beautiful **Lake Naujan**, in a nature conservation area, is the first change in the scenery on the way south; here several species of birds have breeding places. From now on the countryside is more

varied. South of the Dumali Point peninsula one comes to the little town of **Pinamalayan**, from where boats leave for the islands of Maestro de Campo and Banton (Sibali Islands) in the Romblon Archipelago.

Most bus routes finish at **Roxas**. The only reason to visit this hot, dusty hole is to head for the **Dangay** district from where you make the sea-crossing to the islands of Tablas and Boracay (off the northwestern tip of Panay). From November to February, however, there can be heavy seas in the Tablas Strait which is 80 kilometers wide. So even in fairly large outriggers one must be prepared for a rough and wet trip. Dangay itself is in a sheltered bay, where it is not possible to judge the conditions out in the open sea. Under no circumstances should one venture the crossing in a small boat.

Though the distance between them is not great, southern Mindoro has a completely different climate from the north. For months on end it is very hot and dry here, roughly from November until well into June. Uncontrolled deforestation has, moreover, turned large tracts of land into something like a desert. Areas of jungle exist only deep in the interior. The Mangyan people make their home here: some ragged looking characters will come as far as the road and sometimes even ask for lifts. To make contact with the "real" Mangyan, the best place is **Mansalay** and along the road southwards as far as Bulalacao. But one should not go there simply to photograph them and satisfy one's curiosity. These indigenous people do not allow themselves to be so degraded, and should never be confused with the Igorot of northern Luzon, who have lost touch with their roots and live by parading around for tourists.

Mansalay is a scruffy little town at the head of a charming bay. On the north side of the bay several pretty little islands make a striking contrast to the coastline, which is bare to the point of ugliness in

Above: Deserted beaches stretch right along the east coast of Mindoro.

parts. A seemingly endless, if not quite snow-white beach stretches along the southern edge of the bay, giving way mountainous cliffs. Only scattered villages are to be found in this direction.

At the time of writing the road from **Bulalacao** to San José is still in terrible condition; adventurous is the best word to describe it. The mountainous terrain, and the sort of obstacles that this throws up, especially in the rainy season, mean that the inhabitants of the two towns prefer to keep in touch by boat.

San José, an important town that also has an airport, holds few charms for the tourist. Nevertheless, many travelers spend a day here as it is the starting-point for boat journeys to Boracay and Palawan. Those who do so can find distraction and a modest tropical charm on the islands of **Ambulong** and **Ilin** – and Ambulong has a beach with amenities. There are also diving trips to the **Apo Reef**, a long way off the east coast, where, despite considerable environmental damage, lovers of underwater sport can still find pleasure. Tours inland from San José are also possible, such as the two-day trips via the **Queen's Ranch** to **Mount Iglit**, where up until a few years ago some of the last remaining dwarf buffalo (*tamaraw*) were still to be found.

North of San José, between the South China Sea and the high mountains of the hinterland, stretches a savannah reminiscent of the South African veldt. Roughly half-way up the coast, at the mouth of the river Bagong-Sabang, lies the little town of **Sablayan**. It is a good starting-point for expeditions to the idyllic Pandan Islands, the Apo reef and the interior of the island, for example, to **Mount Baco**, Mindoro's second highest peak, 2488 meters high. Mangyan tribesmen live in its forests but are shy people who prefer to avoid contact with strangers. Beyond Sablayan, beaches extend as far as the eye can see, punctuated by rivers which, in the rainy season, flow deep and wide.

Provided one has the stamina and a good pair of trekking-boots, it is possible to walk the whole of the west coast from San José to Mamburao, allowing for the occasional river-crossing by boat.

Mamburao, the capital of **Mindoro Occidental Province**, does not have much more to offer than San José, except a nicer atmosphere. There is a lovely drive to **Paluan**, along Paluan Bay, which forms the prominent hook in Mindoro's northwest corner, with **Mount Calavite** to the north behind it. The journey round the island continues from Mamburao along a pot-holed road to **Abra de Ilog** on the north coast. From the nearby coastal town of **Wawa** there are ferries to Batangas City on Luzon, and boats also leave, irregularly, for Puerto Galera. Since a road to Puerto Galera does not yet exist, those with sufficient energy can walk to Puerto's western **Talipanan Beach** along a 21-kilometer-long footpath. It runs right along the coast, past wonderful, lonely beaches and rushing jungle streams.

The **Lubang Archipelago**, in the northwest, comprises Lubang itself and the smaller islands of Ambil, Cabra and Golo. Administratively they form part of Mindoro. Lubang has no tourist facilities apart from air and sea connections with Manila, but it briefly hit the headlines in 1974 when a stray Japanese soldier was found, left over from the Second World War. Rather than surrender, he had gone into voluntary jungle exile. The most recent of these long-suffering heroes of the Rising Sun re-emerged in 1980, in the Mount Halcon region of Mindoro.

MARINDUQUE

Lying rather inconspicuously between Batangas and the Bondoc peninsula, half embraced by southern Luzon, the island of Marinduque enjoys a very quiet, rural existence. Apart from iron ore, gold and silver, the main mineral to be worked and

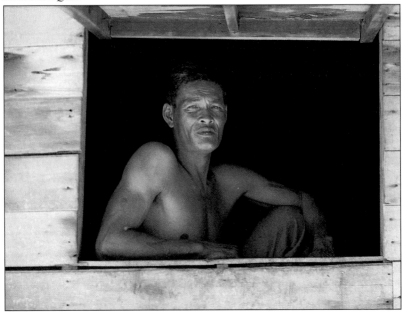

exported is copper. The Marinduqueros, most of whom originally came from Batangas and Quezon, grow rice and also live from the innumerable coconut-palms, the fruit of which is processed into copra. Fish abound in the waters around this mountainous island, where life is by and large peaceful and idyllic.

During Holy Week, however, peace reigns no longer, when the three small coastal towns of **Boac**, **Gasan** and **Mogpog** celebrate the *Moriones* festival, and are transformed into bustling stages for a Passion Play production. Crowds of townspeople dress up as Roman legionaries and figures from the Bible. The emblems of the island, masks combined with helmets, called *moriones*, are brought out and the "bloody melodrama" begins. And in fact real blood flows when a number of flagellants flay each other's backs. The man playing the part of Christ hangs on the cross, and then it is the mo-

Above: Waiting for the annual Passion Play to begin. Right: A wedding on Marinduque.

ment for the entry of Longinus, the principal role in the Marinduque version. Just as described in the Bible, the Roman centurion runs Jesus through with his spear. Blood spurts from the wound and splashes the soldier's blind left eye, whereupon he fully recovers his sight. The miracle converts Longinus to Christianty, much to the annoyance of Pontius Pilatus. A man-hunt ensues as Longinus is pursued over Marinduque's paddyfields and rivers, and up into the hills. Three times he is caught, and three times he manages to escape. The fourth time, he does escape: his captors drag him to the execution-block and triumphantly chop off his head – actually, his wooden mask.

For visitors there is no doubt that watching a baying mob masked as Romans giving chase to the unfortunate Longinus makes for an exciting spectacle. Bearded Europeans are especially sought after for walk-on parts. But the role of the hero must always be reserved for a local actor. In recent years, the festi-

val of *Moriones* may indeed have degenerated into something more akin to a carnival, but it continues to attracts hordes of visitors from the Philippines and abroad, and brings a handsome financial bonus to the island. The artistically carved *moriones* came originally from Mexico. They are popular as souvenirs, and selling them brings in some useful pocket-money for the actors. A resourceful craftsman extended the wood-carving business to wooden birds, and today whole flocks of these creatures keep a thriving cottage-industry busy. They are exported overseas by the container-load.

After the festival, the hectic activity on the island dies down very suddenly. Only a few jeepneys provide transport between the various communities, so one has good reason to explore the island on foot. The road from Boac, the provincial capital, to **Torrijos** on the east coast, is quite stunning. And at the other end the best beach on the island awaits with good spots for snorkeling. Marinduque's reputation as an excellent place for scuba-

divers to make for, is based particularly on the **Islands of the Three Kings** in the southwest and **Elefante Island** in the south. In 1980 the wreck of a junk, some 200 years old, was discovered off Gaspar, and Marinduque hit the international headlines. Divers came up with valuable pieces of Chinese porcelain. There are thought to be other ancient wrecks around Marinduque.

You can explore the depths of the earth in the **Bathala Caves** outside **Santa Cruz**, the largest town on the island. Santa Cruz has an imposing church, dating from 1714. If you prefer to scale the heights, you can climb the 1157-meter-high dormant volcano, **Mount Malindig**, starting at Buenavista.

THE ROMBLON ARCHIPELAGO

South of Marinduque, between Mindoro and Masbate, lies the **Romblon Archipelago**. The province consists of the three main islands, Romblon, Tablas and Sibuyan, and about 15 smaller ones.

The little town of Romblon is its undisputed center, officially called "Romblon on Romblon in Romblon." Fittingly, the motto of the locals is: "We're rumblin' on." And they seem to "rumble on" very happily. The place is one of the prettiest in the Philippines; the panoramic ocean views are reminiscent of the Mediterranean. The town nestles amid tropical greenery, with some delightful buildings from the colonial period, which immediately make the visitor feel welcome. **St Joseph's Cathedral**, founded around 1650 and completed at the end of the 18th century, is a fine example of classic Spanish architecture.

Romblon island is the country's main source of marble. Not always pure white, but often colorfully "marbled," the stone is quarried in great quantity and either shipped straight out or dressed here first. Fortunately the marble industry is very clean and does no damage to Romblon's largely unspoilt environment. This is particularly good news for the most beautiful part of the island, the beach and coast around **Bombon**, which is just three kilometers from Romblon town and can easily be reached on foot.

In nearby **Agnay** one can rent airy tree-houses right beside the sea and enjoy the sound of the waves and the chirping of cicadas. The rest of the island is very rural and not developed for tourism, so it is best to find somewhere to stay in Romblon town, Agnay or San Pedro, which is also a good base for excursions. The little islands of **Alad**, **Langen** and **Bansud**, off the north coast, are good for day-trips. There are also the islets **Lugbung** and **Cobrador**, adorned by white, peaceful beaches and with a few cottages.

Tablas, though the largest island in the archipelago, is less interesting. Travelers on their way to or from the more southerly holiday island of Boracay frequently break their journey – not always volun-

tarily – in **Odiongan** or **Looc**. North of **Alcantara**, **Tugdan Airport** provides the fastets connection between the Romblon Archipelago and Manila. On Tablas itself, however, there is little to see. The interior is mountainous and in places very bare. Only in the north does the coast have a certain charm. Here also are the **Hidden Lakes** near **Calatrava** and the **Mablaran Falls** near **San Andres**.

The mango-shaped island of **Sibuyan**, third largest in the Romblon group, consists principally of the **Mount Guiting-Guiting** massif. With a height of 2050 meters, it is scarcely in the alpine class, nevertheless it is considered very difficult to climb, and was not conquered until 1982. Near the summit, the mountainside has crumbled away in places leaving precipitous drops hidden by thick, moss-covered overhangs. These make treacherous obstacles for any climber. Sudden shifts in the weather are a further danger and have claimed a number of lives. This may have given rise to the legend that a huge magnet is hidden inside the mountain, which pulls in mountaineers, and even aircraft, to be engulfed in the moss.

Magdiwang, the island's main port and largest town, is the base for mountain-climbers. Those who shun the heights can set out from **Taclobo** on the south coast and walk through the glorious **Valley of the Cantingas**, or dive to the corals of the tiny island Cresta de Gallo.

The smaller islands, **Banton**, **Maestre de Campo** and **Simara** are also part of the Romblon Archipelago. Banton is known for its catacombs. Bamboo and coconut-palms grow on the islands and the islanders are genuinely hospitable. Boats leave for these islands from the harbor at Pinamalayan on Mindoro.

MASBATE

On the map, the island province of Masbate looks rather like a beat-up

Right: After a day's work, in a fishing village.

boomerang. Being so close to the Luzon provinces of Albay to the north and to Sorsogon to the northeast, Masbate Island and its two satellites, **Ticao** and **Burias**, politically form part of the Bicol region; geographically, though, they belong to the Romblon Archipelago.

The Spanish explored Masbate early on in the 16th century, and discovered a little gold. Later their galleons often called in at Ticao, before setting out for Mexico. Part of the forest on Masbate was cut down for ship-building and the ship-builders of the island enjoyed a good reputation in the colony. When gold-fever broke out near Aroroy, in the northwest, in 1900 the population began to increase dramatically. Today, although gold is still mined, the great days of prospecting for this precious metal are long past.

The island can certainly be called one of the most backward regions of the Philippines, but in a good as well as a pejorative sense. Their unaffected, rustic way of life, steeped in tradition, makes the is-

landers very endearing. But at the same time, the political and economic situation has earned Masbate the nickname of "Wild West." And that really means something in a country which is itself frequently decribed in those terms. The fact that Masbate goes in for cattle-ranching in a big way and that the island has become the main meat-producing region of the Philippines, only goes part of the way in explaining the cowboy image. The rough, tough reputation is reinforced by the prevailing code among the "Mister Bigs" – landowners, cattle barons and the like – whereby they settle differences of opinion, without further ado, by sending in their trigger-happy henchmen. Needless to say, the majority of Masbateños are hardly helped by this. The province is invariably near the bottom of the scale when the contributions of the different regions to the national GNP are compared.

That is not likely to change in the near future. Unlike the surrounding islands, Masbate does not have a particularly at-

117

tractive landscape. As a result of large-scale deforestation, to clear land for cattle-raising, the interior has for a long time not been as pleasant and green as the area around the provincial capital, **Masbate**. Some parts of the island bear a strong resemblance to the prairies of the American West, while elsewhere you might think you were in the arid Sahel zone.

Now and again one comes across stretches of coastline with attractive beaches, for instance near **Mobo** in the south of the island, or near the capital's suburb of **Tanod**; but there is no comfortable accommodation or half-way convenient transport for tourists.

So the population which consists predominantly of people from Luzon and the Visayas remains undisturbed and continues to make a living from fishing and farming

Above: A pedicab-driver waits for passengers. Right: A fishing-village in the north-west of Samar.

THE VISAYAS

The national flag flutters proudly in front of town halls all over the Philippines. This flag, first hoisted by Aguinaldo on June 12, 1898, is intended to symbolize the virtues of the Filipinos. A white triangle against a blue and red background, a sun with its rays and three shining stars. The color blue stands for peace, red for courage, and so in time of war is at the top of the flag, and white of course means purity. The sun represents freedom, and its eight rays are the eight provinces which rebelled against the Spanish. Luzon, the Visayas and Mindanao, the three islands groups of the Philippines, are portrayed as three stars.

The region of the Visayas has every right to be part of the national emblem. After all, its many islands and islets make up more than half the entire archipelago. In places they are distributed so thickly that even a small isle can be surrounded by host of yet smaller ones. The large masses of Panay, Negros and Cebu lie al-

most side by side. Together with the rounded Bohol they form the political region of the western and central Visayas. The twin islands of Samar and Leyte constitute the eastern region.

A mixture of peoples, languages and customs is found here. Peace and idyllic village life prevail, but urbanization is spreading.

Grinding poverty is driving many inhabitants of the coast and its hinterland out of their backwardness and into the bustling centers, as well as to other provinces. People from the Visayas are found all over the Philippines. They are noted for their sing-song way of speaking; and their love of life is proverbial. The almost fanatical dedication of the menfolk to cock-fighting, and the amused and studied casualness with which they confront the grim reality of life, are characteristics which other Filipnos smile at and perhaps secretly admire. This combination of an appealing mind set and a rich array of geographical advantages, has given the Visayas a head-start in the tourism race.

Apart from Samar and Leyte, the central and western islands have an extremely favorable climate. The year generally divides neatly into a dry season and a rainy season, with only occasional disturbances from typhoons or their accompanying troughs of low pressure. This tends to keep foreign visitors happily spending their money here for a good long season. The fact that several international airlines now run direct flights into Cebu, the hub of the island's transport network, underlines the key role of the Visayas in the tourist market.

Even the name "Visayas" originally came from abroad: migrants from the southwest settled on the central Philippine islands as early as the 13th century. They had fled from the tyranny of the Sultan of Borneo, a land which lay within the sphere of influence of the great Indianized empire of Sri Vijaya. The early settlers are known to have brought other things with them besides the name Visayas: they enriched the native dialects with words from Sanskrit and Tamil.

119

SAMAR

Samar, the third largest island of the Philippines, was the first point of land in Asia sighted by the lookout of Magellan's fleet in 1521. However, abiding by the principle of cautious reconnaissance in the smaller islands first, the European explorers sailed on past Samar and steered for the island of Humunu, now Homonhon, off its south coast. The shores of Samar must have seemed to Magellan too inhospitable to provide anchorage. And in that respect little seems to have changed.

Despite rich treasures beneath the earth and enormous expanses of forest, which until the beginning of this century still covered almost the entire island, and despite a wealth of fish in its waters, Samar is one of the poorest regions of the Philippines. The island is separated from South

Above: Rattan furniture – a lucrative home industry in the Visayas. Right: Blossom in the virgin forest on Samar.

Luzon by the treacherous **San Bernadino Strait**, and joined to Leyte in the south by the two-kilometer-long **San Juanico Bridge** and is very thinly populated, with around 2 million inhabitants. It is divided into the three provinces of East, West and North Samar. These include about 180 smaller islands.

There is very little tourism; the island lacks the superb beaches found elsewhere, and except for the concreted main road running along the west coast and on across to Leyte, the transportation network seems to have changed little since Magellan's day. Besides lying exposed to the typhoon belt, Samar also gets a great deal of rain throughout the year, except in May and June. Not surprisingly, travel turns out to be a muddy experience. As the activities of the NPA in Samar, as in the rest of the contry have dwindled away almost completely, Samar is given little attention or publicity by the local media.

Nevertheless, the raw charm of the island can win over the traveler who is not looking for luxury resorts and sensational attractions. The roaring breakers on the east coast, dense jungle in the interior, the lovely diving waters in the south – there is plenty to discover.

Traveling by land and sea, you normally come on the car-ferry from Matnog in South Luzon, landing either at **San Isidro** or **Allen** in northwest Samar. The three largest towns, **Catarman**, in the north, **Calbayog** and **Catbalogan** in the west, are not very inviting in themselves, but are good places from which to make excursions. Off the west coast lie the many little islands which dot the Samar Sea. Several good discoveries can be made here, for example, Dalupiri (San Antonio) southwest of Allen, where an Italian runs a beach facility.

In the middle of the untouched northeast coast, **Palapag** lies on a picturesque bay, where in earlier days sailors from Spanish galleons could stretch their legs after the stormy Pacific crossing.

The southeast coast more closely resembles the picture-book image of the tropical island, which Samar, right on the edge of the South Pacific, should ideally be. The little coastal town of **Borongan**, linked to the highway in the west by a new road, has a bay of clear water for swimming, and offshore islands where genuine solitude can still be found. Here and there the mangroves, which turn long stretches of Samar's coastline into impenetrable swamp, give way to long inshore reefs and silent lagoons.

The scene then becomes perfectly "South Pacific" on the narrow island (really a peninsula) which is linked to the mainland by low bridges south of the pretty little town of **Guiuan**, with a very beautiful church. Reaching out into the ocean, it rather resembles a worm-cast. Dangerous reefs with huge breakers surging over them alternate with quiet stretches of beach. On **Caliocan Island** practically the only people around are divers; risking life and limb, they bring up golden cowrie-shells. This "Blue Mauritius"

among shells can bring the finder a nice reward, assuming he emerges safely from the raging surf and swift currents.

From Guiuan you can also get to **Homonhon Island**. Here even the crunch of the sand under your feet has historic echoes, and everything seems just as it was when Magellan first set foot on the beach in March 1521. Halfway to the island magnificent reefs rise from the sea.

The rest of Samar's south coast is less varied. In **Balangiga** western visitors might be surprised at the friendly reception they receive, as it was the scene of a notorious massacre by American soldiers in 1901. In revenge for an attack by townspeople on their garrison, in which half the soldiers were slain, the colonial forces killed 10,000 Filipinos and terrorized Balangiga for two years. The commander responsible, General Smith, was dismissed after a public outcry in the USA. A memorial plaque recalls the brutal event, which seems in a grim way to have been a foreshadow of similar atrocities in Vietnam.

Basey in the southeast is the departure-point for the river trip to **Sohoton National Park**. This impressive system of stalactite caves has become Samar's leading tourist attraction. The Sohoton cave formations are among the most beautiful in the country; the journey there takes about five hours by river, followed by a short walk. Unfortunately the Samar islanders do not derive much revenue from the caves. Most visitors arrive directly from Tacloban on Leyte, which is no great distance, and pay for the trip there before they start.

But the Samareños are used to this sort of thing. Outsiders have always dropped by and grabbed whatever was in the way. In Marcos' time Samar was divided up like a cake so that its natural resources could be exploited. A highly profitable deal for some people, no doubt, but none of the proceeds ended up in the Samareños' pockets. Instead every year the ty-

Above: Primeval nature in Sohoton National Park. Right: One of 7107 islands.

phoons strike with monotonous regularity, and the birth-rate in Samar is soaring at an alarming rate. The poverty-stricken emigrate as far as Manila, where they become even poorer. The third largest island in the Philippines faces an uncertain future.

LEYTE

With an area of around 8,000 square kilometers Leyte only ranks eighth in size among the Philippine islands. However, it has contributed more than its share of important dates to the nation's history. At the beginning of April 1521 Ferdinand Magellan arranged for the first Catholic mass ever to be read on Philippine soil, on the island of Limawasa off Leyte's south coast. Several centuries later a certain Imelda was born here, destined to marry another Ferdinand. In 1944 General Douglas MacArthur waded ashore on the east coast, true to his promise that he would return and drive out the Japanese. In 1991, disastrous floods at Ormoc cost at least 7,000 lives, providing the nation and the world with conclusive proof that the wholesale felling of the rain forests would have to stop.

The island is rich in history, but offers a poor livelihood to the three million Leyteños. For the interior is taken up by an almost inaccessible mountain range, forcing the majority of the population to live on the coasts. Their chief source of income is copra production, along with the timber business and fishing. The inhabitants of Leyte belong to two linguistic groups: in the northeast and east they speak *Waray-waray*, while in the south and west, and in the neighboring islands, the language is *Cebuano*.

The capital and commercial center is **Tacloban** in the northeast. It is well worth paying a visit to the bustling harbor, and to wander round the market. Thanks to some good hotels and restaurants, a longer stay can be pleasant, and

Tacloban can even offer a bit of night-life. On the little offshore island of **Dio** stands a house once used by the Marcos family for entertaining guests: it is poss-ibly the most ostentatious of the many they built around the country. After the coup of 1986, people dug long but fruit-lessly for a treasure that the dictator was supposed to have buried here. Now this rather sinister house can be visited by the general public.

South of Tacloban, the east coast is not particularly interesting. In **Palo** you might think you see World War II sol-diers striding ashore: it is group of bronze statues depicting **MacArthur and his troops** – knee-deep in the sea – and com-memorates the beginning of the battle for the Philippines. **Tolosa**, where the former First Lady, Imelda, was born into her glit-tering world, is rather a dull little place.

Near **Dulag** you can start to explore the interior of the island. Cars drive as far as **Burauen**; after that you follow the footpath to Ormoc City on the west coast, about 40 kilometers away at the foot of the 1349-meter-high **Mount Lobi**.

Starting from Lake Danao, the route leads 40 kilometers along the picturesque lakes Casudsaran and Imelda to Lake Mahagnao in the Mahagnao volcanic Na-tional Park near Burauen.Tourism began here in 1981. Originally the trail, how-ever, rather like the Ho Chi Minh Trail in Vietnam, ended up mainly being used as a supply route for the NPA guerillas. The best starting point for walkers is the park entrance, which can be reached by bus from Tacloban and motor cycle taxi from Burauen.

About 20 kilometers south of Dulag, near **Abuyog**, the road leaves the cliff-girt coast, and heads into the mountains. Near **Sogod** the road divides. The eastern branch ends at the impressive high-level bridge across to **Liloan** on the island of **Panoan**. The other road, down the west side of Sogod Bay, brings you to **Padre Burgos** at the southern tip of Leyte. If

you want to tread in Magellan's footsteps again, you can be ferried from here to **Li-masawa Island** and there meditate on how that first mass, held by Magellan, determined the fate of the whole archipe-lago.

On the west coast, **Maasin**, the capital of South Leyte Province has some fine Spanish churches, as do **Hilongos** and **Baybay**. The next large town on the coast is the hapless **Ormoc City** in northern Leyte. Things are back to normal now, but even so the effects of the flood in 1991will be felt for many years to come. For the first, exemplary for the Philip-pines, blame was placed on environmen-tal sinners.

In the north the rural island of **Biliran**, since 1992 a province in its own right shapes the landscape. A bridge spans the narrow channel. The 1187-meter-high **Mount Biliran**, an extinct volcano, can quickly be climbed, if you take a jeepney ride to the can. From there it is only about one hour to the summit. And the romantic bay near **Almeria** is worth visiting.

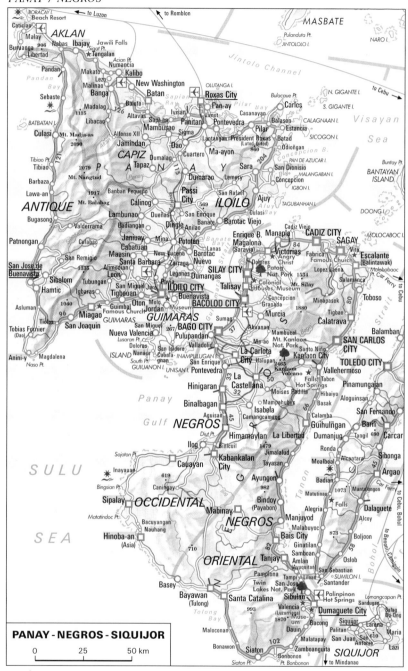

PANAY - NEGROS - SIQUIJOR

0   25   50 km

PANAY

Panay, the largest of the Visayas Islands, with an area of 11,700 square kilometers was one of the main goals of pre-Hispanic migrants. It comprises the four provinces of Iloilo, Atique, Aklan and Capiz. A number of offshore islands and Guimaras Province also belong to it. Topographically, Panay is divided into the inaccessible mountains of the western half, a large lowland plain in the center, and some moderately high mountains in the north-east. Rice is the chief product of the three million inhabitants, and Iloilo in particular, the largest province, is known as the southern "rice-bowl" of the Philippines. Sugar cane and the plentiful fish from the sea are also important sources of revenue for the island.

Culturally, the island is very varied. No less than four main dialects are spoken in different regions: *Hiligaynon* and *Kiniray-a* are spoken in Iloilo and Antique, *Capicenoño*, a mixture of these two, in Capiz province, and *Aklanon* in Aklan. However, the provinces do have one common denominator: They were all settled by migrating Malays, and the indigenous Ati subsequently migrated into the hinterland. Negotiations then took place for the valuable land, and folk-memories of these events can still be traced today, when they come alive in colorful annual festivals like the *Ati-Atihan* in Aklan, the *Dinagyang* in Iloilo and the *Binirayan* in Antique.

The Spanish, who first settled in 1566, at Ogtong, the present-day Oton, clearly did well for themselves on Panay, though ruined fortifications and massive churches along the south coast are a reminder that they frequently had to fend off attacks from envious Muslims and Europeans. The production of rice, and more importantly of sugar from the neighboring island of Negros, made Panay's capital, Iloilo, into a major port and trading center. As the tourist office there is careful to point out, the people of Iloilo were trading with Chinese, Arab, Persian and Indian merchants "long before Magellan was even going to kindergarten in Portugal." Under Spanish rule Iloilo thrived and became the second most important city in the colony after Manila. In 1896 it received the honorary title of *Muy Leal y Noble Ciudad* ("Most Loyal and Noble City").

Under US administration, Panay's star continued to ascend; agriculture and the infrastructure were developed and a railroad was built the along the length of the island. The Americans, too, gave Panay a title: "The Alaska of the Philippines," which referred to the lucrative fishing industry of the region. The chronicles of war would have been proud to say that the Ilonggos never submitted to Japanese occupation; indeed a bitter guerilla war raged throughout the island for the duration of the war.

Today **Iloilo City**, with over 400,000 inhabitants, is of course stricken by the same economic blight as the rest of the country. Many elegant Spanish villas from the heyday of the sugar trade have fallen into ruin. The railroad from Iloilo City to Roxas in the north was closed in the mid-1980s. The slum districts by the harbor are no different from those of any other big city in the archipelago. And yet you cannot overlook the symbols of habitual prosperity and the hope for better times to come. New hotels and department stores are being built, the airport and harbor are being modernized. Dense crowds jostle every day in the heart of the city, along **J.M.Basa Street** and its side-streets, under the arcades of old, mainly Chinese-owned shops; the intersections are jammed with hooting cars – and yet the pace is far from hurried. Amidst the traffic is one of the trade-marks of Iloilo: the Cadillac-styled jeepneys with their proudly gleaming chrome. These are gradually being replaced by trendily stripped-down vehicles, with limited

seating comfort and chiefly notable for the volume of their stereo equipment. Whether you opt for nostalgia or modernism, the jeepney is an excellent means of exploring Iloilo. The city likes visitors and even the gate of the prison on Bonifacio Drive has a sign saying "Welcome"!

Your tour of the city should start with a visit to the **Museo Iloilo**, also on Bonifacio Drive. The collection of ethnographic and historical items is presented in an easily understandable way, giving you a good overview of the region's past. Pride of place goes to the gold-leaf death-mask which was among the pre-Hispanic burial gifts found near Oton. You can also see some of the cargo of a 19th century English sailing ship that sank off Guimaras.

The **market** in the city center, on the corner of Iznart and Rizal Streets offers a wealth of local handcraft products, and

Above: At the Dinagyang festival the Ilonggos become exotic warriors. Right: A former Spanish villa near Fort San Pedro, Iloilo City.

needless to say a hive of activity around the fish and vegetable stalls. The nature-healers always have their conglomeration of native medicinal cures spread out on the pavement. In the little food stalls in the outer walls of the covered market you will be served *Batchoy*, the nourishing meat and noodle soup which is an Iloilo speciality popular throughout the land.

From the market you come into Rizal Street, which leads westward into Gen. Hughes Street, and on to **Fort San Pedro**, on the seaward side of Iloilo City. All that remains today of the fortress, built in 1617, are a few walls between which an open-air restaurant is situated.

Here, and in many other places, big crowds gather on the last weekend of January each year to celebrate the city's *Dinagyang* festival. A glittering parade of tribal groups in masks and costumes marches past, to remind local inhabitants and visitors of the ancient bargains struck between the Malays and the Ati. Not surprisingly, a Christian dimension has been added in the form of *Santo Niño*, the Christ-child. Another high point is the *Paraw* regatta, which takes place on the third weekend in February. This is an occasion for the helmsmen of the outriggers to show their skills as they skim swiftly across the Strait of Guimaras.

Historic buildings are rare in Iloilo City, but some beautiful Spanish colonial houses can be seen in the northern suburb of **Jaro**, where **Jaro Cathedral** also stands, dating from 1874. A little further north, outside the city, is the village of **Pavia**, where on May 3 each year the exciting *Carabao Carroza*, a race between water-buffaloes, takes place.

In the suburb of **Molo**, in the west of Iloilo City, there is a **church of coral stone**, which merits a visit. It was built in 1831 in a mixture of neo-Gothic and Renaissance styles. As you leave Molo going west, it is well worth visiting the **Asilo de Molo**, an orphanage, where the girls make very decorative handcraft

items from pineapple and abaca fibers (*piña* and *jusi*). In the village you can also buy delicious snacks. Just as the *Batchoy* soup belongs to the La Paz quarter, the local broth here is *Pancit Molo*, a tasty soup with stuffed pasta pockets. All buses and jeepneys stop at the **Panaderia de Molo** on the way to the to the south coast at this, for it is the oldest bakery in South Philippines and sells delicious pastries. The suburb of Villa Arevalo is famous for its flowers and for embroidery using natural fibers, to be seen at the **Sinamay Weaving Workshop**. Here the Spanish, early on, built shipyards and arsenals for their frequent campaigns against the Muslims. In the late 16th century the town was the administrative headquarters of the western Visayas.

Guimaras, the Mango Island

It only takes 20 minutes by ferry from Iloilo City to reach **Jordan.** And if you happen to arrive on Good Friday, this biblically named capital of Guimaras, a

Province of Panay, provides a New Testament attraction well worth seeing: the *Ang Pagtaltal sa Guimaras* – a local version of the Passion Plays. Although it involves no actual crucifixions as in other places, the actors and audience give an impressive demonstration of how deeply they have absorbed the Easter story.

Other religious sites on the island include **Balaan Bukid**, a place of pilgrimage on **Bondolan Point**, marked by a large cross, and, in the nearby village of **San Miguel**, the only Trappist monastery in the Philippines.

On the list of natural attractions are the **Daliran Caves** outside **Buenavista,** north of Jordan. But to get a real experience of the landscape you need to take at least three days to tour the island in a rented jeepney. As soon as you leave Jordan you plunge into deeply rural country. The track into the hilly interior takes you through fields of cassava, and past innumerable mango trees – whose delicious fruit have earned Guimaras the nickname "Mango Island." You cannot

127

help noticing the poverty of the islanders. There are scattered settlements where many aboriginals, the Ati, still live.

Anyone keen on snorkeling should visit the little offshore island of **Tandug** in the southwest, where the coral reefs are still alive. However, the once popular waters around Taklong Island, off the southern tip of Guimaras, have been devastated by dynamite-fishing. Quite near the tiny village of **Nanaur** there is a huge and ancient mango tree.

There are some beach resorts on offshore islands such as **Tatlong Pulo** near Jordan, or **Isla Naburot** off the west coast, and the little island of **Inampulugan** in the southeast. They offer accommodation in various styles. It is worth visiting the bungalows on **Nagarao Island**, near **San Isidro** on the south coast where you can not only stay in comfort and go on excursions, but also book into a "study course in environmental tourism." The resident "king of the island," a German called Martin Stummer, has managed to turn the hitherto barren island a luxuriant green, in a few short years. His persistent complaints to the authorities have stopped the blasting and poisoning of the coral and given it a chance of survival. In the dry months from February to May, the salt-farmers from San Isidro to Sebaste harvest sea salt in the traditional manner. Look out for their windmills which pump water into the salt-pans.

Panay's Coast of Churches

Back in Iloilo City again, you take the asphalt road westward into Antique Province, and soon come to **Oton**, the first Spanish possession on Panay. In the neighboring towns of **Tigbauan** and **Guimbal** stand old churches built from sandstone and blocks of coral, but which have been rather spoilt by the use of ugly concrete walls and corrugated iron roofs. The beach at Guimbal is overshadowed

Above: Water-buffalo fighting at the Fiesta of San Joaquin. Right: Religious devotion during the "Pagtaltal" on Guimaras.

by three weathered **watch towers,** from which a lookout was kept for pirates.

Warning of an attack was given from the bell-tower of **Miagao church**, a perfect example of "earthquake Baroque," whichhas been included in the UNESCO World Cultural Heritage. It was built in 1787 and looks more like a fortress than a sanctuary. It dominates the little town and is chiefly notable for the artistic bas-relief on its frontage which shows St Christopher, surrounded by tropical vegetation, carrying the Christ-child and – with unambiguous symbolism – bringing salvation to the heathen souls.

As you leave town, you can observe on the beach how the descendants of those converted heathens live today. Most of the fishermen and their families are obliged to reside on their little sailing-boats, called *barotos.* They have to compete with the *basnigan,* large outriggers with powerful engines, which return from nocturnal fishing trips and anchor off the south coast of Panay. In the dry season, salt is gathered in a very special way on

the beaches between Guimbalk and Miagao: the salt-farmers collect the sea water in long troughs made of bamboo and every evening, when the water has evaporated in the sun, they "harvest" the white crystals.

High above the coast the coral-stone church of **San Joaquin** exhibits a definitely martial demeanour, less in its construction than in the bas-relief on its façade. It depicts the Battle of Tetuan (North Morocco), a punitive expedition by the Spanish against the Berbers of the Rif Mountains in 1859 – just ten years before the church was built. The stone bridge in the middle of a rice field a few miles outside San Joaquin, was constructed at about the same time by the engineer Felipe Diez. At the edge of town there is also a **cemetery,** dating from 1892, which is of historical interest. The ancient petrified coral on a steep slope below the school is of course very much older.

The sleepy town is scarcely recongnizable during the second weekend of

January, when the locals celebrate *Pasungay*. The festival reachs its climax with water-buffalo fights behind the church. Bets are placed on the outcome, when two *carabao* bulls, excited by a buffalo cow, charge each other and lock horns with a crack that can be heard far and wide. Treasure-hunters may strike lucky here too. For so far the *Golden Salakot* has never been found: it is a golden hat which was said to have been handed over to the Ati in the 13th century by three *Datus* from Borneo in exchange for land near San Joaquin, an act known as the "Bargain of Panay."

If you take the winding road through the foothills into Antique Province, stop in the market town of **Tiolas** for the superb view out to sea, to Guimaras and Negros. In **Anini-y**, in the far southwest of Panay, there is another **church** built of dazzling white coral (1880). You can

relax in **sulphur springs** from which the water is fed into a swimming pool.

Beginning in Anini-y, **Antique Province** stretches over a large part of the mountain chain of Panay. From the provincial capital, **San José de Buenavista,** a poor road runs northwest along the narrow coastal strip. The mountains close by were for years a favorite hideout for NPA guerillas, hence the few visitors to the west coast. However, mountaineers revere the still thickly-wooded **Mount Madja-as**, at 2090 meters, the highest peak in the island. At its foot lies the town of **Culasi,** the best place from which to set out for **Maraison Island**, which lies just offshore.

From the village of Pandan in the northwest corner of Panay, the main road continues straight over to Kalibo on the north coast, while a narrow, winding road goes right out around the coast to **Catiklan**, in the very north of the island. Now you have reached the harbor from which you can sail to the nearby "dream island" of Boracay.

Above: A wedding in the church at Miagao.
Right: A peripatetic "dentist" gives consultations at the weekly market.

From Secret Hideaway to Package Tour Destination – Boracay

Boracay, which is barely more than seven kilometers long, is a jewel that has lost something of its sparkle in recent years, due to the flood of tourists. At the beginning of the 1980s travel-weary globe-trotters were happy to drink warm beer on the mile-long beach of sugar-fine sand and enjoy the majestic sunsets. But since then hundreds of tourist bungalows have sprung up between the coconut-palms. Restaurants, windsurfing- and diving-schools tout for trade everywhere, and discotheques and massage parlors have been opened. Electricity may have brought the benefits of civilization, but it has also brought the noise. The concrete main road has made it easier to move goods and people about, but the increasing motorization is not to everyone's taste. The sand on White Beach is no longer so white, and the 5000 islanders are no longer as friendly. Nevertheless, someone landing on Boracay for the first time would doubtless believe he had reached a longed-for tropical paradise.

Boracay is administered by the national tourist authority, which has been trying for years to make the island Southeast Asia's premier vacation resort. Exclusive hotels and restaurants have been built, but now cooled drinks are also available in the less expensive accommodation. If you want, you can spend every evening in front of video machines in the beach bars and forget why you came here at all. The focus of tourist activity is around the villages **Angol** and **Balabag**. There are smaller, quieter beaches in the north: Din Iwid, Balinghai and Punto Bunga. The villages **Manoc-Manoc** on the southern tip, and **Yapak** at the Puka-Shell Beach in the north are popular with snorkelers. But there is in fact more variety underwater off the rocky east coast.

Boracay is most visited in the dry season, from December to May. And except for parts affected by a strange recurring carpet of algae, the sea that laps the beaches is calm and crystal clear, ideal for swimming, surfing and sailing outrigger boats. And in the evening when the roaring motor boats have fallen silent, swarms of fruit-bats fly over from the island to the mainland, and the sun sinks glowing into the sea – then you can still sense the magic feeling of what Boracay once was like.

Colorful festivals

The effects of the boom on Boracay have also rubbed off on **Kalibo**, its supply center with an airport serving Manila and Cebu. However, the fame of the capital of Panay's **Aklan Province** long ago spread through the nation, thanks to the colorful *Ati-Atihan* festival, which literally drums the sleepy coastal town out of its lethargy annually on the third weekend in January. Visitors from all over the world are drawn by the carnival-like abandon, and the fantastic costumes and masks worn by the townspeople – in these four days one pays four times more than usual for board and lodging. Business with the foreigners is blossoming, perhaps echoing the deal made back in the 13th century between the simple-minded Ati and the cunning foreigners from Borneo. This event which is commemorated by the *Ati-Atihan*, when the immigrants blackened their faces in order to deceive the dark-skinned Ati into parting with their fertile land. The Ati of today are certainly no better off now than they were then. While the people of Kalibo and the tourists dress up as Ati, the true aboriginals come to the town to beg, while the town celebrates the unholy trinity of Malay tam-tam, catholic piousness and western commercialism.

You can cool off at the **Jawili Falls** near **Tangalan**, about 20 kilometers northwest of Kalibo. If you still feel like more celebrating, you can join in the "real," i.e., scarcely commercialized, *Ati-Atihan* which takes place a week later in the town of **Ibajay**. When one arrives in **Roxas**, it is hard to understand why this dreary little town should have been given the added title of "City." Perhaps it was an attempt to counteract the image of **Capiz Province** as a haunt of *Aswang*, witches and blood-sucking monsters. Be that as it may, in the suburb of **Pan-ay** you can see the biggest church bell in Southeast Asia.

Roxas used to be the terminus of the Panay Railway from Iloilo, which has been closed for years; but if the rumors are to be believed, it is to be re-opened. It would certainly be more pleasant to cross the island from north to south in a comfortable excursion-train, than making the five-hour trip in cramped buses, along the road – though this is nearly all surfaced – through Dao, Passi and Pototan.

The east coast of Panay has a charming

Right: Souvenir-sellers on the famous beach at Boracay.

landscape. From **Estancia** in the northeast, boats leave for the many offshore islands. The exclusive resort on the enchanting **Sicogon Island** was once internationally famous, but closed its doors several years ago. On the islands **Gigante Norte** and **Gigante Sur** there is only basic accommodation. On the other hand there are numerous caves and a very beautiful beach to explore. The neighboring islets Cabugao Norte and Cabugao Sur are also idyllic.

Rising out of Concepcion Bay, east of of **San Dionisio**, is the Philippines' answer to Sugarloaf Mountain, an island called **Pan de Azucar**. It is surrounded by several other islands which have little in the way of infrastructure; they are a refreshing change from Boracay with delightful people who are happy to offer you a room, and who in unspoilt surroundings reflect Panay's genuine charm.

NEGROS

Scarcely any region in the Philippines reveals the social dichotomy of the country as much as Negros, the fourth-largest island, with an area of 12,750 square kilometers. For over a century, sugar cane has been the underlying cause of the crude division of society into many poor and a few rich and powerful people. On Negros, the sugar barons rule. Although more than half the island is under sugar cultivation, the problem lies not just with plantation ownership: the feudal structure of the monopoly also creates this yawning gulf. The *sacadas*, or harvest-workers, are at the bottom of the social ladder and are the poorest of the poor. Their plight has become worse since the steep drop in the world price of sugar in 1985, and the growth in demand for artificial sweeteners.

The island was called *Buglas*, before the Spaniard Esteban de Rodriguez landed here in 1565. His countrymen then christened it Negros, no doubt im-

pressed by the dark-skinned aboriginals, whose descendants live today in the remotest parts of the island's interior. After 300 years of colonial obscurity, the island's destiny took a new turn in 1856, thanks to one Nicholas Loney. This British consul and business-man persuaded the *mestizos* of Panay, who had grown rich from the manufacture and export of textiles, to invest in sugar plantations on the neighboring island of Negros. Loney prepared the ground by undercutting the textile producers of the Visayas with cheap imports from Manchester. The world had developed a sweet tooth and the boom began. The peasants were talked into parting with their land for wholly inadequate prices. A memorial in Iloilo City still honors Loney as the "Father of the Sugar Industry." Since then vast *haciendas* have scarcely declined in size, and the empire of the sugar barons which grew up in those days has lost none of its political influence. With the increasing destitution of the population, Negros developed into a stronghold

of the NPA. Whatever the army and the government may claim to the contrary, the rebels used to enjoy great support from the islanders. Exploitation, poverty, hunger and sickness mark the plight of the agricultural laborers of Negros, and bear witness to previous governments' inability to improve the situation. However, it seems it is now understood that, in the long run, not even the rich will benefit from the sugar monoculture. On the coast, prawn-farming is being developed and proving very profitable, with Japan as a large and reliable customer.

In 1890 the island was divided politically into the provinces of Negros Occidental in the west, and Negros Oriental in the east. This corresponds not only to the geographical division created by the range of mountains down the center of the island, but also to the socio-cultural influences from the neighboring islands, from where most of the sugar-workers originate. This is why the language spoken in the west is chiefly *Hiligaynon* of Panay, and in the east *Cebuano*.

133

Negros owes its fertile soil to volcanic activity: the north of the island is dominated by two dormant volcanoes, Silay (1,534 meters) and Mandalagan (1,880 meters), and by the active Kanlaon volcano which at 2,465 meters is the highest peak in the Visayas region. Apart from sugar cane, the Negrenses live mainly by fishing; other activities include the mining of gold, copper, sulphur, silica and manganese, growing copra and vegetables, and timber-felling. As in Panay, the dry season runs from January to April, but in recent years the Visayas have suffered long periods of drought.

Bacolod City, the capital of **Negros Occidental,** with a population of around 360,000, is one of the largest cities in the Philippines. As it first grew up along with the sugar-boom, Bacolod has scarcely any venerable buildings to look at. The streets are laid out in a flat, chess-board pattern. However, the **City Plaza** really is nicely designed, a green space with a music pavilion where the music of Haydn, Mozart and Beethoven is performed – clear evidence of the aspirations of the upper class whose sugar revenues allowed them to indulge in western tastes. While in the Plaza, you should also look at the **San Sebastian Cathedral,** built in 1876, and the **Palacio Episcopal** (Bishops' Palace), with its interesting art collection.

The *palenque* or **Public Market,** on the southeast side of the City Plaza, is a maze of many small booths selling a fascinating variety of fish and fruit. Further west, a futuristic city is arising from ground that has been reclaimed from the sea. To the south, Bacolod has been spreading out for a long time. There you will find the **Golden Field Commercial Complex,** an entertainment district with many restaurants, casinos and hotels. The frontage of the **Convention Plaza Hotel** has been designed to emulate the famous Manila Hotel, in an effort to polish up

Above: Sugar cane, the destiny of the island of Negros. Right: San Sebastian Cathedral in Bacolod City.

Bacolod's modern image still further. The rich of Negros, pampered during the years of the sugar-boom, are not about to give up their extravagant life-style.

Every year in October the city celebrates the **Mass-Kara Festival** with great gusto. Wearing colorful costumes and smiling masks the inhabitants parade noisily through the *City of Smiles,* anxious not to be outdone in the festive department by the neighboring cities of Cebu and Iloilo. Bacolod is also famous for its ceramics, which are produced in potteries around the edge of the city.

Although it is a pleasant place to be based for excursions into the surrounding area, Bacolod has hardly been discovered by tourists. This is largely due to the lack of good beaches in the vicinity. **Bago City**, 21 kilometers south of Bacolod, has an interesting past. Due to the determined resistance of the *mestizo* clans, this is one of the few cities in the Philippines where the Chinese were never able to gain a foothold. The renovated **Araneta House** is symbolic in two ways. Firstly, it exemplifies in its architecture and decor the opulent lifestyle of the ruling families. Secondly, it is the birthplace of the leader of the Negros Revolution of 1898, General Juan Araneta. He was a member of the well-to-do intelligentsia, who first opposed the Spanish and then hurriedly declared their support for the Americans – in the hope of early independence and the protection of their own well-paid positions.

In the nearby town of **Valladolid** the 19th-century church is worth a visit.

East of Bacolod the sugar cane fields of **La Carlota** and Ma-ao stretch interminably from the coast to the fertile slopes of the **Kanlaon volcano**. Here and there, old steam locomotives puff along the narrow-gauge plantation railroads, which make up a total network of nearly 300 kilometers.

About 30 kilometers east of the capital lies the health resort of **Mambucal**, at the

foot of Kanlaon. The air here at 400 meters above sea level is pleasantly cool. Several hotels and pensions, hot sulphur springs, cold springs, swimming pools and waterfalls make this a popular weekend retreat for city-dwellers. From Mambucal, a five-kilometer-walk brings you to **Mount Kanlaon National Park,** and the beginning of the climbing trail up this impressive mountain. To climb it from this side you should allow three to four days.

In the summer of 1996 the volcano gave signs of becoming active again. You can find more information and arrange for a guide through the information bureau on City Plaza in Bacolod, which also organizes an Easter climb every year.

A good road runs along the west coast southwards as far as Ilog. Southeast from there is the town of **Kabankalan**, where every year on the third weekend in January the *Sinulog* festival is celebrated with jousting and processions. About half way across to the east coast, Dutch and

Belgian speleologists made an exciting discovery in 1990. In the limestone region of the interior, near the village of **Paniabonan** in the **Mabinay** district, they found the **Odloman Cave System**. Almost nine kilometers long, this is the second largest cave system found in the Philippines.

The rest of southwestern Negros is undeveloped and the roads are in a poor state. This is also true of the beautiful beaches and diving waters near **Sipalay** and **Hinoba-an**. The gold rush of 1982 thrust the village of Nauhang, in the hinterland of Hinoba-an, into the world's headlines, and attracted adventurers from at home and abroad. The sensational gold discoveries were soon followed by murder and mayhem, until the government put its foot down and closed the area to private prospectors. Now the rights to ex-

Above: The fireman on a steam engine of the Victorias Milling Co. Right: In scorching heat women laborers plant sugar-cane seedlings.

tract the precious metal have been granted to an Australian-Philippine consortium. If you can negotiate the potholes on the road to Zamboanguita, the scenery of the south coast is delightful.

The drive through the north of Negros Occidental is more comfortable and no less interesting. About seven kilometers north of Bacolod City, just outside **Talisay**, you can see the well-maintained **House of General Ancieto Lacson**. He was a revolutionary hero who became president of the revolutionary government of Negros. Unfortunately, you are not allowed inside this 19th-century house, even though it is a protected monument. It has been bought by a sect of publicity-shy monks.

The little town of **Silay** is another historic landmark, with some 30 *Balay Negrense*, colonial-style houses dating from around 1860. In those days Silay was the cultural center of the sugar island and known as the "Paris of Negros." You can see how the sugar barons lived by visiting the **Gaston Museum**, the former residence of the wealthy Gaston family, of French origin, who still live in Silay.

All this history can be helped down with delicious cookies made of rice and coconut sold at the **Ideal Bakery** in the main street. The sugar they use is locally produced in what is said to be the largest sugar-refinery in the world, near **Victorias**. The **Vicmico** (Victorias Milling Company) is one of 18 sugar-mills in Negros. There is a guided tour over the 50-hectare plant, which takes you through all the stages of production. If you are lucky, you can get to ride on one of the "Iron Dragons," the old-fashioned steam locomotives that run on the factory's private railroad.

In the center of the sugar-manufacturing town is **St Joseph's Chapel**, with its internationally famous altar painting of the "Angry Christ." It is not easy to guess the meaning of the grim expression on the face of Christ, but at least it makes a

refreshing contrast to the usual sentimental portrayals of Jesus seen in this country. At the same time, the "Angry Christ" and the saints who are portrayed in paintings inside and stained-glass mosaics outside the chapel, all have unmistakably Filipino features. Faced with the bitter harvest of Negros' sugar, Christ does not have much to smile about. The painting was sketched in 1960 by the Belgian-born artist, Ade de Bethune, and completed by Alfonso Ossorio, son of Vicmico's founder, Miguel Ossorio.

Offshore from **Cadiz City,** on the north coast, lies **Llacaon Island** (Lakawaon) with a pleasant bungalow resort on a clean beach. A few kilometers before you reach Escalante, a bumpy track runs through a typical bit of Negros country, where it is plain to see in what poverty the smallholders and casual laborers live, compared to the feudal luxury of the *hacienderos*. At the end of a five-kilometer stretch of track you reach the little village of **Vito**, with its surprisingly attractive **Church of San Vicente Ferrer,** built in 1866. The wooden statue of its patron saint is said to possess healing powers, and on the first Friday of each month the faithful come from far and wide to make pilgrimages here.

The little port of **Escalante** recently came to prominence as a victim of state-sanctioned brutality. A memorial recalls the day in September 1985 when Marcos' soldiers violently broke up a demonstration by sugar workers, and killed 20 of the protesters.

The east coast road now heads southward to **San Carlos City**, a quiet place with little to offer other than a magnificent view of Mount Kanloan glowing in the setting sun. But on the offshore coral island of **Sipaway**, it is tempting to linger and enjoy the wide, flat beaches, clear water and friendly locals. The fermented juice of the coconut-palm, called *tubá*, tastes particularly refreshing here. And provided the many notices warning against drug-abuse and dynamite fishing have some effect, the little island should remain an idyll.

We now enter **Negros Oriental Province**. The minor road climbs through fields of sugar cane, sometimes terraced, until it reaches **Kanlaon City**, nearly 900 meters above sea-level. In the vicinity of this friendly little town there are hot springs and picturesque waterfalls. Even Mount Kanlaon seems near enough to touch and lures one to attempt the climb. According to legend, a seven-headed dragon once lived on the mountain and terrorized the islanders, until the god *Khan Laon* in human form, and with the help of ants, bees, and eagles, cut off the fire-breathing heads of the monster. However, the volcano that was named after the hero has by no means been robbed of its power. Between 1978 and 1998 it flung ash and sulphur into the heavens on at least ten occasions. Kanlaon has one extinct and one active crater; according to vulcanologists the mountain's behavior is relatively tame, but even so it is watched round the clock by three observation stations. From this side it can be climbed in a single day; the steep path is nine kilometers long and requires considerable effort. The vegetation is less luxuriant than on the western route from Mambucal. However, the panorama from the 2,260-meter-high "roof of the Visayas," and the glimpse down 300 meters into the seething crater, is an unforgettable experience. A trained guide is essential. A European who once tried to tackle the dragon-mountain on his own was found dead in a crevasse.

Traveling south along the east coast, anyone who loves animals should avoid **Jimalalud** if the date happens to be January 15. This is the day of the annual fiesta when the townsfolk organize fights between horses. This bizarre and (for the animals) often fatal "sport" is also staged in the La Libertad (April 27), Tanjay (July 24) and Bais City (September 10).

Right: Fertile land on the lower slopes of Mount Kanlaon, by the banks of a river.

From **Tampi** and **San José** there are daily ferries to Cebu. **Dumaguete City**, capital of Negros Oriental and founded in 1890, is an attractive seaport with a population of about 65,000. The first university in the Philippines outside Manila was opened here in 1890. The internationally known **Silliman University** is the only Protestant college in the country. It was founded in 1901 by Dr Horace B. Silliman. Currently more than 20,000 students are enrolled here. An interesting place to visit is the small **ethnographic museum**, which contains art objects from the 18th century, aboriginal artifacts and objects culled from nearby excavations. Even the building itself is a museum piece – it is a New York theater which in 1903 was dismantled, shipped over and reassembled in Dumaguete.

A lot of things combine to make Dumaguete one of the most pleasant cities in the Philippines: it has a number of good restaurants and hotels, a well-kept waterfront promenade, clean beaches of dark sand to the north, and enchanting scenery between the sea and the backdrop of mountains which culminates in the extinct volcanoes of Cuernos de Negros and Mount Talinis. Last but not least on this list of plusses is the warm-heartedness of the local people.

The surrounding area is equally endowed with tropical charm and places to visit. Northwest of the city, via San José, are two crater-lakes, Balinsasayao and Danao, which lie deep in the jungle at a height of about 800 meters. One must hope that this idyll, called **Twin Lake**, does not fall victim to plans for a hydoelectric plant, as has been proposed.

A visit to the geothermal power-station at **Palinpinon**, near **Valencia**, where hot springs are converted into current which supplies the whole of Negros, is interesting. One can refresh oneself in the swimming-pool of the **Banica Valley Resort,** and above Valencia there is a magnificent view from **Camp Lookout**.

In **Bacong**, which is back on the coast, stands a church with an ancient altar and equally venerable organ. From the bell-tower, the villagers were once warned of marauding pirates with cries of *Bacon, bacon!* ("To arms, to arms!"). At **Dauin** the beach is guarded by centuries-old watch-towers, and a there is church worth visiting. Just before the town of Zamboanguita is the village of **Malatapay** (Maluay) where a colorful and busy market is held right on the shore every Wednesday. Livestock changes hands, delicious-smelling suckling-pigs roast on the spit, fish of every color lie ready to be bought, the *tubá* flows freely, and the quack-doctors do a roaring trade.

From **Zamboanguita** boats leave for **Apo Island**, which lies eight kilometers off the coast. Its unique undersea life is protected by the Marine Biological Laboratory of Silliman University. If you want to dive around Apo Island, you should beware of the very dangerous currents. If you prefer, you can just enjoy life in one of the two resorts on the white beach. right in the south of negros, the Tambubo Bay is a rewarding destination to the difficult trip via Siaton; two pleasant beach resorts are already in existence.

SIQUIJOR

It is no surprise that Siquijor has scarcely been heard of, since tourists on Negros and Cebu are warned not to visit the smallest island province of the Visayas. But the threat does not come from rebels – it is from witchcraft and voodoo. The island is known to be a center of black magic. And that in a country were superstition can move mountains! It may be that a few dozen of the 80,000 inhabitants of Siquijor are *Magbabarang*, capable of bringing about misfortune or death by the use of "black" magic. But then there are the more popular *Mananambals,* faith healers of both sexes, who use "white" magic to effect miraculous cures.

Even the Spanish found the isle an eerie place; bewildered by the mysterious

139

glow it gave off, they named it *Isla del Fuego*. Legend, too, calls Siquijor a "fire-island" – it is said that it suddenly rose out of the sea with a flash of lightning and a clap of thunder. However, adventurous travelers who risk the trip from Dumaguete City to Siquijor, will find themselves on a perfectly tranquil island. Friendly locals wave their welcomes from the jetty in the harbor of **Larena**. A generally good road runs along the coast, which often rises high above the sea, making way for mangroves and inviting beaches.

Like Larena, **Siquijor**, the provincial capital, is a peaceful town. Near **San Juan**, on one of the best beaches on the island, the newly completed **Coco Grove Beach Resort** offers comfort and many a flaming sunset, which turns Siquijor and Negros, looming on the horizon, into true islands of fire. The presence of other beach complexes at **Palitan**, and **Salag**

Above: Not a witch's brew, but cooking in the market of Malatapay, Negros Oriental.

Do-Ong in the east and **Sandugan**, north of Larena, show that Siquijor wants to break out of its "bewitched" isolation.

Of historical importance is the monastic school at **Lazi**, the largest and oldest in the Philippines, founded in 1891. It's an austere place, with creaking floorboards and harsh discipline. But if you want to probe the mysterious creeds of the Siquijodnons, you should visit **San Antonio** in the mountainous interior during Holy Week. This is where the *Mananambals* meet and brew plants and insects into an elixir for the next magical year. On Crocodile Mountain, in the country behind Lazi, people gather on warm nights when the moon is full for a witch's feast, and the villagers perform a ghostly dance around a big medicine cauldron.

CEBU

Four hundred and seventy one years elapsed between Magellan's landing and the opening, in 1992, of the international terminal at Cebu Airport on the little satellite island of Mactan. Since 1521, Cebu Province, with its capital, Cebu City and its 167 adjacent islands, has retained its importance in the Philippines. Yet long before the Europeans arrived, the settlement of *Zubu* on the east coast was already an important port of call for ships from Asia, India and Arabia. Magellan's landing was followed by the conversion of Humabon and his people. The cross which was erected then – or what is left of it – is still honored as a sacred national treasure. Who knows, perhaps in 2021 the "Discovery of the Philippines" will be just as hotly debated as was the 500th anniversary of Columbus' discovery of America. However that may be, modern Philippine historians now describe the appearance of the Spanish as "the misfortune of liberation," – even though the death of Magellan on Mactan in 1521 was initially followed by a breathing-space of four decades. But when Miguel Lopez de Legazpi promoted the settlement of *Zubu* to *La Ciudad del Santissimo Nombre de Jesus* ("City of the most sacred name of Jesus") in 1565, it became the colonial capital until the conquest of Manila in 1571. This does not in any way mean that the Cebuanos, who did not have much time for Magellan, were willing to play second fiddle. Quite the opposite. The Spanish strove with cross and sword to develop the island into a base for their expeditions into the surrounding region. Under the US administration, Cebu City, as it was now called, retained an important role as headquarters of the regional civil and military authorities. Then for a brief period the Japanese governed the Visayas from here.

During the Vietnam war, US bombers took off from Mactan airport, while GIs on leave sunned themselves on the many beaches, thus laying the foundations, from the 1970s on, of Cebu's reputation as a tourist island. Resentment against

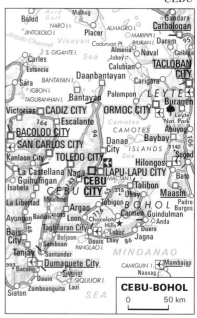

foreign power has a long tradition, and today's effort by Cebu City to develop into a potential rival to Manila, is the form which it now takes.

The island is 220 kilometers long and nowhere more than 40 kilometers wide. A range of mountains, rising to 1,000 meters, runs right along the island to the northernmost point. The population of almost three million live from mining – the biggest copper-mine in Southeast Asia is being exploited near Toledo, gold and silver are also worked – from fishing and from wheat- mango- and maize-growing. And of course from tourism, and supplying the tourists with items such as rattan furniture, shell- and coral-decorations. The exporting industries of Cebu rely on Mactan airport to move goods to their markets.

With almost 700,000 inhabitants, **Cebu City** is the third largest city on the Philippines. Being the oldest Spanish settlement it claims several superlatives: it is the oldest Christian city in the Far East; and **Colon Street**, the oldest street in the

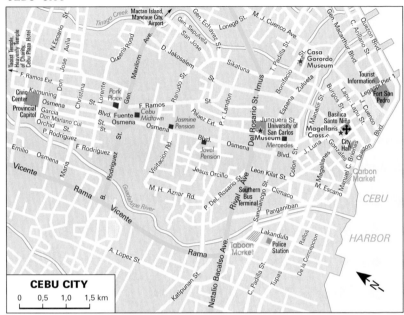

country, named after Columbus (who was really Cristobal Colon, of course) s here. Today the heart of **downtown** Cebu is crammed with shops and department stores

As early as 1595 Cebu's **University of San Carlos** was the first college to be founded in the Philippines. (It is well worth visiting the adjoining **ethnological museum,** which also has exhibits from other neighboring countries.)

The **Basilica Minore de Santo Niño** is the oldest church, and **Fort San Pedro** is the first and smallest fortress in the country. Founded as a wooden stockade in 1565 and named after Legazpi's flag-ship, it served for a long time as a defence against pirates. At the end of the 1960s the fort was turned into a charming little park and now houses the **National Museum**.

From here it is not far to another of the city's emblems: **Magellan's Cross** in Magellanes Street. In a pavilion near the city hall, the remains of the original are said to be incorporated in a later cross of tindalo wood. A painting on the wall vividly depicts how the first momentous baptism on Cebu on April 14, 1521 might have appeared.

A true shrine of Philippine piety is the **Santo Niño Church**, only a few steps from Magellan's Cross, also in downtown Cebu. In the stone basilica, built in 1740, a small figure of the Christ-child draws large crowds of faithful every day. The precious statue is said to have been presented by Magellan to the wife of his blood-brother Humabon on the occasion of his baptism. Legend has it that one of Legazpi's soldiers rediscovered it in 1565. The *Sinulog* or *Fiesta Señor*, Cebu's biggest festival, takes place annually on the third Sunday in January. Santo Niño church is then encircled by processions of people in colorful costumes, dancing to the wild rhythm of drums. Walking in southerly direction toward the sea, you cross Quezon Boulevard and come to the colorful **Carbon Market**, which not only sells food of all kinds but also a wide variety of handcrafted items from Cebu and the neighboring islands.

In 1990 Cebu City, the "Queen of the South," was hit by a typhoon, during which the 860-meter-long bridge across to Mactan Island was damaged by a drifting ship. It has since been repaired while the rapidly growing city profited from the opportunity to carry out some well-planned modernization.

Clinging to the hillsides, the **uptown district** has been improved by new roads, luxury hotels and good restaurants. By the harbor, part of the foreshore has been reclaimed to create a successful shoppers' paradise and entertainment district. However, in the downtown area, traffic chaos and dirt have increased. The boom has added a growing number of private cars to the existing jeepneys and *tartanillas,* the horse-drawn carriages of Cebu, and the streets seem forever clogged. Another unfortunate consequence of all this progress has been to bring vagrants, beggars and petty criminals flooding into the downtown area.

None of this has much effect on **Beverly Hills**, the millionaire's enclave in the suburb of Lahug. Up here the **Taoist temple** looks down over Cebu City. Along with the **Heavenly Temple of Charity**, a little lower down, it is the religious focus of the Taoist community and evidence of the Chinese presence: they account for 15 percent of the population.

The way the Spanish aristocracy lived a century ago is vividly presented in the **Museum Casa Gorordo** in Lopes Jaena Street. This former residence of the Gorordo family is the only reminder of the elegance of this once exclusive district.

Making your way through the confused swirl of traffic in the town of **Mandaue**, which is a continuation of Cebu City, you cross the bridge over to Mactan Island. The capital of this flat, bare coral island is **Lapu Lapu City**, formerly Opon, where a little monument commemorates Lapu Lapu, the man who killed Magellan, and thus became the Philippines' first national hero.

In **Maribago,** on the east coast of Mactan, guitars, mandolins and ukuleles are made in the traditional way. Outriggers ply the seas to and from Olango Island, which is known as a health resort, but through the efforts of an environmental organization, the *Asian Wetland Bureau*, it has been declared a nature-reserve for migratory birds and mangrove fauna.

All the beach hotels, some highly exclusive and expensive, are on the east coast of Mactan. Broad, white beaches invite you to laze in the sun. Sadly, the interior of the island is no tropical idyll, since it is severely polluted by refuse.

On **Punta Engano**, the northeastern tip of the island, lies **Magellan Bay**, where the historic battle took place in 1521. Memorials have been erected to both protagonists. The one to the Portuguese circumnavigator has stood there since 1866. The one depicting Lapu Lapu in a martial pose is of more recent date.

Every year, on April 27, the humiliation of the Spanish is vividly recreated, when amateur actors take the parts of the ferocious opponents and belabor each other in the warm sea water.

Cebu boasts a fair deal of experience in the tourism industry and has a reasonably well-functioning infrastructure. But what has been irrevocably lost are its forests and intact marine life. Even in the once popular beach resort of **Moalboal**, in the south-west, underwater enthusiasts have no choice but to make for the distant **Pescador Island** if they want to see anything of special interest on the sea bed. In 1984, a typhoon along Cebu's coast literally ground to pieces any of the coral reef that had not already been destroyed by dynamite-fishing. However, on Moalboal's **Panagsama beach** diving lessons are still offered, exploring the slowly-recovering corals. A few kilometers further south a few resorts have grown up at

Lambug and on Badjan Island, around a lagoon-like bay. An excursion to **Matutinao**, south of Badian, is also attractive. After a short trek inland, you can see, besides the refreshing **Kawasan Waterfalls**, one of the last pockets of tropical rain forest on Cebu. Almost at the southwest end of Cebu, within sight of Negros is the village **Samboan**, where whales and dolphins are frequently sighted and a coral reef attracts snorkelers.

From Badian, a mountain road crosses the island diagonally to **Dalaguete**, a beach paradise on the east coast. But on Cebu the mountain roads frequently fall victim to the monsoon rains; so it may be that you have to start out from Dalaguete in order to reach the cool mountain village of **Montalogon** (about halfway across the island), with its colorful vegetable market and fields of chrysanthemums all around.

From the south coast, ferries sail across to Negros. Leaving from **San Sebastian**

Above: A Chinese temple in Cebu City.

you arrive in Tampi, and from **Liloan** or **Santander** you land at Sibulan.

The offshore **island of Bantayan**, in the northwest, certainly has a future in tourism, as here the beaches are superb. The surrounding islets could definitely attract hermits and others in search of solitude. The islet Malapascua, until recently almost unknown, which lies off the northeast tip of Cebu, has become famous for its friendly inhabitants and idyllic bays. It is only to be hoped that its charm endures and the completely un-paradise-like dynamite fishing can be stopped.

BOHOL

Bohol is famous for two things: the "Chocolate Hills" and the dwarf-maki or *Tarsius*, a rare mammal. The Chocolate Hills are not about to melt, but this smallest prosimian species on earth – only found on Bohol, Leyte and Mindanao – will soon be extinct unless protected.

It is the beaches of the neighboring island of Panglao which have increased

Bohol's fame, but apart from this, the tenth largest island in the Philippines has so far remained rather off from the tourist track. The visitor to this tranquil island with its very friendly and industrious people, and unique landscape, may hope that it will long remain so. A fertile plateau covers the interior, and the south coast drops steeply to the Mindanao Sea. Off the more gentle western, northern and northwestern coasts are 72 smaller islands belonging to the province.

The island population of about 900,000 lives mainly by growing maize, rice and coconut- and nipa-palms.

Bohol is well provided with monuments from the colonial period. But the history of settlement in the island stretches much farther back. Recent excavations have brought to light prehistoric graves, boat-shaped coffins and Chinese porcelain dating back 600 years. Another remarkable fact in Bohol's history is that the little island succeeded for 85 years, from 1744 to 1829, in maintaining independence from Spanish colonial rule. The leader of the rebellion was a certain Francisco Dagohoy, who was able to mobilize 20,000 men against the Spanish, after his brother, who had been executed for the murder of a policeman, was refused a Christian burial. Surprisingly, Bohol's contact with the west had begun on a very hopeful note: The treaty of brotherhood which Legazpi concluded with Datu Siktuna has gone down in history as the "Blood-pact of Bohol." This took place in the village of **Bo-ol** only three kilometers east of the present capital, Tagbilaran City. A stone relief on the coastal road commemorates the alliance.

Tagbilaran City, on the southwest coast, is the commercial hub of Bohol, with an airport and ferry terminal. The lively Torralba market, the spacious plaza with its decorative church, the airy restaurants on stilts by the pier, which serve delicious seafood dishes – all combine to make your stay pleasant.

Close by Tagbilaran City, two bridges link Bohol with **Panglao Island.** In Panglao's main town, **Dauis**, the high altar of the 18th-century church has a spring of sparkling water, said to possess healing properties. In the southwest of this small island a number of resorts have sprung up by the beautiful beaches of **Alona** and **Doljo.** There are excursions to be made to tiny islands or to the cool lake in the **Hinagdanan caves.** Offshore from Panglao, **Balicasag Island** is popular with environmentally conscious divers and snorkelers, since its coral is under conservation. South of Bohol, **Pamilacan Island** also has attractive beaches and colorful marine life. Some locals offer their services as guide on whale-watching trips (especially from April to July).

Like so many of the Philippine islands Bohol also had trouble with pirates, as can be seen by the **Punta Cruz watchtower,** built in 1796, near **Maribojoc,** fifteen kilometers north of Tagbilaran. The large **church** in **Loon,** dating from 1753, is decorated with interesting ceiling-paintings. Inland, the Sunday market in the village of **Antequera** shows off the skill of the villagers in basket-weaving.

The **church** in **Baclayon**, about 10 kilometers east of Tagbilaran City, is a national monument. Built in 1595, it is the oldest church on Bohol and one of the first in the whole of the Philippines. Its characteristic, large belltower was used as a refuge during pirate attacks. The interior is notable for its carved pulpit, altar and centuries-old paintings, all depicting "inner values." In the adjoining monastery, articles used by the early monks are exhibited. Sadly, lack of funds has prevented much-needed restoration work from being undertaken.

Another interesting church can be seen in **Loay,** at the mouth of the river Loboc. From there a road runs upstream into the highlands. In **Loboc** the **Church of San Pedro** was built in 1602 but is particularly notable for its 19th-century ceiling

paintings. A boat trip on the idyllic River Loboc, between banks of lush vegetation makes, in the truest sense of the word, a refreshing alternative to visiting the venerable church buildings.

The road to **Carmen**, in the center of the island, does not seem to have been much improved since Spanish colonial times. But the bumpy road will be willingly endured by those who wish to see and experience the **Chocolate Hills** of Bohol.

This is a curious landscape of little hills – 1,268 of them, none more than 40 meters high – which rise shoulder to shoulder from the earth. In the dry season the scorched grass turns them a chocolate brown shade. There are various explanations for their shape. They are marine rock formations worn smooth by millennia of wind and weather. Or so most geologists assume. One popular belief is that they are missiles hurled by quarreling giants. Or more romantically: they are the petrified tears of the giant Arogo, shed in grief over the death of his earthly beloved, Aluya.

It is no legend, but absolutely true that in the village of **Taytay**, near **Duero** on the south coast, 130 families of the Eskaya tribe still keep up their ancient customs and beliefs, and have preserved their tribal literature in its ancient pictographic script. Relaxation on the beach can be found further east at the village of Anda, where there are now two attractive resorts awaiting guests.

In the north, **Talibon** is the jumping off point for Cebu and the islands offshore. On **Jao Island,** there is an ideal anchorage for yachts and a small bungalow-hotel run by a Canadian of German origin. All around, the sea is dotted with small, low-lying islands, where fishermen live out their peaceful lives far from the maddening crowd, and where birds of passage – not only the feathered kind – are lured by the mangrove covered sandbanks and gather strength for the next leg of the journey.

Above: The "Chocolate Hills" of Bohol.

MINDORO ISLAND
Accommodation

MEDIUM: **PUERTO GALERA: Puerto Galera Resort**. Near town: **Villa de la Chance**. Towards SA-BANG: **Encenada Beach Resort**. **Tanawin Lodge**, Tel: Manila 5254374. **SABANG BEACH: Terraces Garden Resort**. **SMALL LA LAGUNA: El Galleon Beach Resort** (diving). **BIG LA LAGUNA: La Laguna Beach Club** (diving), Tel. Manila 5212371. **Coco Beach Resort** (diving), Tel: Manila 5215260. **ANINUAN BEACH: Tamaraw Beach Resort**. **SAN JOSÉ: Sikatuna Beach Hotel**, Airport Rd. **MAMBURAO: Tayamaan Palm Beach Club**.

BUDGET: **PUERTO GALERA: Malou's Hilltop Inn. Melxa's Beach House**, Balete Beach. **El Canonero Marivelis Hotel**, at the jetty. **Villa Margerita Bamboo House**. Many basic cottages and lodges, some with diving, outside Puerto Galera and at the beaches: Sabang Beach (discos, bars), Small La Laguna Beach (quieter), Big La Laguna Beach (snorkeling), White Beach (very crowded), Aninuan Beach (quiet) and Talipanan Beach (quiet). **CALAPAN: The Traveller's Inn**, Leuterio St. **Riceland Inn**, Rizal St. **ROXAS: Santo Niño Lodge. Catalina Beach Resort**, Bagumbayan. **SAN JOSÉ: Jolo Hotel**, Rizal St. **Sikatuna Town**, Sikatuna St. **SABLAYAN: Emely Hotel**, Rosario St. **NORTH PANDAN ISLAND: Pandan Island Resort**, Res. Tel: Manila 5222911. **MAMBURAO: Traveller's Lodge. LUBANG:** Only private lodgings

Getting There / Means of transport
BY AIR: PAL several times weekly Manila-San José, Manila-Mamburao, Pacific Air several times weekly Manila-Lubang.
BUS: Manila BLTB to Batangas, then ferry. Ferry tickets: Hotel Centrepoint, Ermita. From Puerto Galera to the beaches: jeepney, boat or on foot. Bus or jeepney to Calapan-Roxas-Mansalay-Bulalacao, in the rainy season from there by boat to San José, also a connection San José-Mamburao. *SHIP:* Manila-Tilik (Lubang Island) and San José-Tilik, then by ship to Coron (Calamian Islands).

MARINDUQUE ISLAND
Accommodation
MEDIUM: **GASAN: Sunset Garden Beach Resort**, Pangi (2 km north) Tel: Manila 8016369.
BUDGET: **BOAC: Boac Hotel**, Nepomuceno St. **Aussie-Pom Guest House**, Caganhao. **CAWIT: Sunraft Beach. STA CRUZ: Model's Lodging. BUENAVISTA: Three Kings Cottages. TORRIJOS:** Private, near beach, Rendevous Cottages.

Getting There / Means of Transport
BY AIR: PAL flies daily from Manila to Boac.
SHIP: Daily Lucena - Santa Cruz, Balanacan.

ROMBLON ARCHIPELAGO
TABLAS / SIBUYAN / MASBATE
Accommodation
ROMBLON ISLAND: *MEDIUM-PRICED:* **Palm Beach Resort**, Lonos (c. 4 km s. of Romblon town). *BUDGET:* ROMBLON (town): **Marble Hotel**. **AGNAY: Selangga Tree House. D'Marble Beach Cottages**, San Pedro. **TABLAS ISLAND:** ODION-GAN: **Shellborne**. LOOC: **Morales Lodging**. TUG-DAN: **Airport Pension**. **SIBUYAN ISLAND:** SAN FERNANDO: **Bernie's Inn**. **MASBATE ISLAND:** MASBATE (Town): **St. Anthony**, Quezon St. MANDAON: **Mesa's Lodging** (at beach).

Getting There / Means of Transport
BY AIR: PAL several times per week Manila-Tugdan, Legazpi-Masbate; daily Manila-Masbate.
SHIP: To Manila, Lucena, Batangas. Regular service Cebu - Masbate. Between the islands by outrigger.
BUS: From Masbate to Mandao, otherwise jeepneys.

SAMAR ISLAND
Accommodation
BUDGET: **CALBAYOG: Seaside Drive Inn**, Nat. Highway. **ALLEN: Laureen's Lodge** (market). **BORONGAN: Domsowir**, Real. St. **CATARMAN: Joni's Hotel** (market). **CALBAYOG: Calbayog Hotel**. **CATBALOGAN: Maqueda Bay Hotel**, at waterside. **GUIUAN: Villa Rosario Lodge**, Concepcion St. **DALUPIRI ISL:** Flying Dog Resort .

LEYTE ISLAND
Accommodation
MEDIUM-PRICED: **TACLOBAN: Leyte Park**, Magsaysay Blvd., Tel: 3256000. **Asia Stars Hotel**, Zamora St., Tel: 3214942. **Manhattan Inn**, Rizal Ave.,Tel: 3214170. **Tacloban Plaza**, J. Romualdez St., Tel: 3255850. **PALO: MacArthur Park Beach Resort. BAYBAY: Plaza Hotel**, Uptown Center, Tel: 3352412. **ORMOC: Don Felipe**, Bonifacio St., Tel: 64661.
BUDGET: **TACLOBAN: Cecilia's Lodge**, 178 Paterno St. **Leyte State College House**, Paterno St. **PALO: City Lodge. BAYBAY: Ellean's Lodge**, A. Bonifacio St. **MAASIN: Verano Pension**, Mantahan. **ORMOC: Pongos Hotel u. Lodge**, Bonifacio St. **PANAON ISLAND:** LILOAN: **Liloan Hillside Lodge**, behind the jetty.

Tourist Information
TACLOBAN: DOT, Children's Park, Sen. Enage St., Tel: 3212048.

BILIRAN ISLAND
Accommodation
BUDGET: **NAVAL: LM Lodge**, Vicentillo St. **ALMERIA: Agta Beach Resort**.

Getting There / Means of Transport
BY AIR: PAL, Cebu Pacific: Manila-Catarman, Cal-bayog, Cebu City-Tacloban, Ormoc several times weekly; Manila-Tacloban daily.
SHIP: From Cebu City, Masbate, Leyte, Manila-Cat-balogan, Calbayog, Allen.
BUS: (Philtranco) Manila-Catarman, Catbalogan, Cal-bayog, Tacloban (approx 26 hours).

PANAY ISLAND
Accommodation
LUXURY: **ILOILO: Day's Hotel**, Gen. Luna St., Tel: 3368000.
MEDIUM: **ILOILO: River Queen**, Tel: 3376667. **Castle Hotel**, Tel: 81021; both: Bonifacio Drive. **Hotel del Rio**, M. H. del Pilar St., Tel: 3351171. **Manfred's Inn**, Tel: 73788. **Casa Plaza Pension**, Tel: 3373461. **Chito's Iloilo Penn**, 180, Jalandoni St. de Leon St., Tel: 3376415. **Sarabia Manor**, Tel: 3351021; all: Gen. Luna St. **Amigo Terrace**, Iznart St., Tel: 3350908. **KALIBO: Glowmoon**, Tel: 2663073, S. Martelino St. **Hibiscus Garden**, Andago, Tel: 8684488. **ROXAS CITY: Marc's Beach Resort**, Baybay, Tel: 6210103. **ESTANCIA: Pa-on Beach Club**, Tel: 444.
BUDGET: **ILOILO: Madja-as Hotel**, Aldeguer St., Tel: 3372756. **SAN JOAQUIN: Talisayan Beach Resort**. **S. J. DE BUENAVISTA: Annavic Plaza**, Tel: 558. **KALIBO: Garcia Legaspi Mansion**, 159 Roxas Ave., Tel: 6623251. **ROXAS: Halaran Ave. Pension**, Roxas Ave. **Halaran Plaza**, Rizal St., Tel: 6210649. **ESTANCIA: Terry & Em Lodge**, Clemet St. **CON-CEPCION: SBS Iyang Beach Resort**.
GIGANTE ISLANDS: private, also in San Dionisio.

Museum / Tourist Information
ILOILO CITY: Museo Iloilo, Bonifacio Drive, daily 9 am - 12 noon and 1 - 5 pm.
DOT, Bonifacio Drive, Tel: 3375411.

GUIMARAS ISLAND
Accommodation
MEDIUM: **Isla Naburot Resort** (Info from PAL, Iloilo City). **Costa Aguada Resort**, Inampulugan Island. **Nagarao Island Resort** (Info: Seminario St., Jaro, Tel: Iloilo 3206290).
BUDGET: **Gonzaga Family**, Cabalagnan.

BORACAY ISLAND
Accommodation
LUXURY: Resorts such as: **Club Panoly, Friday's, Sundance.**
MEDIUM: **Paradise Garden Resort. Palm Beach Club**, both in Mangayad. **Crystal Sands**, Balabag. **Nirwana Beach,** Mangayad.
BUDGET: Approx. 160 lodgings in and around Angol, Mangayad and Balabag; also many restaurants.

Getting There / Means of Transport Information
BY AIR: PAL, Air Ads, Pacific Air etc. daily Manila-Ioilo City, Kalibo, Roxas; Cebu City-Iloilo City. Manila-Ca-tiklan (also charters). *SHIP:* Manila-Iloilo City, Kalibo, Roxas, San José de Buenavista. Zamboanga, Minda-nao, Cagayan de Oro-Iloilo City. Ferry, outrigger boat: Iloilo City-Jordan (Guimaras).
BUS: (Ceres Liner): Iloilo City-Kalibo, Catiklan. Buses or jeepneys link all towns; on Guimaras jeepneys.
Tourist Information: Mangayad, Tel: 2883089.

NEGROS ISLAND
Accommodation
LUXURY: **BACOLOD: Goldenfield Garden**, Golden-field Complex, Tel. 4333111. **Convention Plaza**, Magsaysay Ave./Lacson St., Tel: 83551. **L'Fisher**, Lacson St./14th St. Tel: 4333731.
MEDIUM: **BACOLOD: Bascon**, Gonzaga St., Tel: 23141. **Sea Breeze**, S. Juan St., Tel: 24571. **DU-MAGUETE: Habitat**, Hibbard Ave. Tel: 2252483. **El Oriente**, Real St., Tel: 2250539. **Sta Monica Beach Res.**, Banilad (4 km south), Tel: 2250704. **El Oriente Beach Res.**, Mangnao (3 km south), Tel: 2250668. **Panorama Beach Resort**, Sibulan (6 km north), Tel: 0912-5150275. **El Dorado Beach Resort**, Dauin (16 km south), diving courses, Tel: 2257725. **ZAMBOAN-GUITA: Salawaki Beach Resort**.
BUDGET: **BACOLOD: Pension Bacolod**, 11th St. **Palm Inn**, Locsin St. **Ester Pension**, Araneta St. **MAMBUCAL: Mountain Resort. KABANKALAN: Friends Inn** (north). **HINOBA-AN: Mesajon**, Gatus-lao St. **CADIZ: Lakawon Resort** (by boat from Cadiz). **SAN CARLOS: Van's Lodging Hs.**, at jetty. **Skyland Hotel**, Broca St. Coco Crove, Ylagan St. **CANLAON: City Lodge. DUMAGUETE: Casa Lona**, Real St. **Opena's**, Katada St. **Plaza Inn**, Locsin St. **Al Mar**, Rizal Ave. **INSEL APO: Apo Island Beach Resort**.

Tourist Information / Museum
BACOLOD: Tourist Office, City Plaza Tel: 29021. **DUMAGUETE: Tourist Office**, Capitol Area, Tel: 3218. **Anthropological Museum**, Silliman University, Administration Bldg.

SIQUIJOR ISLAND
Accommodation
BUDGET: **SAN JUAN: Coco Crove**, Paliton Beach. **LARENA: Luisa & Son's Lodge**. Sandugan. **Para-dise Beach** 6 km north of Larena. **SIQUIJOR** (town): **Beach Garden Mini**, Catalinan. **Dondeezco Beach Resort**, 2 km w. **Kiwi Dive Resort**, Sandugan Beach

Getting There / Means of Transport
BY AIR: PAL etc. daily Manila-Cebu City - Bacolod, Dumaguete.

SHIP: Several times daily Iloilo City-Bacolod; several times per week Manila-Bacolod, Cagayan de Oro, Dapitan (Mindanao)-Dumaguete. Daily ship / boat Dumaguete-Larena, Cabalagnan (Guimaras)-Valladolid (Negros). *BUS:* Bacolod-Cadiz-San Carlos-Dumaguete: Ceres Liner, via Escalante to Cebu City. S. Carlos-Canlaon. Dumaguete-Zamboanguita-Hinobaan. Bus, jeepney, tricycles on shorter routes. On Siquijor Island: Jeepney und tricycle.

CEBU ISLAND
Accommodation

LUXURY: **CEBU CITY**: **Montebello Villa**, Banilad, Tel: 2313681. **Cebu Midtown**, Fuente Osmeña, Tel: 2539711. **Cebu Plaza**, Nivel Hills, Lahug, Tel: 2311231. **SOGOD** (NE-Cebu): **Alegre Beach Resort**, Tel: 2311231. **BADIAN**: **Badian Island Beach Hotel**, Badian Island, Tel: (Cebu City) 2536452. **Green Island Golf & Beach Club**, Lambug, Tel. (Cebu City) 95935.
MEDIUM: **CEBU CITY**: **Pacific Tourist Inn**, V. Gullas St., Tel: 2532151. **Hotel de Mercedes**, Tel: 2531105, Pelaez St. **Centrepoint**, Plaridel St/Osmeña Blvd., Tel: 2531831. **Park Place**, Fte Osmeña, Tel: 2531131. **West Gorordo**, Gorordo Ave., Tel: 2314347. **MOALBOAL**: e.g. **Moalboal Reef Club**. **Philippine Dive & Tour**. **Savedra**. **Serena Beach** Club (all: diving). **LILOAN** (east coast): **Franziskas Beach Resort**, Jubay. **LILOAN** (southern tip): **Manureva Beach Resort** (diving). **ARGAO**: **Bamboo Paradise** diving. **SOGOD Club Pacific**, diving, Tel: 2531229. **OLANGO ISLAND**: **Resthouse** (Booking at Kukuk's Nest Pension, Cebu City). **BANTAYAN ISLAND**: **Santa Fe Beach Club**, Talisay.
BUDGET: **CEBU CITY**: **McSherry Pension**, Pelaez St. **Jovel Pension**, 24-K Uytengsu Rd. **Jasmine Pension**, 395 Osmeña Blvd. **Kukuk's Nest Pension**, Gorordo St., Tel: 2315180. **MOALBOAL**: **Pacita's Nipa Hut**. **Pacifico's Cottages**. **Sunshine Pension**. **MATUTINAO**: **Kawasan Falls Cottages**. **ARGAO**: **Luisa's Place**, beach. **BADIAN**: **Lambug Beach** (diving). **BANTAYAN ISLAND**: **Admiral Lodge**, Bantayan, Rizal Ave. **MALAPASCUA ISLAND**: Blue Water Beach Resort. Cocobana Beach Resort.

Immigration Authority
CEBU CITY: **Immigration Office**, Customs Bldg. Quezon Blvd. (Fort San Pedro), Tel: 2534339.
Hospital
CEBU CITY: **Cebu Doctors Hospital**, Osmeña Blvd., Tel: 2537511.
Museums / Zoo
CEBU CITY: **Casa Gorordo Museum**, Lopez Jaena St., Mon - Sat 9 am - 12 noon, 2 - 6 pm. **San Carlos Museum**, Del Rosario St., Mon - Fri 9 am - 12 noon and 2 - 5 pm. **Zoo**, Beverly Hills.

Tourist Information
CEBU CITY: **DOT Office**, GMC Bldg., Plaza Independencia, Tel: 2542811; Mactan International Airport, Tel: 3408229. Info in the magazine *What's On* (airport, hotels).
Tourist Police, Tel: 2547317.

Getting There
Means of Transport
BY AIR: International airlines to Cebu City. PAL, Cebu Air, Grand Air etc. daily Manila-Cebu City, Flights from Visayas and Mindanao-towns to Cebu City. Pacific Air, Aerolift: Lahug Airport.
SHIP: Regular services to and from Manila and from the south Philippine ports to Cebu City.
BUS: Going north: Northern Bus Terminal, Soriano St. Going south: Southern Bus Terminal, Bacalso Avenue, ABC-Liner Terminal (bus and ferry to Negros), San José Street.

MACTAN ISLAND
Accomodation

LUXURY: **PUNTA ENGANO**: **Shangri-La's Mactan Island Resort**, Punta Engano Rd., Lapu-Lapu-City, Tel: 2310288. **Mar y Cielo Beach Resort**, Tel: 2532232. **MARIBAGO**: **Maribago Bluewater Beach Resort**, Tel: 2537617, (all with watersports).
MEDIUM: **MARIBAGO**: **Hadsan Beach Resort**, Tel: 72679. **Club KonTiki**, Tel: 3400310 (for divers, no beach).

BOHOL/PANGLAO/JAO ISLANDS
Accommodation

BOHOL ISLAND: *MEDIUM:* **TAGBILARAN**: **Bohol Tropics Resort**, Tel: 4113510. **Coralandia**, Tel: 4113445; both: Graham Ave. **Gie Gardens**, M. H. del Pilar St., Tel: 4113182. *BUDGET:* **TAGBILARAN**: **Sea Breeze**, C. Gallares St. **CHOCOLATE HILLS**: **Chocolate Hills Complex**. **TALIBON**: **Lapyahan Lodge**. ANDA: Bituon Beach Resort, Basdio (diving).
PANGLAO ISLAND: *MEDIUM:* **Bohol Beach Club**, Tel: 4115222 (diving). **JUL Resort**, Bingag, Tel: 4112697 .**Alona Kew White Beach**. **Bohol Divers Lodge**, (Alona Beach). **Bagobo Beach Resort**, Libaong. *BUDGET:* **Alonaville** (diving); **Pyramid Resort**; both Alona Beach.
BALICASAG ISLAND: *MEDIUM:* **Dive Resort**.
JAO ISLAND: *BUDGET:* **Laguna Escondido Resort**.

Getting There / Means of Transport
BY AIR daily. Manila-Tagbilaran (Bohol), Cebu -Tagbilaran. *BUS* Tagbilaran-Panglao: minibus from Agora Market, Bus from Noli Me Tangere St.; Bus from Tagbilaran - Carmen (for Chocolate Hills: have bus stop before here) - Talibon.

MINDANAO
THE TROUBLED
SOUTHERN ISLAND

NORTHERN MINDANAO
EASTERN MINDANAO
SOUTHERN MINDANAO
WESTERN MINDANAO

With an area of 95,587 square kilometers, Mindanao, the second largest of the Philippine islands forms a topographical counterweight to Luzon. It is characterized by numerous peninsulas and deep bays, and has several mountain ranges, mainly running from north to south. Mount Apo, the highest peak in the Philippines, rises from the Central Cordillera to 2,956 meters near the city of Davao. East of the Pacific Cordillera, the sea is 10,540 meters deep, the second deepest ocean trench in the world. The bow-shaped western side is dominated by mountains nearly 1,500 meters high. A high plateau extends from the center of the north coast to the center of the island, while the Agusan river in the east and the Buluan and Alah rivers in the south have created two vast lowland plains.

This "Promised Land" owes its reputation to the rich mineral deposits of nickel, gold, silver, copper and iron ore, the cultivation of large plantations, a rain forest which is still thriving, and a climate virtually free of typhoons; it enjoys rainfall that is spread fairly evenly through the year, and with 14 million inhabitants its

Previous pages: Campo Muslim and Rio Hondo, Zamboanga. Left: Young Magindanao woman from Cotabato playing the Kulintang or kettle-gong.

population density is relatively low. The island owes its name to the river Pulangi or Rio Grande de Mindanao, the second longest in the Philippines, which rises in the Central Cordillera and on countless occasions has transformed the lowland area of Cotabato into *magindanao* – "flooded land."

The Philippine singer, Freddie Aguilar, performs a melancholy song in Tagalog called *Mindanao*. It mourns the fratricidal war between Filipinos, the centuries-old suffering which intolerance and the struggle for power have brought to this large and rich island. Mindanao is in fact an area of religious strife: 75 percent of the population are Christian, but there is a substantial 20 percent Muslim minority, while the remaining 5 percent are believers in primitive animism and other faiths. Immigrants from Luzon and the Visayas have apparently adopted the ethnocentric behavior of the earlier colonial masters, and any resolution of the religious conflict in Mindanao seems no more than a pipe-dream in the light, for example, of Islam being denounced from some Catholic pulpits as the "number one enemy of Christianity," having supplanted Communism, now that the latter has experienced a worldwide collapse. Christian Filipinos do not want to admit that the teaching of Mohammed had ar-

153

rived in Mindanao at least 140 years before Magellan – four centuries of Catholicism, and a modern cultural policy that is firmly rooted in it, have definitely left their imprint. It seems to matter little to the central government and the clergy, that Islamic sultanates once united most of the southern islands, and even Manila itself, and parts of Luzon, were under Muslim control.

The Muslim struggle for autonomy is being carried on not so much in the hope of regaining lost territory, but rather as a reaction against cultural, economic and political discrimination in the regions where they now live. *Moros* is the disparaging name that was given by the Spanish to the Philippine Muslims, recalling the Moors who were driven out of the Iberian peninsula. But the Muslims now put this nickname proudly on their banners as a symbol of their struggle for freedom.The MNLF (Moro National Liberation Front) was founded in the late 1960s and was still trying to achieve self-determination for the Muslim population by armed force until the middle of 1996.

The social and political motive behind the revolts was certainly the massive influx of settlers from Luzon and the Visayas. The Muslims in Mindanao saw themselves reduced to less than a quarter of the population in their own homeland and, in a subsequent referendum on the question of autonomy, the Moros were the losers. Covered by a declaration of martial law in 1972, Marcos fought the rebellion by sending in heavily armed forces. From being a powder keg, Mindanao turned into a battlefield and then a graveyard for tens of thousands.

In 1976 Imelda Marcos went to Libya to negotiate the Tripoli Agreement with the MNLF leader Nur Misuari, who was living in exile there. Under international pressure the Marcos regime agreed to grant partial self-government to West and Central Mindanao. However, this treaty did not progress beyond recommenda-

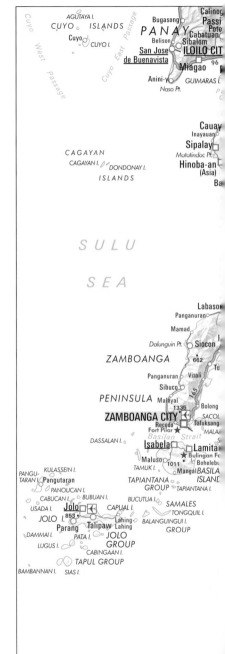

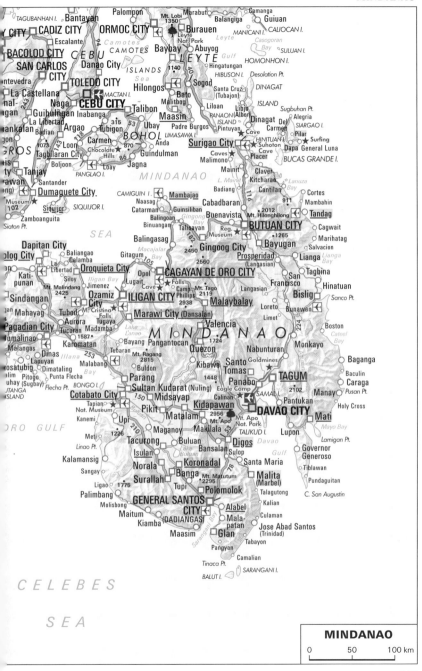

MINDANAO

0   50   100 km

tions on paper concerning the extension of semi-autonomy to 13 provinces.

Nevertheless a cease-fire was agreed between the MNLF and the army.The peace treaty signed between Nur Misuari and Fidel Ramos in September 1996 in Manila certainly dampened the radicalism of the Muslims' strivings for autonomy, and gives hope of a more peaceful future on Mindanao, even if radical splinter groups on both sides continue to carry out kidnappings and bomb attacks.

The political situation has naturally hindered tourism. Yet Mindanao has a fascinating cultural and physical diversity. Most attractive to its visitors are undoubtedly the Islamic elements combined with the cultural and geographical proximity to Indonesia and Malasia. Though foreigners do get embroiled in the troubles on occasion, it is too much of a generalization to simply describe Min-

Above: A banana-leaf provides effective protection in the rainy season. Right: Fishermen, south of Placer in Suriago del Norte.

danao as dangerous. Those who travel to the "Land of Promise" soon realize that all sections of the population earnestly desire peace.

NORTHERN MINDANAO

Viewed on a map, the extreme north of Mindanao looks like an index-finger pointing accusingly at the rest of the Philippines. At its tip lies **Surigao City**, the capital of **Surigao del Norte Province**. It is the principal transport and communications hub for the whole region and is thus known as the "gateway to Mindanao." Anyone arriving here at the turn of the year must expect a very damp welcome, since from December to February Surigao holds the record for rainfall in the Philippines, with an average of 1570 millimeters. Apart from these months, when typhoons may also be expected, the town is genuinely worth visiting as a base for many interesting excursions and adventures. There is bustling activity at the market and the harbor offers all kinds of

distractions. The islands to the north and east of Suriago are of greater interest.

Dinagat Island, which is about 50 kilometers long, offers wonderful walks and a beautifully clean sea for swimming. Nickel was mined on a large scale on **Nonoc Island** until 1987.

The largest island to the east is **Siargao Island** with **Dapa** as its principal town. The road runs alongside wonderfully picturesque bays and surfing beaches in the south of the island; there are reports of crocodiles being spotted in Siargao. you can also visit the fascinating mangrove forest near the village of **Pilar**.

Not far from Surigao City are several limestone caves with stalactites and stalagmites. They include the **Buenevista Cave**, the **Mapawa Cave** and the **Sohoton Cave**, with an underground river.

One of the two routes out of Surigao City to the south is on a well-built road which passes the charmingly situated **Lake Mainit** ("Hot Lake"), before reaching **Butuan City**, the capital of **Agusan del Norte Province**.

An important harbor and an influential cultural center grew up here many centuries ago, at the mouth of the Agusan, Mindanao's second longest river. Butuan was in the news in 1976/77, when parts of two pre-Hispanic boats were found in the Libertad district of the town. A connection was quickly established between these boats and the *balanghai*, which was the type of vessel described by Magellan's chronicler Pigafetta, in 1521. Planks dating back 600 or possibly 1000 years were found in a site which indicated the position of the original waterfront; taken together with skeletal remains, burial objects, jewelry and Chinese porcelain, they reinforced the archeologists' supposition that Butuan was not only an important pre-Hispanic port, but also the oldest urban settlement in the Philippines. The notion, long held by the people of Butuan, which used to be called Masawa, that the Spanish held their first mass here, and not in Limawasa, has not been proved. On the other hand, the discovery of the boats has strengthened the

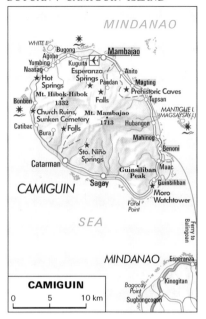

conviction of archeologists specializing in ancient sea-travel, that the Austronesians, ancestors of the Malay-Polynesians and Madagascans, undertook their long voyages over the Pacific and Indian Oceans in boats of similar construction. For the Butuan boats appear to have been constructed by "sewing" the planks together in a manner we know to have been done as early as the 3rd century B.C. A partially restored boat may be seen in the **Balanghai Shrine** at the excavation site, about five kilometers outside the town center, and some of the finds are now exhibited in the **Regional Museum** at the City Hall in Butuan, although most are to be found in the Museum of the Xavier University in Cagayan de Oro.

Camiguin, Island of Volcanoes

The good coastal road from Butuan brings you quite quickly to Gingoog City

Right: The volcano Hibok-Hibok and the beach at Agoho, Camiguin.

in **Misamis Oriental Province**. To the northeast of it lies the fishing port of **Balingoan**, from where ferries leave for **Camiguin Island**. Since 1998, when the airport on this fertile, mountainous island was extended, the previously tranquil atmosphere of the island has naturally changed to some extent. Nevertheless, Camiguin has retained much of its rural charm which, until recent years only a few foreign visitors had experienced.

Camiguin is a small island – only 300 square kilometers in area – but it has magnificent scenery. Seven volcanoes dominate the landscape in the middle of the island. The highest of them is **Hibok-Hibok**, (1,332 m), one of three which are still active. At once beautiful and threatening, it looms up behind the small capital town of **Mambajao**, which was almost obliterated by a major eruption in 1951. The damage it did on that occasion was bad enough. The eruption was visible from 160 kilometers away and about 2000 people lost their lives in the cloud of gas that descended into the valley. Prompted by this catastrophe, a national institution for the observation of volcanoes was established, which now keeps a watchful eye on the unpredictable activity of Hibok-Hibok.

It is better not to attempt an ascent of the volcano until after a visit to the PHIL-VOLC research station, which you will find about 400 meters up the mountainside. There is a wonderful view from its southwest slope. Healthy, primeval forest covers the ground, tree-ferns thrive in the cool shade, and springs bubble out of the ground. The **Tuwasan Waterfall** which thunders down from a height of 30 meters into a natural pool is very impressive.

The hydro-electric plant that was planned here will not now be built, as the electricity supply by undersea cable from Mindanao is more than adequate.

You can drive right around the island in a jeepney in a few hours, a distance of

65 kilometers. But there is a great deal worth staying around for: both natural wonders and sites of historical interest, such as the weathered church ruins and a submerged cemetery at **Bonbon**, a 300-year-old watchtower at **Guinsiliban** in the south, and the prehistoric **caves of Magting**. Then there is the proverbial friendliness of the Camigueños themselves. Delicious fruit, called *lanzones*, ripen at the end of October when Caminguin holds a festival in their honor. There are good hotels and guesthouses in Mambajao and outside the town are tempting lava beaches where several bungalow complexes have been built – some quite luxurious.

The much-vaunted **White Island**, which, when seen from high up on the mountain, looks like a gleaming horseshoe in the blue of the Mindanao Sea, is simply a rather large sandbank with little shade and limited snorkeling. More white sand can be found on **Mantigue Island**, also known as Magsaysay Island. It lies off the eastern coast of Camiguin and can

be reached from Binone, off Mahinog. Unfortunately the coral reefs have been over-fished here, as in so many places. Conservation must be enforced, otherwise visitors will ignore the sound of the island's name: "Come again!"

A Bastion of Christianity

The economic and cultural center of northern Mindanao is **Cagayan de Oro**. It is the capital of **Misamis Oriental Province** and its port serves the hinterland, the mountainous Bukidnon Province and the industries which have settled along the north coast. According to legend, Cagayan de Oro is not a favored place: the Bukidnon settlers from Kalambagohan were driven away by immigrant Maranao into what is today Bukidnon Province. One of their chieftains wanted to wage war to regain their lost lands and urged his people to fight. However, this Datu ironically fell in love with a Maranao princess, whom he soon married. Hostilities ceased, but the Bukidnon felt they had been betrayed. They surrendered their former territories for ever, but not before they had christened the land *Kagayhaan*, "Place of Shame." The name was spoonerized by the Spanish and the words *de Oro* were added when gold was discovered there. Thus the city, now with 400,000 inhabitants, received its name.

The museum of the Jesuit **Xavier University** deserves a visit. Apart from the Butuan finds, the it contains neolithic items from the nearby **Huluga Caves** and objects from the Bukidnon and Manobo peoples who were the original inhabitants of the region. The "City of Golden Friendship" holds its fiesta on August 27 and 28, with dances, jousting and beauty-contests.

Places you should visit around Cagayan de Oro are the **Macahambus Caves** near Lumbia to the southeast, **Mount Dulang Dulang** and **Mount Kitanlad** for climbing, and the **Catanico Falls** over to the east. There is swimming in the sea at **San Pedro Beach** near **Opo**, a few miles west of the city.

Around **Camp Phillips**, about 35 kilometers southeast of Cagayan de Oro, you will see one of the mainstays of the Mindanao economy: an impressive acreage of pineapple plantations belonging to the well-known American fruit-canning company Del Monte, which has developed the town specifically for its employees. The country club and golf course are open to the more senior employees and their visitors.

Bukidnon, the largest of the northern provinces of Mindanao, borders on the southern part of Misamis Oriental. This part of the high central plateau is little visited by tourists but has some high mountains, such as Mount Kaatoan, (2,938 meters). The provincial capital, **Malaybalay,** lies on a tributary of the long Pulangi river and if there is one time

Right: A Maranao weaving the colored Malong fabrics on her loom.

in the year when it merits a visit, it is during the *Kaamulan* festival in November.

Iligan City, capital of **Lanao del Norte Province**, to the southwest of Cagayan de Oro, is the industrial hub of the southern Philippines. Outside the port are cement, steel and fertilizer factories; chemicals, car tyres, flour, coconut oil, pipes and biscuits are also produced here. The hydroelectric power station, built in the 1950s on the **Maria Cristina Falls**, provides the energy for Iligan and distant regions of Mindanao. One of the town's landmarks, it is situated about 8.5 kilometers to the southwest. The falls are worth visiting, even if you have no interest in engineering. The waters, fed by the river Agus, the only outlet of Lake Lanao plunge in a dramatic, vertical drop of more than 80 meters.

The area, densely populated by Cebuanos, is besieged every year on September 29 by people attending the *Sinulog* festival. The Higaonon people, descendants of the earlier inhabitants of the hinterland, come to dance in honor of Santo Niño.

A Muslim Stronghold on Lake Lanao

When you make the journey from Lanao del Norte to **Lanao del Sur**, from the predominantly Christian Iligan City to the almost exclusively Muslim **Marawi City**, you only travel 30 kilometers, but you cross an invisible frontier from one culture to another. The capital of the southern Lanao province, which is officially autonomous, represents the cultural metropolis of the Philippine Muslims. The indigenous Maranao people were the latest converts to Islam but are also its most devout adherents, and, after the Magindanao and Tausug, are the third largest Muslim community in the whole archipelago.

Lake Lanao lies more than 780 meters above sea level between high mountains. **Mount Ragang**, at 2,815 meters is the

highest active volcano in the Philippines. The lake is the second largest in the country, with an area of 357 square kilometers and is the subject of many legends. The state tourist board woos visitors with the tale of St Francis Xavier, who is said to have tried hard to effect the conversion of the warlike Maranao people. It is said that he unfortunately lost a sandal in the lake, and only when the sandal is found again will the population convert to Christianity and peace will reign in Lanao!

The Maranao country is still an area of tension so independent travelers should make the effort to obtain detailed information about the current situation. It is nevertheless a fascinating place, which reminds one of Indonesia; each village is dominated by its mosque, and every house and domestic utensil is decorated in *okir,* the typical art of the Maranao, featuring the magic bird Sarimanok and other motifs.

In most other parts of the Philippines, women like to wear jeans, but here they are rarely seen. The usual form of dress is the *malong,* a brightly patterned cloth worn around the hips. Men wear the typical Muslim headgear, the *kepiah*, to show that they are *hadj,* that is, they have been on a pilgrimage to Mecca.

The exotic and richly stocked **market** in Marawi City puts the average Philippine *palenque* in the shade. There is a particularly large choice of chased brassware – pots, kettles, plates and vases, which are mainly produced in the village of **Tugaya,** 22 kilometers away. You can also buy gongs and other musical instruments, textiles and palm-fibre mats.

Mindanao State University was built in 1962 just outside the city. The small **Aga Khan Museum** on campus, is well worth visiting as a source of information about the rich Islamic culture of Mindanao. Beside the **King Feisal Mosque** and the Institute for Arabic Studies, the tallest minaret in the Philippines soars above the university.

The nearby **Marawi Resort Hotel** offers not only comfortable accommoda-

tion but also a wonderful view over the lake. There is an important "Holy mountain" on the road from Iligan to Marawi. Anyone who climbs it, it is said, including foreigners, will meet misfortune. Far more appealing is watching Maranao dances, which are famous all over the country. They are distinguished by particularly graceful movements, like the *kini-kini*, the proud, swaying motion of the women as they walk. Other typical features are the elaborate costumes and the *singkil*, an astonishingly nimble dance between two bamboo poles, while they are struck against each other. These exciting dances are reason enough to attend the Maranao festival of *Kalilang*, in the heart of the oriental Philippines.

EASTERN MINDANAO

The region to the southeast of Surigao City is a particularly exciting place, but is

Above: Goldminers dig deep into the earth near Lianga, Surigao del Sur.

completely undeveloped as far as tourism is concerned. Both provinces of Surigao have endured much poverty and suffering – they were the stronghold of the NPA rebels. In some areas, such as those around Tandag and Lianga, to the south of the gold-mining town of **Placer**, another force – the so-called *Lost Command* – holds sway. This tightly organized private army recruits mainly from members of the military and the police who have either been dishonorably discharged or have deserted. They live in considerable comfort with their families in military villages and control the local economy: they hire entire villages to dig and pan for gold, take a percentage from illegal tree-felling and from the fishing catch; they bribe the authorities, and are frequently behind the ambushes that occur on the poorly surfaced eastern coastal road. In addition, they fight alternately against the army and the rebels, or against both at the same time.

Not surprisingly, visitors are rarely seen in this really "Wild East." To explore this strange, labyrinthine coastline with bays, full of islands, lonely beaches and mountainsides clad in dense virgin rain forest would be an unforgettable experience. But up to now the local people have had no reason to share the "adventure" of having to live in this state of insecurity. This is particularly true of the Manobo tribespeople living in the hinterland of **Tandag**, the provincial capital of **Surigao del Sur**. For years they have been caught in the crossfire of the rebels, soldiers and large landowners, a precarious situation which they share with other ethnic minorities, especially on Mindanao. There is little in the way of traffic between Tandag and Mati, far to the south of **Davao Oriental Province**. The answer to the anxious question as to whether one will make it along the appalling road, is always limited to the little word *siguro* – "maybe." Consequently, little has changed on the Pacific coast since Spanish seafarers like Ruy Lopez de Villalobos established the first ports of call here in the 16th century, and the terrain proved too bleak, inhospitable and uncivilized even for them. Should a modern traveler find himself in this isolated region he can at least enjoy the wonderful landscape. There is jungle, unfortunately very much exploited around **Bislig**, a center of the timber industry; there are beaches and a coastline where mountains alternate with mangrove swamps. One reward at the end of a journey through the "Wild East," is a feast of juicy and vitamin-filled pine-apples which grow in plantations around **Mati** on Pujada Bay.

The highway out of Surigao City towards the south runs past Butuan City to Davao City. Buses complete the 350 kilometer journey through **Agusan del Sur** to **Davao del Norte** in record time, since this north-south route across Mindanao is one of the few decent, long stretches of road in the Philippines. Military requirements and the availibility of plenty of concrete in the area are the reason for

this. However, the bus does stop now and then, for instance in **Tagum**, 50 km before Davao City, where hordes of passengers get aboard, among them some pretty tough-looking characters. This is no surprise when you know that the notorious **Diwalwal gold mines** are near the town, a place that has been combed by many a prospector and which still yields a considerable quantity of the precious metal. But at a price! Over the years, hundreds of miners have lost their lives in landslides, collapsing tunnels and shootings. Trivial disputes over land-claims are still settled with the *bolo*, a kind of dagger, while drink and prostitution are the cause of many a skull being smashed. For a long time Diwalwal was synonymous with lawlessness and violence, like the American West during the great gold rush. Now the gold fever has subsided somewhat and a little order has been brought to bear. But the place is by no means tame and Diwalwal is just the place for someone looking for full-blooded adventure.

SOUTHERN MINDANAO

With almost 900,000 inhabitants **Davao City** is the largest city in Mindanao and the second largest in the Philippines. Founded in the 19th century as *Nueva Vergara*, this metropolis on the Gulf of Davao is in fact one of the most widespread cities in the world, though it is true that only a small part of its 2,440 square kilometer area is built up. This gives Davao City a constant pioneer atmosphere which has recently earned a name as a "boom-town." Up until a few years ago that term would have been considered utopian. Then the town was notorious for a crime-rate outstripping that of Manila. Furthermore, in the early 1980s Davao City was *the* stronghold of the NPA in Mindanao. The vigilantes, legalized by Aquino when she came to power, and the right-wing death-squads

of the *Alsa Masa* ("People's Rebellion") who, with the blessing of Cardinal Sin, went head-hunting among the leftists, have performed some of their worst deeds here. Fortunately, this reign of terror seems to have come to an end. Davao now attracts both employers and tourists; and since 1991 there are sea and air connections to Manado in North Sulawesi, and an Indonesian consulate in the city.

Like all cities that have grown rapidly, the center of Davao offers little of interest. There is, however, a lovely **fruit-market** (Madrazo Fruit Center) downtown at the intersection of Bangoy and Mabini Streets. The dominant "scent" here is the rather offputting smell of the durian. This large fruit is the size of man's head and is covered with spines. It is said to "stink like hell and taste like heaven" and has given Davao the nickname "City of Durian;" as well as its

Above: Durians and rambutans on sale at the fruit-market in Davao. Right: Billing and cooing in the Eagle Camp near Malagos.

own **Durian Monument**, situated on the Plaza Rizal.

The **Davao Museum** deserves a visit. It is in the **Lanang** district of the city, close to the exclusive **Insular Century Hotel**. The different ethnic groups of the region are represented in the museum: the Manobo, Mansaka, Mandaya and Bagobo. In the neighboring **Ethnica Dabaw Center** a Mandaya princess organizes the sale of native ethnic art.

Lon Hua Temple, the largest Buddhist place of worship in Mindanao, was built in 1965 for the large Chinese population. It stands on Cabaguio Avenue in the north of the city. For anyone who enjoys flowers the nearby **Puentespina Orchid Garden** is a wonderful place to stroll. The garden covers an area of less than 3,800 square meters and has many varieties of orchid including the famous Waling-waling (*Vanda Sanderiana*). A wonderful view over the city and the Gulf of Davao can be had from the **Shrine of the Holy Infant Jesus of Prague**, dedicated to the protector of

Davao, which is five kilometers south of the city. Davao City is suitably provided with hotels, restaurants, discos and nightclubs for those who care for nightlife.

The offshore islands of **Talikud** and **Samal** have been designated as "tourist zones." The two flagship resorts on Samal are called **Paradise Island** and **Coral Reef** and are intended to enhance the re-born tourist destination Davao City with their leisure facilities and the marvellous diving reviers. But it must be said that the beaches near Davao itself are very polluted since untreated sewage from this big city flows right into the sea.

Eagle Camp at Malagos near the town of **Calinan**, 35 kilometers northwest of Davao, is an important environmental tool. Dedicated workers of the *Philippine Eagle Conservation Foundation* are trying to rescue the monarch of the Philippine skies from imminent extinction. The known population of the second-largest eagle species in the world – only the South American harpy eagle weighs a little more – amounts to approximately 77 birds, including those born in captivity. The Philippine eagle is called, rather misleadingly, *Pithecophaga jefferyi* (monkey-eater) but usually hunts other prey. Since something like 2,000 square kilometers of Philippine forest disappear every year, the bird has scarcely any natural habitat left.

Some distance from Davao City, the "grandfather of the mountains," **Mount Apo** rises to 2,956 meters, a major challenge to mountaineers. It is surrounded by a vast National Park covering 70,000 square kilometers but even this can scarcely protect the virgin forest from plunderers. Back in the Marcos era there was an attempt to take a chain-saw to the forest, a scandal which was only just prevented by international protest. Even now, the reserve is continually being depleted by illegal felling and slash-and-burn (*kaingin*). In spite of more protests, construction of a thermal power station in

the middle of the park was started in 1992. This project, described as "absolutely clean" by those responsible, is an answer to the constant power shortages which Mindanao has suffered for some years, due to frequent droughts. Before this, the highest peak in the Philippines had already become known to the world's press in 1988 and 1989, when groups of mountaineers where held prisoner for a short time by NPA rebels. The tourist authorities still recommend that anyone considering a mountain trek should check at their office in Davao City for information about the current security situation.

Really dedicated climbers should not be daunted by alarming headlines. The ascent of Apo has to be one of the most beautiful experiences in any tour of the Philippines. There are three routes to chose from. Most people start from **Kidapawan** on the western slope. There is now a basic infrastructure on this route. Helpful local people organize guides and porters.

The trek leads up past the picturesque **Lake Agko** and ends at the equally delightful **Lake Venado**, about 500 meters below the summit. A second trail begins at **New Israel** in the southwest. As the name suggests, this is the headquarters of a curious sect who, among other things, believe that the human race originated in the Philippines. This will present no problem for climbers, since the villagers, who worship Mount Apo, provide useful services in return for cash. The last leg to the summit passes **Lake Macadac.** The third path starts at **Cabarisan**, which can be reached by jeepney from Davao City. Halfway along this route the **Tudaya Falls** offer a refreshing diversion. In the summit region night-time temperatures of about 4°C are the norm.

South of Davao City, a peninsula tipped by Cape Tinaca stretches far out into the Celebes Sea, away from modern

traffic routes. The coastal road drawn on many maps ends in fact at **Malita**, and the numerous villages that lie along the Davao Gulf in **Davao del Sur Province**, are only connected by footpaths, if at all. Motorboats provide a link with the big city, but in the spring, when the strong northeast monsoon is blowing, it is often impossible for them to land on the open coast. Life is very lonely here and the hospitable inhabitants welcome any visitor. At **Glan** a road begins that will take you back to more "civilized" parts, specifically to the area around Sarangi Bay and **General Santos City**, capital of **South Cotabato Province**.

Pioneers of the South

General Santos City, situated on the estuary of the Buayan river, is also known by the name *Dadiangas* ("thorn bush"), and can of course be reached more quickly by highway from Davao City, by way of Digos, than across the peninsula of Davao del Sur. As early as 3,500 B.C.

Above: Mt. Apo, Grandfather of all Philippine mountains. Right: T'boli women at Lake Sebu.

Sarangani Bay was a sheltered harbor for seafaring people and was used by the immigrant proto-Malays. In the 15th century a Muslim community led by Sharif Kabungsuan settled in the fertile lowlands of southern Mindanao. Some of the indigenous tribes such as the B'laan, Tagabili, and T'boli moved up into the surrounding mountains, out of reach of Islamic teachings and, initially, those of Christianity as well. Much later, the pioneers from the Visayas and Luzon arrived. The town was renamed in 1968 in honor of General Paulino Santos, hailed as the "hero of progress," who brought the first large group of settlers here in 1939. The pioneering spirit also prompted the big fruit companies of Dole and Stanfilco to flatten vast areas of South Cotabato Province to grow pineapples and bananas. This fast-growing city of over 200,000 inhabitants has a rather bland appearance, underlined by the grid layout of its spacious streets. The enlargement of the harbor and construction of an airport are intended to entice industry and investors

to a new economic hub of the southern Philippines.

A road through **Polomolok,** where the **Dole Pineapple Plantations** are located, brings you into the foothills of the 2,295-meter-high Mount Matutum and to the town of **Koronadal.** This is the name given by the Magindanao to their provincial capital, but it is called **Marbel** by the other long-established tribal group, the B'laan. The only reason to stop here is to change to the bus or jeepney which takes one to Lake Sebu, home of the T'boli (with another change at **Surallah**). Several kidnappings by Muslim extremists in recent years make it essential to enquire here or in General Santos City about the current security situation! **Lake Sebu** is in fact a series of three connected lakes – Sebu, Lahit and Siluton – stretched out in an enchanting setting. It seems a veritable haven of peace in the midst of the troubles of Mindanao. The lake is surrounded by a lush, green landscape; the air up here at nearly 900 meters is cool and fresh; there is a spectacular waterfall

cascading down seven levels as the water leaves the northern end of the lake, and everywhere a restful quiet prevails. For many years, the world of the150,00 or so members of the T'boli tribe in the Tiruray mountains was in order. But economic development in the province has meant that ever-growing numbers of Ilonggos, Bicolanos and Cebuanos are forcing their way into the hinterland. Their excuse is that they have come to "bring civilization" to the T'boli but all they do is buy up their land. Ever since gold was discovered in the area, the rich traditional culture of the mountain people has been under increasing pressure.

Around the lake and in **Lake Sebu Town,** as the newly established administrative seat is called, the resident Santa Cruz Mission is stoutly defending the rights of the T'boli. Several simple private guesthouses provide lodgings for visitors, and a walk round the lakes and

Above: The T'boli are justifiably afraid of losing their land and their traditions.

into the mountains will still reveal something of the modest and hospitable lifestyle of the T'boli people. The Saturday market in Lake Sebu gives the scattered T'boli the best opportunity to exchange goods and information. The sight of the T'boli in their colorful traditional costume, chewing betel nut and deep in conversation with one another, makes the presence of the traders who have come up from the lowlands with their synthetic materials, plastic toys and blaring cassette players, all the more incongruous and disturbing.

The dilemma of cultural adaptation is something another minority in southern Cotabato is currently having to contend with: the two dozen members of the Tasaday tribe who were "discovered" in 1971. For 15 years they were described to the rest of the world as the "last Stone Age people." They lived, and continue to live, in caves in an inaccessible region of the Tiruray rain forest to the west of Lake Sebu, which, as a protective measure, the Marcos government declared a reservation, sealed off and shielded from the outside world. In 1986 these tribespeople were at the center of a provisionally shelved (but still unresolved) dispute about the authenticity of their neolithic way of life (see p.212).

Whether one continues the journey beyond Surallah or Koronadal depends on the current assessment of the security situation. The two Cotabato provinces, the province of Sultan Kudarat which lies between them, and the northwest of Maguindanao Province, are all relatively tense and dangerous areas. The locals will happily advise travelers to board the Muslim-run buses and jeepneys, and assure doubters that these would never be the target of one of the sporadic ambushes one hears about...

Islamic Roots

In the 17th century Sultan Kudarat was a powerful ruler who held sway over Mindanao and Sulu. The province which bears his name was separated from Cotabato in 1973. It's a fertile agricultural region producing rice, maize, coconuts, fruit, vegetables, sugar cane, and the extremely useful fiber-yielding crops of abaca and ramie. In addition, rubber planations have been established, and the famous Waling-waling orchid thrives here.

Cotabato City, the capital of **Maguindanao Province**, is the second Islamic center in the southern Philippines. *Kuta wato*, from which the name is derived, means "fort of stone" in the Magindanao language. Muslims who came here from Borneo in 1475 built the fort on the delta of the Pulangi, or Rio Grande de Mindanao, at the place which today is known as **P.C.** (for Pedro Colina) **Hill**. A cave was also discovered there, which was last used as an arsenal by the Japanese. The broad gateway of Illana Bay faces Indonesia, and Islam arrived in the Philippines this way a good century before the founding of Cotabato, a city which still

retains its Muslim character today. Not until 1872 did Spanish Jesuits succeed in building a church at Tamontaka, some seven kilometers to the southwest, as a symbol of Christian influence. The church was partially restored following the 1976 earthquake.

Today the large university town of Cotabato has a population of over 100,000, of which roughly 60 percent are Christian and 40 percent Muslim. Cotabato's role as an important hub of trade and transport is enhanced by its political significance as the seat of autonomous government for the whole of Region XII, that is to say Central Mindanao (Maguindanao, Sultan Kudarat and North Cotabato).

The **National Museum,** which is housed in the **Regional Autonomous Government Center,** provides good insights into the cultural history of the region. The **City Hall** on the Plaza in the lively lower part of town was built about on hundred years ago in Islamic style, with numerous spires, turrets and curved roof sections. The city is proud of its modern supermarket complex, but there is a much more authentic atmosphere in the **Old Market** down near the Pulangi river. This is the Muslim quarter, where women in headscarves and men wearing caftans and caps can be seen everywhere. When you try some of the sweet cakes and pastries from the food stalls, with strong local coffee, and greet the traders with a friendly "Salamu aleikum!" then the bazaar experience is perfect**.**

On the riverfront too, where the ferries dock, the oriental atmosphere seems oddly remote from the modern western ambience around the plaza.

Gleaming mosques rise from the green of the palm trees on both sides of the Rio Grande, slender dugout canoes bustle about between villages built on stilts on the dull brown waters of the river. Beyond the Quirino Bridge lies the suburb of **Lugay-Lugay**, where craftsmen of the **Kalanganan Brasswares Co-operative**

produce brass utensils and bowls, as well as the *kulintang* – a gong-like instrument capable of playing different notes. At home the Magindanao weave the typical *Malong* (a sarong-like garment) and the *Tubao*, brightly checkered head-scarves. You can buy goods from Singapore and Malaysia in the **Cotabato Barter Trade Center** on Gov. Gutierrez Avenue in the town center.

WESTERN MINDANAO

The western part of this large island is shaped like a giant handle, only connected to North Mindanao by a narrow neck of land separating Pagadian Bay to the south from Panguil Bay to the north. The mountainous peninsula of Zamboanga, with the provinces of Misamis Occidental, Zamboanga del Norte and Zamboanga del Sur, is only more densely

Above: A mosque and village of stilt-houses on the Rio Grande, Cotabato City. Right: Idyll between the cliffs – Dakak Beach.

populated along the coast. **Pagadian City**, the provincial capital of **Zamboanga del Sur**, has for years only been linked with Cotabato City by ferry, because the overland route has been partially destroyed by fighting in Lanao del Sur. This hilly harbor town, most inappropriately called "Little Hong Kong," has little to offer the traveler apart from the Public Market a bus service to Dipolog, Oroquieta and Zamboanga, which has started operating again from here. There are, however, bathing beaches on the tiny offshore island of **Dao-Dao** and at **Tucuran**, about 30 kilometers to the east. Caves, lakes and waterfalls can be found inland. Living in the mountains around **Lapuyan**, 40 kilometers to the south, are the Subanon people, among the most ancient ethnic groups of western Mindanao.

The road passes through **Ozamis City**, the economic center of **Misamis Occidental Province**, and leads to the provincial capital, **Oroquieta City**. **Dakak Beach Resort** in the next-door province of **Zamboanga del Norte** close to the little town of **Dapitan City** is making a name for itself. It is idyllically located on a secluded bay between high cliffs. José Rizal stayed in Dapitan between 1892 and 1896, albeit unwillingly, for the Spanish had exiled the unruly intellectual here. The present inhabitants are still grateful to the hero who put this peaceful town on the map and laid out the relief depicting Mindanaou in the plaza. **St James' Church**, beneath blazing red poinciana trees, is worth a visit, as is the well-tended **Rizal Shrine**, the house where he spent his years of exile. A pleasant park and one or two streets named after his novels pay him homage.

Equally unassuming is **Dipolog City**, originally founded by the Subanon and now the capital of Zamboanga del Norte Province. Outriggers leave from here for excursions to **Aliguay Island** for beach-lovers, or for diving expeditions.

Zamboanga – Zone of Tension

More than anywhere else in the southern Philippines, **Zamboanga City** symbolizes the centuries-old tensions between East and West. Yet it also typifies peaceful commerce and a blending of various Southeast Asian cultures. The city lies at the tip of the Zamboanga peninsula and has approximately 450,000 inhabitants, of which roughly 64 percent are Christian and 36 percent "minorities."

The history of Zamboanga City, even in most recent times, has been turbulent.

The Subanon settlers from Malaya must have liked Jambangan, this "Land of Flowers," when their ships dropped anchor here long ago. Their leader, Datu Saragan, is said to have lived on the mountain called **Pulumbato**. Later, sometime before the 13th century, the seafaring Samal and Badjao peoples landed here from the islands of the southwest. Today, as in ancient times, they punt their boats, the nimble *vintas* or

lipas, through the shallow waters along the shore, with the *sabuan,* a wooden pole, which they also traditionally use to moor their boats. It is assumed that the *sabuan* is the origin of the name *Samboangan.* "The place where boats are moored" was certainly a busy trading-post for the Tausug, Samal, Badjao, and Subanon, as well as Chinese and Malays, in the 13th and 14th centuries. According to Pigafetta's journal, the survivors of Magellan's crew also sailed through what is today the Basilan Strait in search of the Spice Islands, and in October 1521 they landed on the southern tip of the Zamboanga peninsula, where they are suposed to have traded two knives for some cloves.

But it was not until 1593 that Christianity gained its first, rather unsteady foothold in this region where Islam was already established. In La Caldera, now called Recodo, to the west of Zamboanga City, Spanish monks set up a Catholic mission, which preceded the fortress, built in 1635 and still preserved today,

171

partially restored, and known as Fort Pilar. This, then was the origin of the town which henceforth was named Zamboanga.

This Spanish redoubt was constantly under attack by Muslims, Dutch, English and Portuguese. As a hub of trade and a place of refuge, Zamboanga attracted settlers from the Visayas, Luzon and the neighboring Sulu Islands over the centuries.

Zamboanga, the *Leal y Valiente Villa* ("loyal and valiant town") did maintain the bridgehead of Christianity on Mindanao, however the missionary work remained limited to the immediate vicinity. The no less persistent Tausug from the Sulu Islands and the other Muslim inhabitants gave the Spanish settlers no peace.

Even the American provincial government learned to fear the resistance of the Moros, and in Marcos' time the "city of flowers" was in fact more like a city of weapons.

Zamboanga has remained a cultural crossroads. Many have left their traces here – not only the colonial powers, but also merchants and missionaries from Arabia to China. History lives on in the old walls and in the faces of their inhabitants. The *Chabacano* (dialect) is a particularly lively reminder of the racial mix.

The Zamboangueños are still a colorful and exuberant people, especially between October 7 and 12, when they celebrate the *Zamboanga Hermosa Festival* with folk music, a regatta and a procession.

If you stay nowadays at the venerable **Lantaka Hotel** you have at least two places of historical interest close by: the port and Fort Pilar. It s especially pleasant to sit in the open Talisay Bar at the harbor and watch the ships plying the Sulu Sea. Beyond the low, sandy island

Right: The Badjao only rig their Vintas in this colorful way for festivals and tourists.

of **Great Santa Cruz**, where the Badjao ("sea gypsies") bury their dead, the shape of Basilan Island can be made out on the horizon.

Not far from the Lantaka, Valderroza Street ends at **Fort Pilar**, where the still incomplete **National Museum** puts on very interesting shows of underwater archeology. Among the exhibits are part of the cargo recovered in 1986 from a British ship which sank off Basilan Island in the year 1761.

On the east wall of the fort the faithful pray daily at the shrine of the town's patron saint, *Señora del Pilar de Zaragoza*.

A little farther to the east are the minaret and mosque of the **Campo Muslim**. From this part of town a wooden bridge crosses to **Rio Hondo** ("deep river"). The people here do not like tourists with their intrusive cameras, but accompanied by a local guide, you may have the chance to meet members of the reserved Tausug, Badjao and Samal.

Returning to the center of town, we recommend you to call in at the office of the **Department of Tourism**, close to the Lantaka Hotel, before going to look at the colonial-style **City Hall**. This was even more of a a landmark during the time when the unforgettable Cesar Climaco was mayor. A resolute opponent of Marcos, he not only vowed never to have his hair cut as long as martial law was in force. Every day, in protest against the passivity of the police and the army, he chalked up on a large board the latest numbers of townspeople to have been murdered, abducted or robbed. Then, on October 19, 1985, this darling of the people, who was always unarmed was gunned down in the street by political opponents.

Plaza Pershing, opposite City Hall, is named in memory of Brigadier-General John "Black Jack" Pershing, who was the first United States Governor of Mindanao. Nearby is the **Public Market**, where not only, fruit, brassware, and colorful Samal

mats are for sale, there is also one of four branches of the **Barter Trade Market**, selling duty-free goods from Indonesia and Malaysia. Adjacent to the Public Market is the lively **Fish Market** (mornings and afternoons).

From the **R.T.Lim Boulevard** there is a particularly impressive view of the sunset over Zamboanga, as the red fireball slowly sinks behind the forest of masts of the enormous *Basnigan* fishing boats that sail in from the Visayas.

About five kilometers north of the town stands the indisputably magnificent and dazzling **Astanah Kasannangan** ("Palace of Peace"), the seat of the Autonomous Government of Region IX, built, appropriately, in the style of a mosque. From its terrace you look away out over the endless, shimmering blue of the Sulu Sea.

Just over two kilometers further north you come to the **Pansonaca Park,** a large leisure complex with swimming pools, an open-air theater and picnic places. It has a **tree-house,** where anyone who

wishes may spend a comfortable night, having obtained the mayor's permission. It is not far from here to the grave of Cesar Climaco in the nearby **Climaco Freedom Park**.

On the west coast, seven kilometers from the city, past the **Zamboanga Beach Park**, lies the **Yakan Weaving Village,** where Yakan people from Basilan Island, demonstrate their fine skills at the loom.

San Ramon Penal Farm, about 22 kilometers west of the city, is a proud experiment in re-education. Minor criminals can live out their sentences accompanied by their families, grow rice and make souvenirs for tourists.

The picturesque waterside village of **Taluksangay**, 20 kilometers northeast of Zamboanga is another Muslim enclave. It is built on a sandbank, but only tourists find it picturesque, as the the Samal and Badjao people, who live here and who were forced from the sea to the land can only scrape together a meagre existence from boat-building and fishing.

173

NORTH MINDANAO
Surigao / Siargao Island
Accommodation

SURIGAO: *MEDIUM:* **The Tavern**, Borromeo St., Tel: 87300. *BUDGET:* **Flourish Lodge**, Borromeo St., harbor area. **Dexters Pension**. **Garcia Hotel**, Tel: 658; both: San Nicolas St. **SIARGAO ISLAND**: *BUDGET:* DAPA: **Lucing's Carenderia**, Juan Luna St. GENERAL LUNA: **Siargao Pension House**. Pisangan **Beach Resort**. **BRC Beach Resort**. **Jade Lodge & Beach Resort**. UNION: **Latitude 9 Beach Resort**.

Butuan
Accommodation

MEDIUM: **Imperial**, San Francisco St., Tel: 2199. **Embassy**, Montilla Blvd., Tel: 3737. **Emerald Villa**, Villanueva St.. **Almont**, San José St., Tel: 3332. *BUDGET:* **Hensonly Plaza**, San Francisco St., Tel: 3196.

Museum / Tourist Information

Regional Museum, nr. City Hall. **DOT**, City Hall, Tel: 82041.

Camiguin / Mahinog
Accommodation

CAMIGUIN ISLAND: *MEDIUM:* **Paras Beach Resort**, Yumbing, Tel: 879008. *BUDGET:* BENONE (ferry port): **J&A Fishpen**. MAMBAJAO: **Tia's Pension**. **Tia's Beach Cottages**, Tapon (out of town). **Tree House**, Bolokbolok (1 km northwest). **Camiguin Seaside**. **Jasmin by the Sea**. **Paradise Palm Pension**. **Caves Resort**; all in/near Agoho (8 km from Mambajao). CATARMAN: **Fisherman's Friend Resort**.

Cagayan de Oro
Accommodation

LUXURY: **Pryce Plaza**, Carmen Hill (4 km from City), Tel: 722791. *MEDIUM:* **Dynasty Court Hotel**, Tiano Brothers/Hayes St., Tel: 724516. **VIP Hotel**, Velez St./Borja St., Tel: 726080. **Philtown**, Makahambus St., Tel: 726295. *BUDGET:* **Nature's Pensionne**, T. Chavez St., Tel: 723718. **Parkview Lodge**, Tiso Neri St., Tel: 723223. **Sampaguita Inn**, Borja St. **Bonair Inn**, Don Sergio Osmeña St., Tel: 725431.

Museum / Tourist Information

Xavier Univers. Folk Museum, Corrales Ave., Mon - Fri 8 am - 12 noon, 2 - 6 pm, Sat 9 am - 12 noon. **DOT**, Pelaez Sports Complex, Tel: 726394.

Malaybalay / Iligan
Accommodation

MALAYBALAY: *BUDGET:* **Haus Malibu**, Bonifacio Drive/Comisio St., Tel: 5714. ILIGAN: *MEDIUM:* **Tinago Residence Inn**, nr. Tinago Falls. **Maria Christina**, Mabini St., Tel: 20645. **Iligan Village**, Palao (a little outside), Tel: 21752. *BUDGET:* **Iligan Star Inn**,

Quezon Ave. **MC Tourist Inn**, Tibanga Hwy.

Marawi
Accommodation

MEDIUM: **Marawi Resort Hotel**, MSU Campus, Tel: 520981.

Museum / Tourist Information

Aga Khan Museum, Mindanao State University (MSU), Mon-Thu 9 -11:30 am, 1:30 - 5 pm, Fri 9 -10:30 am, 1:30 - 5 pm. Closed holidays.
DOT, Ford Guest House Nr. 2, MSU.

Getting There / Means of Transport

BY AIR: PAL etc. daily Manila-Cagayan de Oro; several times weekly Manila-Butuan, Cebu City-Cagayan de Oro. Cebu City-Camiguin Island. Davao-Cagayan de Oro; Cebu City-Surigao, Butuan, Iligan-Cotabato. *SHIP:* regular services Manila-Cagayan de Oro, Cebu City-Surigao, Butuan, Cagayan de Oro, Iligan, Iloilo (Panay)-Cagayan de Oro, Maasin, Ormoc (Leyte)-Surigao. Daily Surigao-Dapa (Siargao Island), Liloan (Leyte)-Surigao. *BUS:* Manila-Tacloban (Leyte)-Cagayan de Oro. Daily Surigao-Butuan, Cagayan de Oro, Iligan. Cagayan de Oro-Malaybalay. Surigao, Butuan-Davao. Cagayan de Oro-Davao. Cotabato, General Santos-Davao. Jeepney/shared taxis: several times daily Iligan-Marawi.

EAST AND SOUTH MINDANAO

In Placer, Tandag, Lianga, Bislig, Mati und Tagum there is no touristic infrastructure. Private lodgings may be found with or through the mayor.

Davao
Accommodation

LUXURY: **Durian**, J.P. Laurel Ave., Tel: 2220600. **Insular Century Davao**, Lanang, Tel: 2343050. **Apo View**, J. Camus St., Tel: 2216430. **Grand Men Seng**, A. Pichon St., Tel: 2219040. *MEDIUM:* **The Manor Pension House**, A. Pichon St., Tel: 2212511. **Maguindanao**, Claro M. Recto Ave., Tel: 2212894. *BUDGET:* **El Gusto Fam. Lodge**, 51 A. Pichon St. **Le Mirage Fam. Lodge**, San Pedro St. **Royale House**, 34 C. M. Recto Ave.

Museum / Arts and Crafts

Davao Museum (ethnic artefacts art and crafts), **Lanang** (nr. Insular Hotel) Tue-Sun 9:30 am - 5 pm. **Dabaw Etnika**, Mandaya Weaving Center, Insular Hotel, Lanang, 8 am - 12 noon, 1 - 5 pm.

Touristen-Information

DOT, Magsaysay Park, Tel: 2216955, 2216798.

Samal Island
Accommodation

LUXURY: **Pearl Farm Beach Resort**, Res. Tel:

2219970. *MEDIUM:* **Paradise Island Beach Resort**. **Coral Reef Beach Resort**. **TALIKUD ISLAND** (west of Samal). *BUDGET:* Info: from the mayor.

General Santos
Accommodation
MEDIUM: **Hotel Sansu**, Pioneer Ave., Tel:5527219 **Matutum Hotel**, P. Acharon Blvd., Tel: 5522711. **Phela Grande**, Magsaysay Ave., Tel: 5524925. **T'Boli**, Nat. Hwy., Tel: 5523042. *BUDGET:* **Concrete Lodge**, Pioneer Ave. **La Azotea Inn,** Salazar St.
Tourist Information
City Tourism Office, City Hall, Sergio Osmeña St.

Koronadal / Surallah / Lake Sebu
Accommodation
MEDIUM: **KORONADAL: Marvella Plaza,** General Santos Dr. *BUDGET:* **KORONADAL: Alabado's**, Alunan/Rizal St. **SURALLAH: Bonns House**. **V.I.P. Trading LAKE SEBU: Bao Ba-ay Village Inn. Hill-side View Park & Lodge** (at lake). **Punta Isla Lake Resort**.

Cotabato
Accommodation
MEDIUM: **El Corazon Inn**, Makakua St., Tel: 4213035. *BUDGET:* **Padama Pension**, Quezon Ave. **Hotel Filipino**, Sinsuat Ave., Tel: 4212307.
Museum / Tourist Information
National Museum (Islamic regional culture), Regional Autonomous Government Center, Mon-Fri 9 am - 12 noon, 1 - 4 pm. **DOT**, Elisabeth Tan Bldg., De Mazenod Ave., Tel: 4211110.

Getting There / Means of Transport
BY AIR: PAL etc. fly daily from Manila to Davao, Cotabato; from Cebu City to Davao, G. Santos, Cotabato; Cagayan de Oro-Cotabato. Several times weekly Cagayan de Oro-Davao. Once a week Iloilo-G. Santos. *SHIP:* Regular service Manila-Davao (via Zamboanga City-G. Santos), Cebu City-Davao. Davao-Samal Island: boats from Lanang. Boats Samal Island-Talikud Island. Daily Cotabato-Pagadian.
BUS: To Butuan, Surigao (Bachelor Express), Manila (Philtranco), Cagayan de Oro (Ceres Liner, Bachelor Express), Cotabato (Minitranco), Gen. Santos (Yellow Bus), Terminal in Ecoland (2 km south of center). G. Santos-Koronadal (Marbel): Yellow Bus, from Nat. Hwy. (G.Santos) Koronadal-Surallah: Yellow Bus or Jeepney. Surallah-Lake Sebu: Jeepney. G. Santos-Koronadel-Cotabato: Yellow Bus, J.D. Express.

WEST MINDANAO
Pagadian / Ozamis City
Accommodation
PAGADIAN: *MEDIUM:* **Camilla**, Bonifacio Dr., Tel:

2142934. **Pagadian City**, Rizal Ave., Tel: 214285. **Guillermo**, Rizal Ave., Tel: 42062. *BUDGET:* **Peninsula**, Jamisola St. **OZAMIS CITY:** *MEDIUM:* **Holiday Tourist Inn**, Blumentritt St., Tel: 20073. *BUDGET:* **Grand Hotel**, Abanil St./Ledesma St. **Soriano Pension**, Mabini St.

Oroquieta / Dapitan / Dipolog
Accommodation
OROQUIETA: *BUDGET:* **Sheena's**, Barrienta St./G.del Pilar St. **Beach Resort Elvira**, Orbita St. **Plaridel**, 20 km north. **DAPITAN:** *MEDIUM-PRICED:* **Dapitan Resort,** Sunset Blvd. **DIPOLOG:** *MEDIUM:* **CL Inn**, Rizal Ave. *BUDGET:* **Arocha**, Quezon Ave. **Ranillo's Pension**, Bonifacio St. **Ramos**, Magsaysay St. **Village**, Sicayab.

Zamboanga City
Accommodation
MEDIUM: **Paradise**, R. Reyes St., Tel: 9912026. **Paradise Pension**, Barcelona/T. Claudio St., Tel: 9911054. **Zamboanga Hermosa**, Mayor Jaldon St., Tel: 9912040. **Platinum 21 Pension**, Barcelona St., Tel: 9912514. **Marcian**, Gov. Camins Rd. (airport), Tel: 9911874. **Preciosa**, Mayor Jaldon St. Tel: 9912020. **Lantaka**, Valderrosa St., Tel: 9912033. *BUDGET:* **Imperial**, Campaner St. **Atilano's Pension**, M.Jaldon St. **Mag-V-Royal**, D. Basilio Navarro St. **New Pasonanca**, Almonte/T. Claudio St.

Immigration Authority
Immigration Office, Valderrosa St. Nat. Museum, Fort Pilar, Sun-Fri 9 am - 12 noon, 2 - 5 pm.
Tourist Information
DOT, Valderrosa St. (beside Lantaka), Tel: 9910218. Info Zamboanga Province/Sulu Region.

Getting There / Means of Transport
BY AIR: PAL etc. daily Manila-Zamboanga City, Dipolog. Flights to Zamboanga City: Cebu City- Pagadian or Dipolog.From Davao and Cotabato; Several times weekly Cebu City-Zamboanga City. Cebu City-Ozamis. *SHIP:* Nach Zamboanga City: Several times weekly Manila (to Davao/Cotabato). Regularly from Iloilo (Panay), Cebu City (via Dumaguete, Dapitan), Cotabato, G. Santos, Pagadian. Boat rental (in good weather): Dapitan-Dakak. Several times daily ferry Zamboanga City Basilan Island. Irregular ferry service to Jolo, Siasi, Bongao, Sitangkai Islands, from Pablio Lorenzo St. To Gt. Santa Cruz Island: outrigger boats from Lantaka Hotel. *BUS:* To/from Pagadian, Cagayan de Oro, Dipolog, Iligan; from Guiwan (4 km north of Zamboanga City); to San Ramon, Yakan Weaving Village: from Gov. Lim Ave.; to Taluksangay: jeepneys from market. Local transport Zamboanga: jeepneys, tricycles (to airport), taxis.

THE MYSTERIOUS SULU SEA

BASILAN ISLAND
SULU ARCHIPELAGO

Adventure and exoticism can both be found in abundance among the islands to the southwest of Mindanao, but the dangerous waters of the Sulu Sea are better known as a "hotbed of pirates, smugglers and gunrunners from Malaysia," or "the home of the warlike Tausug." For centuries this area has been the black sheep of the Philippines family, yet it has continued to attract settlers from other parts of the country.

Fear of the "saber-rattling Moors" was first introduced from Europe and became widespread in Asia, thus helping the Spanish to secure the loyalty of the Christianized *Indios*. And after independence, the new Philippine government simply perpetuated the old image of the enemy.

For their part, the leaders of the local Muslim community regard the continuing immigration of Christian Filipinos, protected by massive military garrisons, as a threat to their existence. The Muslims, who are ready to fight, meet them with open aggression.

The peace greement of 1996 between the rebels and the government has scarcely improved the reputation of the Sulu Islands. Pirates frequently attack

Previous pages: A Yakan woman selling textiles. Left: A Badjao boy near Great Santa Cruz Island.

ferries and sailing yachts. Before travelling in this touristic "grey area" (which includes the island of Basilan) it is advisable to enquire at a responsible quarter about the current security situation (see page 185).

BASILAN ISLAND

Even the island of Basilan, a province with about 250,000 inhabitants, lying to the south of Zamboanga, has suffered from this negative image ever since the 1970s, when Muslim separatists took up arms against the Philippine government. The majority of the population, which also includes Chabacano, settlers from Visayas and Chinese, is made up of the peace-loving Yakan, the aboriginal Austronesian inhabitants, who, in the 14th century, were driven into the island's hinterland by Muslim migrants from Sumatra and Borneo. The Yakan were once semi-nomadic but now, converted to Islam, they live in settled farming communities. On important occasions they wear expensive traditional costumes, woven in materials that are among the finest in Southeast Asia. Equally prized by both men and women are the characteristic *sinaluan*, striped trousers in muted colors, which are narrow below the knee.

179

The north of this mountainous island has a temperate climate with rainfall distributed evenly throughout the year, whereas the south is very hot and dry between the months of November and April. Basilan has a number of agricultural products, the most important of which is timber and latex from rubber plantations, which are in some cases managed by foreign companies. The island also exports coffee, cocoa, pepper, abaca, copra and palm oil. Wealthy Basilanese, and others from Visayas and Luzon, have invested in the island and, as big landowners, they control its economy. That is why, for almost 100 years, the Yakan have been farming the land for others – land which they had owned since time immemorial. The unjust distribution of property is one of the major factors underlying the continuing conflict, although the offcial version maintains that it is purely of a religious nature.

Above: A Yakan girl at the festival of Lami-Lamihan in Basilan.

Outside Isabela there is a rubber processing plant which is part of the large plantation belonging to the Menzi family. Tours of the plant are possible, except at weekends.

The little capital of Basilan, **Isabela**, lies on the north coast, right in the lee of the offshore island of **Malamaui**. The ferry that arrives from Zamboanga City passes close by the houses built on stilts by the Badjao and Samal people, who have settled on this small island. The other feature of interest on Malamaui is the beautiful, private **White Beach,** owned by the influential Allano family, but open to foreign tourists.

Lamitan, Basilan's other important coastal town, is about 30 kilometers east of Isabela. It has an interesting market on Thursdays and Sunday mornings, where which the different racial groups of the island congregate. The Yakan proudly demonstrate their culture at the annual celebrate of their traditional harvest festival, *Lami-Lamihan,* every year in late March or early April. There is bathing at **Palm Beach** near **Lamitan**. The **Bulingan Waterfall** is about 712 kilometers inland from the town.

Whether it is safe to visit the very unspoilt fishing village of **Maluso**, on the west coast, depends, like all tours on the island, on the current military situation.

THE SULU ARCHIPELAGO

The 500 islands and islets of the Sulu archipelago stretch 300 kilometers from Borneo to the Philippines, and form both a geological and a historical bridge between the two. The region has scarcely been touched by tourism, and few Filipinos in the north even take much interest in this remote region. Yet, over the centuries, this Islamic corner of the nation has been the source of new cultural impulses, and anti-colonial movements have spread from here to the rest of the Philippines. The best known of the is-

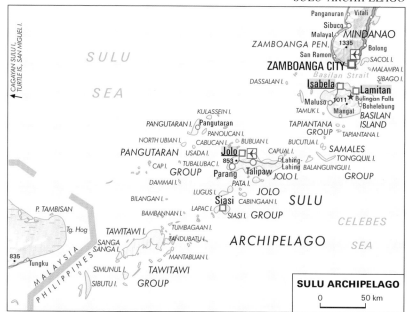

SULU ARCHIPELAGO

0   50 km

lands are Jolo and the Pangutaran, Tapul and Tawi-Tawi groups.

The inhabitants of Sulu province are the *Tau Sug*, or "people of the current," and they call their home *Lupah Sug* – "land of the ocean current." Across the sea, in the wake of migrations from Southeast Asia, came the "wave of culture" that was to make Sulu so powerful. Muslim seafarers had reached the islands as early as the 12th century. In 1380, Karim al-Makdum became the first Arabic scholar to set foot in the region that was later to become the Sultanate of Sulu, feared even by the Spanish.

Ten years later Raja Baginda came from Minangkabau in Sumatra and converted the islanders to Islam. Then, in 1450, Abu Bakr, also from Malaya, came and expanded the sultanate that Baginda had founded, into a mighty nation. The Spanish tried three times, to invade the islands, without success; at the fourth attempt to break the power of the *Moros*, in 1638, troops led by Governor-General Corcurera succeeded in occupying the

town of Jolo – but they could only hold it for eight short years. From then on, until the Spanish built a fortress in 1876, the Sulu islands remained under the crescent flag.

When the Americans arrived at the turn of the century, they wanted to impose their "progress" on the Philippine Muslims, just as they had on the Indians back home, but had as little success as the Japanese occupiers. The USA did, however, incorporate the Sultanate of Sulu into the Philippine Commonwealth in 1940. The Tausug, who have up to now resisted every foreign power, are now, letting their neighbors, the less numerous Samal and the Badjao, feel their claim to domination of the Sulu Sea.

The Sulu Archipelago stretches like a boundary wall between the Celebes and Sulu seas. Some 430,000 people live on the islands, 95 percent of them Muslim. Their main occupations are boat building, fishing, weaving fiber mats, and the growing and processing of coffee and fruit.

Jolo Island

The island of Jolo, with its provincial capital, Jolo town, is the political and commercial center of the Sulu Archipelago. Several abductions of foreigners, which made headlines in recent years have significantly diminished the attraction of this volcanic isle for tourists. Unlike other islands, where travel is once again possible without permission, travel on Jolo, especially to the interior, is only allowed with permission of the military.

In **Jolo** town the destruction caused by the fighting during the 1970s is all too clearly visible. Nothing but ruins remain of the old Walled City, once famous for being the "smallest fortified city" and the palace of Sultan Jamalul Kiram has virtually disappeared. The cultural focus of this predominantly Muslim town is the **Tulay Mosque**. The fish market by the

Above: Even ashore, the Badjao live a marine life, as here in Rio Hondo near Zamboanga. Right: An old Badjao, Tawi-Tawi.

harbor is still busy, as much-needed goods from Borneo are landed here and offered in the **Barter Trade Market**.

The lovely **beaches** of **Quezon, Tandu** and **Tandjung** are near the town. About one kilometer outside Jolo, there is (its future was uncertain) the only **museum** in Sulu province, with exhibits of Tausug ethnography. The first Islamic ruler of the Sulu Islands, Raja Baginda, is buried in **Bud Datu,** about nine kilometers south of the town. The highest point on the island is **Tumantangis**, the "crying mountain." Its 853-meter-high peak is nearly always wreathed in cloud.

The Tawi-Tawi group

While a visit to the island of **Siasi** in the **Tapul group**, the other Tausug stronghold, is currently also rather dangerous, the southwestern **Tawi-Tawi Islands** are relatively peaceful. Nevertheless, the one-hour flight from Zamboanga City is still to be recommended, in preference to a day-long trip by boat, with the chance

of being attacked by pirates. The early Asiatic migrants called the islands *Jaui Jaui* – "far away." Seen from the air, set in the turquoise Sulu Sea, they look like everyone's dream of a tropical paradise. The strong military presence in Bongao does have a sobering effect on the visitor.

The province of Tawi-Tawi comprises 308 islands and islets, including Turtle Island, the sea-gull colony San Miguel, and the islands grouped around Cagayan de Tawi-Tawi (Cagayan Sulu), which lie nearer to Palawan. The population numbers around 230,000. It is 90 percent Muslim, and governed from Bongao on Bongao Island. The largest ethnic group are the Samal, who can be found all over the archipelago working as fishermen, traders, farmers and boat builders. A group of Samal, called Jama Mapun, live in the area between south Palawan and Cagayan de Tawi-Tawi, and are renowned as superb seamen and boat builders. Spreading outwards from Jolo, the Tausug have settled chiefly on the main island of Tawi-Tawi, where they

cultivate the land and run a lucrative trade in agar-agar, a sea-weed used in chemical processes. They occupy influential administrative posts, while at the same time quite a number are no doubt involved in smuggling and piracy. Right at the bottom of the social ladder are the poor Badjao, who are known, sometimes contemptuously, sometimes sentimentally, as "sea-gypsies," though they prefer to call themselves as "the men of the sea."

Since its military occupation, **Bongao Island** has been one of the few refuges for the sea-gypsies, and is also one of the less safe islands for tourists in the vicinity of the main island, Tawi-Tawi. The market in the town of **Bongao** and the colorful bustle on the pier are just what you would expect in a faraway port, which draws in people from remote islands on the horizon. Stalls are laid out with all sorts of handicrafts, hats made from palm leaves, colorfully patterered mats, spices and plastic toys. There is much trading in fish, brought in and out again by heavily

laden sailing and motor-boats. Children splash in the clear water of the harbor and the narrow strait between Bongao and the neighboring island of Sanga Sanga. There is a beautiful beach on Bongao's west coast. Along the shore of the harbor bay, below the provincial capitol, the houses of the "resident" Badjao huddle closely together on stilts. The authorities want to lure them away from their rootless aquatic life on house-boats, and turn them into land men, with corrugated iron roofs and rough wooden walls.

Bongao Island is dominated by **Mount Bongao**, a wooded outcrop of rock, 314 meters high, which can be climbed from the village of **Pasiagan**. But take care, because a royal ancestor, Anjaotal, lies buried on the summit of the holy mountain. On the way you may encounter the equally revered monkeys, who are said to serve a white monkey-king. The locals say it brings bad luck if you touch them.

Above: A Samal fisherman transports seaweed in a dugout canoe, Bongao.

Between the islands of Bongao and Simunul lies the alluring **Sangay-Siapo Island**, with a fine beach and coral reef. On **Simunul Island** one treads holy ground: in the year 1380 Sheikh Karim al-Makdum ordered the building of the Philippines' first mosque in the village of **Tubig Indangan**. Its four wooden pillars have survived, and the Sheikh himself is buried in Tandubanak on Sibutu Island.

Both the north of **Sanga Sanga Island** and the main island, **Tawi-Tawi**, where pirate gangs and rebels hide out, are off-limits to visitors. Nonetheless, in 1984, **Port Languyan** on Tawi-Tawi was the starting point for a daring enterprise by some adventurous Europeans. In an outrigger, named *Sarimanok*, built locally using wood from the rain forest, they set sail on the route of prehistoric Austronesian seafarers and crossed 7,000 kilometers of the Indian Ocean, to reach Madagascar. In order to achieve this the expedition was able to rely on the great boat-building tradition of the Sulu people.

Good boat builders also live on the long, flat **Sibutu Island**, south of the Tawi-Tawi group. Their strong, fast, single-hulled boats, called *kumpits*, have long been feared far and wide as the trade-mark of the pirates. More recently, foreign yachtsmen have been ordering them in a sleeker design. Mostly you will see them all through the archipelago, working as motorized ferries or freight transporters.

Sibutu's twin island, **Sitankai**, lying on the edge of a broad chain of reefs, is known as the "Venice of Southeast Asia." Both islands are strongholds of the Badjao, who here live in settlements of stilt-houses, but also still often dwell in roomy houseboats called *lipa*. These nomads of the sea have been sailing Southeast Asian waters for thousands of years; they reached the Philippines just ahead of, or in the wake of the immigrant fleets, but nowadays they are no more than flotsam on the stormy and confusing seas of politics.

In order to survive, the Badjao, who a re peaceable people, keep clear of conflicts. They are submit to the domination of theTausug, who treat them as *luwaan* ("people you can spit out") by cloaking their animistic beliefs in Islam. These seafaring people have never totally overcome their aversion to dry land, which they believe is the seat of all earthly evils and to which they traditionally only make their final journey, to be buried. Although some of them have moved into humble stilt-houses, the Badjao remain true to their element. They live mainly by catching fish, but are also excellent divers, bringing up sea-snails, pearl oysters and sea-cucumber, which they sell to Chinese or Tausug merchants. The Badjao embody the ancient physical harmony of man, sea and boat, which originally made it possible for the early Austronesians to embark on their great colonizing voyages to Polynesia and over the Indian Ocean to East Africa.

BASILAN ISLAND / JOLO ISLAND

Accommodation / Restaurants
BASILAN ISLAND: *BUDGET:* ISABELA: **New Basilan Hotel**, J. S. Alano St. (near jetty). **New International Restaurant**. MENZI: **Menzi Guest House** (reservation necessary), 3 km outside town in the Menzi Plantation. LAMITAN: Traveller's Inn Estabilio Home Stay (Nalamar Restaurant), Pedro Cuevas St. **JOLO ISLAND**: *BUDGET:* JOLO (Town): **Helen's Lodge & Restaurant**, Buyon St., Tel: 104.

Getting There / Means of Transport
BY AIR: PAL daily flight Zamboanga City-Jolo.
SHIP: Several ferries daily Zamboanga City-Isabela, Lamitan (Basilan), 2 hours.
Rented Boat: Isabela (Basilan)-Malamawi Island. From Basilan to the other Sulu Islands: irregular, unsafe connections. Daily ferries (unreliable): Zamboanga City-Insel Jolo (at least 10 hours). *BUS:* On-Basilan Island: Several times daily Isabel-Lamitan. Bus/jeepney: Isabela-Maluso. On Jolo Island: Rented jeepney or tricycle (for short distances).

Security
Before travelling to the islands, it is essential to obtain up-to-date information. Enquire at **DOT**, the Office for Muslim Affairs in Zamboanga City and the military Southern Command Headquarters. Advise them of your planned itinerary. Do not leave the larger towns. **SIASI:** Insecure island, a visit here is not advisable.

SITANGKAI AND BONGAO ISLANDS

Accommodation / Restaurant
BONGAO ISLAND: *BUDGET:* BONGAO (Town): **Peping Cuarema's Residence**, Muslimin St. **The Southern Hotel**, Datu Halun St. **Stonehills Hotel**, Nalil. **Private lodgings**, Info: Mr. Annal Tadus c/o LTG Marketing, Ridjiki Blvd., also info on boat rentals. **Jane's Fastfood & Restaurant**, Muslimin St. **SITANGKAI ISLAND**: Info. about private lodgings from the school or from **DOT** in Zamboanga City.

Getting There / Means of Transport
BY AIR: PAL daily Zamboanga City-Bongao Island.
SHIP: Daily (not always reliable) Zamboanga City-Bongao, Sibutu, Sitangkai Islands (via Jolo and Siasi Islands). Arrival/departure from: Commercial Pier, Bongao Island. Smaller ferries and outrigger boats from Bongao to the surrounding islands, irregular timetables. Arrival/departure: Chinese Pier, Bongao Island.
JEEPNEYS / TRICYCLES: From the airport on Sanga Sanga (6 km from Bonago Island) and within Bongao.

PALAWAN
ALMOST PARADISE

AROUND PUERTO PRINCESA
SOUTHERN PALAWAN
NORTHERN PALAWAN
CALAMIAN ARCHIPELAGO

Many people who know the Philippines will agree that of all the regions of the archipelago, Palawan possesses the greatest and most varied natural beauty. Alone from a geographical standpoint the province is remarkable: the main island, 435 kilometers long, is only 40 kilometers across at its widest point, and lies like a huge rampart between the South China Sea and the Sulu Sea. Only a few miles separate its southern tip from Borneo. In the north, Palawan ends in a ragged confusion of bays, deep inlets and hundreds of islands, large and small. With more than 1,770 islands in all, and a total length of 650 kilometers, Palawan is the largest province in the Philippines.

When local political leaders mutter darkly about the "Republic of Palawan," they are only partly joking. Palawan has always enjoyed a certain independence from the Philippines. This starts with the flora and fauna, still largely unaltered, whose origins can be traced to Borneo. It seems that in the mists of time the two neighboring islands were joined together. Palawan has been considered the "cradle of Philippine civilization," since the discovery, in 1962 in the Tabon Caves near

Previous pages: Diving in Cayangan Lake, on Coron Island, in the Calamian Archipelago. Left: By jeepney through Palawan.

Quezon, of human bones around 22,000 years old. It is even possible that as far back as 50,000 years ago, *homo sapiens* prowled around the island, as indicated by the stone tools from that period that have also been found here. In the 9th century A.D., Chinese merchants dropped anchor in the place they called *Pa-Lao-Yu* ("land with fine, safe harbor"). Ships also arrived from the sultanates of Brunei and Jolo, to pick up cargoes of hardwood, pearls, mother-of-pearl, honey, resin, *trepang* (dried sea-cucumber), edible swallows' nests and, it must be said, native slaves. From the 16th century onward came the Spanish, British and Dutch, and even during the American colonial period, the Japanese were able to maintain fisheries here, without disturbance.

In 1967 Marcos placed the whole region under a nature conservation order. Alas, as so often, this looked good on paper but in reality meant little. Palawan's maginificent virgin forest, with its abundant animal and plant life has recently been so despoiled that visitors who knew the island in the early 1980s will be horrified to see it now. Not even the splendid coral reefs have been spared from environmental vandalism. A hail of dynamite rained down on the once rich fishing grounds, and the sought-after tropical fish were stunned with sodium cyanide, so that they could be more swiftly exported to western aquaria. By the beginning of the 1990s, 150 tons of this dangerous poison were being poured out annually around the islands. There was a national outcry – finally – when a foreign company set up on the hitherto untouched Tubbataha reef. They wanted to cultivate algae there – what harm could 60 families growing algae do to the nature reserve and the world-famous diving waters? An international cheer went up when a Philippine eco-group drove out the intruders.

Fortunately only parts of Palawan have been plundered and deforested. Sizeable tracts of primeval forest are still standing because they are too inaccessible for the greedy chain-saws. Financial and practical assistance, much of it from abroad, is helping to protect the threatened areas. These are the places which the indigenous people, traditionally in contact with nature, have made their home since prehistoric times. Finally, the greatest ray of hope is the gradual realization by the Filipinos that tourists will only come and spend money here, if the much-vaunted experience of nature in the"last frontier" of Palawan really is possible.

Awareness of the problem is growing. Time will show if the expansion of the road network will turn out to be a threat to nature. A coastguard, the *bantay dagat* patrols the waters in outriggers keeping an eye out for dynamite fishers, and a "forest guard" prowls the land to prevent illegal felling of trees. Setbacks do occur. Additionally, the pressure of a growing population is already noticeable. Every day people arrive from the poor regions of Visayas, especially from Negros, for Palawan has begun to replace Mindanao as the "Land of Promise."

In spite of these side-effects, there is still a great deal in Palawan for nature-enthusiasts to feast their eyes on. Trekking tours though the mountainous island have lost none of their excitement. The ever-present combination of forest, beach and water gives them a unique quality. The waters of the South China and Sulu Seas are almost always crystal clear, and anyone wanting to walk long distances on foot is not only alone for hours on end, but is also safe. For, apart from a small area in the far south, Palawan has no problem with rebels.

There is food in abundance. Cheap and simple it may be, but also fresh and delicious. Fish and seafood are always at the top of any Palawan menu. Sea-grass is a speciality, and even jelly-fish are "harvested" and processed for export, and for Chinese palates.

AROUND PUERTO PRINCESA

The friendly capital of **Puerto Princesa**, on the sheltered Puerto Princesa Bay of the same name, lies halfway down the long, narrow island, and is the starting-point for expeditions in every direction. The town of about 65,000 inhabitants, named the "Princess among ports," was hewn out of the virgin jungle as recently as 1872. The extensive but straightforward layout of the city offers little to look at, other than the **Cathedral** beside **Rizal Park**, which was built to replace the original church dating from the 1880s. The attraction of the town is found in the places where the relaxed and friendly Palaweños gather: at the **harbor**, surrounded by fishermen's stilt-houses, and at the **market**, by the junction of Malvar and Burgos Streets, where you can buy anything from safety-pins to rice, wild honey, fish and live pigs. Very near the market, still in the center of towna is **Mendoza Park**, and in it a little **museum** with interesting and informative exhibits from the culture of Palawan's aboriginal inhabitants. Plenty of guest-houses, hotels and restaurants make the town a pleasant place to stay. At any rate, the incumbent mayor E. Hagedorn (of German origin) has made Puerto the cleanest

PALAWAN
0   50 km

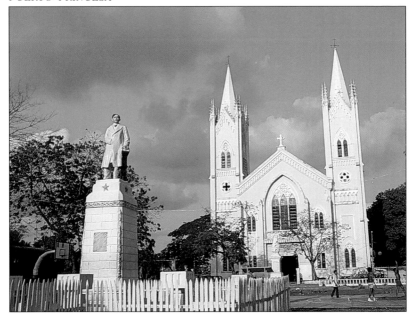

town in the Philippines. Severe regulations have been brought to the streets: failing to use the garbage cans, flicking cigarette butts, or illegally felling trees about can result in a steep fine or even a prison sentence.

You do not have to go very far out of Puerto to find interesting things to do. Pleasant day-long excursions can be made to the host of little islands in **Honda Bay**: **Snake**, **Starfish** and **Cowrie Islands** are very popular with island-hoppers. Mangroves and sandbanks, coral reefs and bathing places all combine to make the bay an attractive spot. A two-hour journey by jeepney, followed by a walk, brings you to inviting **Nagtabon beach**, on the South China Sea, northwest of Puerto Princesa. There is a delightful view out to Cock and Hen Islands. The debit side, it must be said, are the bloodsucking *niknik*, the tiny sand-flies which buzz around so many of the

Above: Puerto Princesa's well-tended park with the cathedral and statue of Rizal.

otherwise paradisical beaches in this country. Heading southwest from Puerto Princesa you will find some other lovely bathing beaches around **Napsan** on the west coast.

If you take the road to Iwahig, 23 kilometers southwest of Puerto Princesa, you will pass a **crocodile farm** in Irawan, which is financed by Japan. In spite of the protective function of the institute, the unfortunate reptiles have to sacrifice their skins as the raw material for extravagant, fashion accessories. There is an impressive five-meter-long skeleton of a crocodile that was caught in Palawan a few years ago.

In the nearby **Iwahig Prison and Penal Farm** some 4000 prisoners from all over the Philippines live and work out their sentences here under open conditions. They plant rice and produce hand-made souvenirs which they are allowed to sell. Many of them work the farm together with their families, and continue to live here after their release. The public is invited to visit this undoubtedly humane establishment, but you should not be deceived into thinking that all Philippine prisons are like this. Conditions in the country's "normal" penitentiaries are pretty dreadful. Further south there is another part of the penal colony, called **Santa Lucia**, from where a walk of seven kilometers leads to a hot spring. Further southwest, via Mangingisda, and rather difficult to reach, is the Turtle Bay Resort, where you can relax by the ocean.

SOUTHERN PALAWAN

The coast of the Sulu Sea, south of Puerto Princesa, is relatively easy to get to. A so-called "highway," very bumpy in parts, runs through Narra to **Brooke's Point**, 150 kilometers to the south-west. From there a rough track continues on to Bataraza.

At **Rio Tuba** the road peters out completely in wild country. For years the far south of Palawan has been a stronghold of the Moro rebels, and can only be reached by boat. Despite its remoteness, the forests of southern Palawan have been grievously damaged. Even on the slopes of **Mount Mantanlingajan**, at 2073 meters the highest peak in the province, men with saws and axes have clearly been hard at work.

A further destination that until recently was much praised, is now also disappointing: the "bird paradise" **Ursula Island**. Lying quite a distance off the coast of Palawan, the island was indeed the haunt of thousands of sea-birds. Then man arrived, and with him – rats, which caused most of the birds to take refuge on the even more distant **Tubbataha reef**. The little islands in the extreme south are all the more attractive. On **Bugsuk**, **Candaraman** and **Balabac** colorful Moslem influence prevails; Borneo is very near. The waters are wonderful for scuba diving but the currents are dangerous.

A long way off the southwest coast of Palawan stretches a chaos of reefs and sandbanks, which sailors have always been careful to avoid. Real atolls, like those on postcards of the South Seas, lie gleaming in the sea. Far to the west lies the **Dangerous Ground**, an even more treacherous labyrinth of coral in the middle of the South China Sea. These fragments of dry land are the object of shrewd territorial claims by all the adjacent coastal states. If oil were to be discovered here, an international crisis would immediately ensue. Indeed the **Spratly Islands** pop up in the headlines every so often, and shots have already been fired over them.

The islands lying closer to the coast of Palawan should, with any luck, be spared such conflicts. Most of them are uninhabited isles, fringed with white beaches and colorful corals. A while back you could meet a "white man" on **Tamlagun Island** ("Frederick's Island") off the coast near Quezon. Frederick, a German, lived for years beneath fruit trees and coconut palms, surrounded by flocks of fowl. Whether he finally died of loneliness (in 1994) no one knows.

Quezon is a sleepy little town, but nearby there is an archeological feature of national importance.You can visit the prehistoric **Tabon Caves** on the hilly **Lipuun Point**, not far away. This complex of 200 caverns is far from fully explored and may yet have some archeological surprises in store. The caves (only seven are accessible) have been placed under state protection, and there is a guardian on the site who will give you a guided tour. The most valuable items, such as a piece of skull from the "first Filipino," more than 20,000 years old, are kept in the National Museum in Manila. Many other caves have been discovered, all on Palawan's west coast. Formerly used as burial chambers, they tell us much about the early settlement of the island and prove Palawan's importance as an early crossroads of trade for the Asiatic peoples.

NORTHERN PALAWAN
St Paul's National Park

Palawan's largest and most famous cavern, **St Paul's Cave**, can only be reached by water. About 50 kilometers north of Puerto Princesa, as the crow flies, the **Underground River** flows through the seven-kilometer-long cave in **St Paul's National Park**, which covers 3900 hectares on the shore of St Paul's Bay on the South China Sea. This subterranean river was first explored and mapped by Australian and Filipino speleologists in the early 1980's. During their explorations they discovered an extremely varied cave system, with some vast caverns, and passages lined with innumerable stalactites. Some way inland, the winding tunnel ends in three vertical shafts connecting St Paul's Cave with the surface. At this point the Underground River disappears into the rock. For mere

Above: Fishermen in southern Palawan.
Right: The mouth of the subterranean river.

mortals, who only want a brief sniff of the underworld, the official tour in a little paddle boat, under the eye of the government ranger, is adventurous enough. During the trip of about four kilometers along the river you can see the "bowels" of the earth: sharp stalactites hanging down to within inches of the water, the dead straight stretch of "subway," the "cathedral," and a "sorrowing Virgin Mary"... These and many other cave-formations, in the light of a kerosene lamp, look either eerie or reassuringly biblical – to say nothing of the thousands of swallows and bats. The boat trip begins and ends at the impressive mouth of the cave, a jagged hole in the cliff. In front of it lies an inviting white bathing beach. Running north from the National Park as far as Port Barton is one of the loneliest but most delightful stretches of coastline on Palawan.

Getting there from Puerto Princesa is difficult but well worth the effort for the picturesque provincial and mountain landscape. It is possible to go overland to **Baheli** or **Macarascas** on Ulagan Bay, and from there be ferried in an outrigger to the cave. However, between June and September the southwest monsoon and high waves rule out the sea trip. Alternatively, you can hire a jeepney to take you directly from the capital to the fishing village of **Sabang**, where bamboo huts at the Central Ranger Station serve as overnight accommodation. *Bancas* then ferry you over to the Underground River. You can find out about current transport charges from the Department of Tourism in Puerto Princesa. To do this trip in one day from Puerto Princesa, you should hire a jeepney or join an organized tour for the sake of time.

Into the Far North

The only road along the coast to the north starts in Puerto Princesa. Until the highway is improved the trip remains ex-

tremely dusty, especially from January to May and runs through varied and, in places, thickly-wooded landscape – for example around **Cleopatra's Needle,** (1,593 meters), the highest mountain in the central-north of Palawan.

This is the home of the Batak. They live mainly along the watercourses which run crystal clear down the mountain, such as the Tanabag and Langogan rivers. These dark-skinned and frizzy-haired people are the most famous of the eight ethnic groups on the island. Living as semi-nomadic hunter-gatherers, whose life depends on the rain forest, the Batak, who in 1996 numbered barely 250 are threatened with extinction.Timber-fellers and slash-and-burn settlers have driven them relentlessly back into the interior of the island. Malaria, tuberculosis and infant mortality are equally serious threats to their existence.

Foreigners who occasionally go out from San Rafael and Tanabag and fight their way through the jungle, find them shy and reticent. Even so, they are not prepared to be photographed for nothing. Anyone who finds his way to their simple huts must give the village chief or head of the family presents such as salt, sugar, dried fish, live poultry or tobacco. Then one can observe how these are distributed in a highly democratic manner. For a brief period, the Batak also had to share the forest with about 100 Aëta people who had been evacuated from the Pinatubo disaster-area. The Negritos had been brought to Palawan by a German aid organization, but the government soon had the refugees shipped back to an emergency camp on Luzon.

Outside Roxas the road branches off to **Port Barton**, north of St Paul's National Park. On Pagdanan bay, dotted with islands, the town draws travelers back again and again, and quite a number of people have forsaken city life to open restaurants, diving-schools and chalet hotels here. Although the island-hopping and diving for which it is famous have suffered from fishing methods using dynamite and cyanide, Port Barton has de-

veloped into a tourist center with an established price structure. The authorities are anxious to secure its future and are becoming more serious in their efforts to prevent damage to the environment. The hinterland still offers stretches of virgin forest, waterfalls and tumbling streams.

More of the same kind of surroundings can be enjoyed further north, near the little town of **San Vicente**, behind the long, palm-fringed shores of Imuruan Bay. Giant trees soar skywards and the chattering of monkeys underlines the jungle atmosphere. A high point, in every sense, is the 1,021-meter-high **Mount Capoas**, which rises up from the rugged peninsula at the northern end of the bay. A climb to the summit is rewarded by a fascinating panorama over the entire island.

Back on the east coast once again, the road takes one through the quiet village

Above: Washerwomen on the Tanabag river. Right: A Batak woman grinding coffee-beans in a wooden mortar.

196

of **Roxas**, overlooking a shoal of low-lying offshore islands. Some of these, like **Pandan Island** with its smart **Coco Loco Resort**, boast coral reefs and lovely beaches

On the large neighboring island of **Dumaran**, northeast of Roxas, tourism is still unknown – despite the immaculate sandy beaches near the main village of **Araceli** and in the south of the island.

Taytay used to be the capital of Palawan. A **fortification** built in 1622 makes an imposing ruin beside the reef-girt sea. The **church**, more than three hundred years old, also bears witness to the long colonial past. However, Taytay's isolated position and very shallow seaward approaches made it unsuitable as a port, and the Spanish later abandoned it. It is still difficult to reach the town overland. The jeepney from Roxas sinks into the sand in summer, and into mud during the rainy season.

There are several excursions to be made from Taytay. Not far to the south lies the picturesque **Lake Danao**. You

can take a boat to the offshore **Pabel-lones Islands** with steep cliffs and caves. The snorkeling is good around **Elephant Island**. The attractions of **Paly Island**, further south, include waterfalls and fine beaches.

The islets of **Calabadian** and **Icadam-banauan** are equally idyllic. Superb waters for diving surround the islands of **Binatican** and **Apulit** north of Taytay. On Apulit, the luxurious Club Noah Isa-belle was opened in 1996, offering ex-pensive vacations in idyllic suroundings. The preservation of the natural enviro-ment has been made an emphasis at the resort.

Almost everywhere you go north of Taytay the underwater world has much to offer. **Casian**, near the fishery station of **Debangan**, is a pretty little island town of this region.

The neighboring islands of **Cagdanao**, **Maobanan** and **Calabugdong** compete with each other in claiming to have the finest beaches. **Flower Island** has a small beach resort which is open to guests.

Iloc Island, almost at the northern tip of Palawan, could be a little Boracay, but without the tourist hordes - fortunately. The further north one goes, the more un-explored and deserted are the islands. In the direction of Linapacan it becomes very lonely indeed.

Well to the east lie the islands of the **Cuyo Archipelago**, scattered acrosss the Sulu Sea yet still part of Palawan prov-ince. Though of interest to divers, the 40 or so islands are unfortunately not very accessible. Only from the main island, **Cuyo**, are there regular boat connections to the neighboring islands of **Bisucay**, **Cocoro** and **Agutaya**.

On **Pamalican Island** in the Quinilu-ban Group, the Soriano family maintains by far the most exclusive vacation com-plex in the country: at 500 US$ per day, it is usually accessed by companies' private planes from Manila.

The administrative capital, **Cuyo**, of-fers an unspoilt, provincial atmosphere, enhanced by old houses and a **fortress church** built by the Spanish in 1677. For

197

a long time, large numbers of Cuyunos have been emigrating to Palawan, where their *Cuyonin* language has become very widely spoken.

El Nido and the Bacuit Archipelago

There is always plenty going on in El Nido, in the northwest of Palawan. The little town on the mainland overlooking the Bacuit Archipelago is the place that visitors to Palawan dream of finding. A road to El Nido was opened recently. It starts at **Embarcadero**, about six kilometers west of Taytay, on Malampaya Sound, and is still liable to be adversely affected by the weather conditions. So the sea trip is preferable, weather permitting. You can either take a boat from **Embarcadero**, or board a larger ship at **Abongan**.

At first you cruise down the Abongan river, past wild mangrove swamps, the habitat of birds and monkeys. Then the

Above: A boat trip in the Bacuit Archipelago.

ship enters the fascinating Malampaya Sound, a fjord-like bay that cuts into the land for a good 40 kilometers. Mount Capoas soars into the clouds, and jagged, rocky islands point the way into the South China Sea.

You should disembark at the important fishing-port of **Liminangcong**. From here you can hire a boat, or take the scheduled service to El Nido. When the sea is calm, this is a pleasant trip past curiously-shaped islands to the cliffs of the Bacuit Archipelago. In 1991 a group of Europeans were drowned while trying to reach El Nido in a howling southwest monsoon. So, if you are traveling to "paradise," take your time.

The Spanish called the place **El Nido** ("nest") because bird's-nests, from which the famous soup is made, "grew" in the limestone cliffs. The town snuggles shyly between the dark marble cliffs and the white, sandy beach. A dream, a glorious "world's end!"

Although the world discovered it quite some time ago, at least the invasion of foreign visitors in the last few years has not robbed El Nido of its friendly charm. Here they have tried not to repeat the mistakes of other tourist centers. The idyll around El Nido has remained astonishingly modest. In the face of such overwhelmingly beautiful natural landscape, any further development would have been both irresponsible and presumptuous. It becomes even more miraculous when you go off to explore the **Bacuit Archipelago**. Cliffs rise like dark ships sheer out of the crystal-clear water, white beaches gleam above colorful banks of coral, lagoons hide behind steep walls of rock.

It is however not always a democratic "paradise." Here a rather unapproachable would-be Crusoe has settled on one of the 30-odd Bacuit Islands, and there watchmen from exclusive resorts shoo undesired guests back into the water. But there are beaches enough for everyone.

THE CALAMIAN ARCHIPELAGO

The **Calamian Archipelago** with the main islands Busanga, Culion and Coron, lies in the northernmost part of Palawan. with some improvement to the infrastructure, modest growth in the field of tourism is now taking place. This does not as yet bring even a basic income for the local inhabitants; they exist mainly from fishing.

It is above all the gracious beauty of the landscape, for which the Calamian Archipelago has become known. It stretches north of the main island from Palawan almost to Mindoro. Nowhere else in the Philippines is a relatively small stretch of sea so densely dotted with islands. The third largest of the Calamians is **Linapacan Island**, off whose west coast significant oil-reserves were recently found. In spite of this the thinly populated island remains as unassuming as before. **Linapacan Town**, at the northeastern end, is a pleasant little place

where a few houses cluster round a church.

Islands are scattered all around like confetti. Everywhere banks of coral glow through the water, despite the vicious attacks on the undersea life. There is even a reef of living coral just offshore from Linapacan Town.

Culion Island is the second largest of the Calamians. In 1906 the island was given the status of a leper colony (now revoked) which was housed in extensive hospital buildings in Culion, the main town on the northeast coast. Since leprosy has now largely ceased to be the scourge it once was, the number of patients, formerly in the thousands, has dropped dramatically. The few hundred remaining patients mostly live quite happily with their families in the colony, which until recently was administered not by local politicians but by doctors. This may explain the amazingly clean and friendly appearance of the town.

Between Culion and Busuanga, the largest island in the group, lie a myriad small and tiny islands. Many are no more than raised coral reefs fringed with gorgeous sandy beaches. Others have massive cliffs, rising sheer out of the sea which are riddled with caves. Because they lack fresh water, most of the islands are uninhabited. Occasionally they are visited by members of the Tagbanua tribe, a nomadic people who roam all over northern Palawan.

Busuanga Island is quite densely populated and fairly well developed. Several decades ago, **King Ranch** was established inland, 40,000-hectare cattle farm – supposedly the largest in Asia – and is now given over to experimental breeding. The island's capital, **Coron**, is full of activity. As befits the "gateway to northern Palawan," the harbor is always busy. A short distance inland there is an airstrip, which, like a second, near to the town, is served by regular flights from Manila.

The Busuanga region is still in the early stages of touristic development Several guest-houses have been opened in Coron, most of them in idyllic settings on the wide bay. On **Dimakya**, a tiny island to the north, the luxurious **Club Paradise** has opened its doors, while more modest resorts can be found in the southwest of Busuanga. There is already regular boat service running between Busuanga Island and Taytay.

The Calamian Islands can be explored comfortably with the cruising catamaran *Lagoon Explorer* (stationed in Coron Town).

The greatest attractions of this island world lie down in the blue depths. The waters round **Sangat Island**, in the south, already have an international reputation among divers. It was here, in 1944, that US aircraft sank a Japanese naval squadron, and a dozen rusting hulks rest at depths of between six and 40 meters.

Above: Life-risiking search for salangana birds' nests, on the cliffs of Coron Island.

Behind the strange looking cliffs of the wedge-shaped **Coron Island**, south of Coron town, more surprises await you: seven turquoise-colored fresh-water lakes lying in a rugged landscape.

Of these lakes, **Cayangan Lake** is relatively easy to reach. More difficult is the ascent to Barrakuda Lake, which s said to be inhabited by a barracuda fish. Otherwise the island's only inhabitants are a few Tagbuana tribesmen. They risk life and limb, clambering barefoot and agile as lizards, up the vertical, sharp-edged cliffs, to gather the highly-valued nests of the Salangana birds, a member of the swift family, which sell at good prices. The nests provide the chief ingredient of bird's nest soup, prized as an aphrodisiac by the Chinese.

The peninsula of **Calauit**, in the northwest of Busuanga, is a good place to see animals. In 1976 Ferdinand Marcos had giraffes, zebras, gazelles and other species from the East African savannah introduced here and the animals are multiplying rapidly.

At about the same time a project was launched to re-establish some of Palawan's endangered species, including the mouse-deer (the world's smallest red deer), the bear-cat, a jungle marten, tortoises and crocodiles. The fellowship of African and endangered native species seems to be developing to their mutual advantage. Even the sea around Calauit was closely guarded and in the mid-1980s the island was like a Garden of Eden.

In the cause of conservation, Marcos had ordered the removal of 250 families from Calauit to Culion Island in 1977, but after his fall from power, these people forced their way back – it was a civil uprising which did not stop short of the use of violence. Now tourists are again permitted to visit "Giraffe Island," after payment of a small fee. The management of club Paradise (among others) organizes excursions.

PUERTO PRINCESA (P. P.)
Accommodation

MEDIUM: **Asiaworld Resort**, National Rd., Tel: 4332214. **Casa Linda**, Trinidad Rd., Tel: 4332606. **Badjao Inn**, Tel: 4332380. **Airport Hotel**, Tel: 4332177, **Palawan Hotel**, Tel: 4332326 all Rizal Ave. *BUDGET:* **Duchess Pension**, Valencia St. **Puerto Pension**, 35 Malvar St. **Sonne Gasthaus. International Guest House**, both Manalo St. **Trattoria Inn**, 353 Rizal Ave.

Museum / Crocodile Farm
Museum, City Hall, Mendoza Park, Mon - Fri 8:30 am -12 noon, 1 - 5 pm. **Crocodile Farm**, Iwaran, Mon - Fri 1 - 4:30 pm, Sat & holidays 8 am - 12 noon, 1 - 5 pm, Closed Sun.

Tourist Information
Provincial Tourism Office, Capitol Bldg., Rizal Ave. / Roxas St., Tel: 4332968; **Airport Office**, Tel: 4332983.

Around Puerto Princesa
Accommodation

MEDIUM: **HONDA BAY: Meara Island Resort**, diving courses. *BUDGET:* **NAGTABON: Pablico's Nagtabon Resort. Georg's Place**. (All with restaurant).

SOUTH PALAWAN
Accommodation

BUDGET: **NARRA: Tiosin Lodging**, Panacan Rd. **BROOKE'S POINT: Silayan Lodge. Cristina Beach Resort. RIO TUBA:** at the jetty. **QUEZON: New Bayside Lodge**, jetty. **Tabon Village Res.**, Tabon beach.
   Getting There / Means of Transport
BY AIR: PAL etc. daily Manila-P. P., Cebu via Iloilo City (Panay)-P. P.
SHIP: Regular service Manila-P. P. 1-2 x monthly. San José de Buenavista (Panay)-P. P. (30 hours). MV Don Julio (Negros Nav.) 1x weekly from Iloilo via Boracay to P. P. Honda Bay: Boat rentals from Santa Lourdes Harbor. P. P.-Santa Lucia. P. P.-Tubbataha-Reef (c. 12 hours). Boat rentals from Quezon to nearby islands. Brooke's Point-Ursula Island. Rio Tuba.
BUS: Several times daily P. P.-Quezon from jeepney terminal. *JEEPNEY:* Honda Bay: from jeepney terminal, Malivar St. Several times daily from v. P. P. to: Crocodile Farm, Iwahig, Nagtabon. Brooke's Point-Rio Tuba (via Bataraza).

NORTH PALAWAN
Accommodation

LUXURY: **near TAYTAY: Club Noah Isabelle**, Tel: Manila 8945644. **Near EL NIDO: Pangulasian Resort., Club Noah El Nido**, diving, Tel: Manila 8945644. **Marina del Nido,** Malapacao Island, Tel: Manila 8311487.

MEDIUM: **SAN VICENTE: Caparii Dive Camp**, (info: airport P. Princesa). **PORT BARTON: Manta Ray Res.**, Capsalay Island. **Near TAYTAY: Flower Island Res.** (info: Pem's Pension). **Near EL NIDO: Malapacao Retreat**,diving courses: Bacuit Divers, El Nido. *BUDGET:* **SABANG: Villa Sabang. Bambua Jungle Cott. Ranger Station. SAN RAFAEL: Duchess Beachside Cott. PORT BARTON: Swissippini Cottages** (diving). **El Busero Inn. Shangri La. ROXAS: Gemalain's Inn** (market). **Coco Loco Res.**, Pandan Island (diving), info: own Office, Rizal Ave., P. Princesa. **TAYTAY: Publico's International Guesthouse. Pem's Pension House. EMBARCADERO: Riverview Guesth. EL NIDO: Austria's Guesth. Gloria's Beach Cott. Tandikan Cott. Marina Garden Cott. Lally & Abet Cott.**

Getting There / Means of Transport
BY AIR: PAL daily, Air Philippines several times weekly Manila-P. Princesa, Soriano Av. Manila-P. P.- El Nido (boat El Nido-Miniloc). Seair: Manila-Taytay.
BOAT: Regular services and rented boats from Palawan to islands and San Vicente (from Port Barton).

CALAMIAN-ARCHIPELAGO / CUYO ISLANDS

Busuanga Island
Accommodation

LUXURY: **Club Paradise**, Dimakya Island, diving course, info: Manila, Tel: 8166871. *MEDIUM:* **BUSUANGA** (Town): **Las Hamacas Resort.** *BUDGET:* **CONCEPCION: Pier House L. CORON: L & M Lodge**, near market. **Sea Breeze Lodge**, on the bay, diving. **Bayside**, good restaurant, diving. **Kokosnuss Resort**, near hospital, good infos. *Diving and cruising:* **Discovery Divers**, Coron (Town). **Lagoon Explorer**, Discovery Cruises, Coron, Tel: Manila 8153008.

Culion Island / Calumbuyan / Cuyo
Accommodation

LUXURY: **CUYO-INSELN: Amanpulo Resort**, Pamalican Island, Tel: Manila 8315876. *BUDGET:* **CULION: New Luncheonette Lodge. Fishermen's Inn**, both near jetty. **TANGAT ISLAND: Sangat Island Reserve**, diving (reservations: Manila 5261295). **CUYO: Suba Resort**, Tabunan Beach.

Getting There / Means of Transport
BY AIR: PAL, Air Ads, Pacific Air several times weekly: Manila-Busuanga. Soriano Av. Manila-Pamalican Island. *SHIP:* Regular service Manila, Batangas (Luzon)-Coron (Busuanga). Port Barton-El Nido (outrigger boat, 5 hours). 2 x weekly Taytay-Coron (M/B Dioniemer, 8 hours). Several ferries weekly Coron-Culion-Cuyo.

A MIXED LEGACY

"We inherited our religion from the Spanish, and from the Americans we got democracy and an educational system." When asked about their national character, educated Filipinos like to frame their reply in this way. What they often omit to say, however, is that even today the lifestyle and values of the Philippines are deeply rooted in Malay culture. This is why the manifestations of their religion, and the behavior of their politicians are regarded with amazement and even disdain by westerners. Their Christianity has a strong blend of superstition and reliance on the powers of spirits and miracle healers. Their democracy seems more like a political façade behind which powerful oligarchy operates, often hypocritical, and ready to resort to violence.

Previous pages: Life on the water – the Badjao of the Tawi-Tawi Islands. A refreshing bath for water-buffaloes. Above: Offering of candles at Santo Niño church in Cebu City.

English is admittedly the language of instruction in all secondary schools and even the syllabus has an American look to it. Yet in everyday life "western education" generally remains in the background. It is truer to say that during the long period of colonization the adaptable Filipinos have taken over certain elements of western civilization and given them an oriental slant. In the west one is liable to judge this, too hastily, as mere imitation, but the Filipinos prefer to see it as a natural assimilation that led to the creation of an independent culture.

The visitor to the Philippines, this land between east and west, is well advised to abandon any western preconceptions and try to adapt to the oriental psyche of the Filipinos. As so often in Asia, sensuality tends to prevail over reason. Truth, justice and duty count for less than that which is beautiful, pleasing or amusing. A good appearance promises success, a smile always helps or at least indicates liking and well-being in a country where hospitality is a matter of personal pride.

Filipinos are only individualistic in a limited sense, for they are brought up to appreciate the value of family ties, and this sets limits on the personal freedom that is so highly prized in the west. Success is measured by how much it benefits the family as a whole. However, this loyalty to the family group can also serve as a very useful excuse for antisocial, immoral and aggressive behavior, whether it be by a pick-pocket, a prostitute, or a big landowner or politician. The need for everyone to live harmoniously in the community dominates every aspect of life. Loners and nonconformists are rejected, or at least regarded with disfavor. The requirement to adapt to group norms and the duties of friendship, known as *sakop*, *taya-tayo* or *pakikisama*, envelop social relationships like a tight, fine-meshed net.

Members of a street gang who raise money to get one of their buddies out of jail, are just as wrapped up in this net as the household help, working in some distant foreign country in order to send money back to feed her family.

The individual's feeling for the community is not, of course, entirely unselfish. The system only works because it is mutual. The saying, "we're all in the same boat," is nowhere more applicable than in Philippine society, which can trace its origins, literally, back to the crews of the ancient *balang-hai* ships.

Loss of face and gratitude

As in the rest of Asia, social and business life in the Philippines is governed by the anxiety not to lose face. Politeness and patience are very important virtues. On the other hand, a too obvious or exaggerated show of sympathy is considered an unwarranted involvement in someone else's misfortune. For the person concerned, whether man or woman, is proud and sensitive; wounded self-respect can lead to thoughts of revenge. The management

ress of an office would never simply fire an incompetent employee; instead, the man has to be persuaded to leave of his own accord and thus be able to "save face." To western eyes such elaborate formalities would seem to be a very obvious obstacle to the development of a "healthy" national economy.

The influence of corruption is similarly great. In a state which guarantees neither a child-allowance nor an old-age pension, and where unemployment and the struggle for survival are the accepted way of life for millions of people, the individual is scarcely interested in an abstract concept of the common good. The only form of social security is the family, to which he is bound all his life. His loyalty is focussed entirely on his family, and the more influential his position, the greater the pressure on him to support his relatives. The resulting corruption is thus tolerated by society; indeed, it is to a certain extent expected. Through the family and through one's circle of friends, everyone, whether man or woman, endeavors to build up a system of favors and debts of gratitude, which can be relied upon in times of need.

The principle of *utang na loob* ("debt of the inner self"), the binding obligation to gratitude and restitution, is so deeply rooted in Philippine culture that it could be described as the Eleventh Commandment, or rather the Commandment surpassing all others. *Utang na loob* is the social putty that binds people together. In fact, it is only thanks to this that the economy and adminstration function at all. It gradually dawns on the foreigner that "corruption" has a very different meaning than in Western concepts of justice.

The Filipinos' strong sense of family is accompanied, particularly among the poor, by a need to have as many children as possible. The logic of this is often misunderstood by foreigners, whether they be tourists or aid-workers. The fact is that raising a child produces the same sense of

security in a Filipino, as contributing to a pension-scheme does for a European, American or Australian. The more children the parents can bring up, the more assured is their old age, which is, alas, for three-quarters of all Filipinos, destined to be a time of poverty and dependence. Having a child is like drawing a ticket in the lottery of life: the more tickets you have, the greater your chances of prosperity. A daughter may marry a rich man; a son could, with any luck, become a policeman. Right at the top of the wish-list for the younger generation is a job abroad. It is hardly surprising that, in all this, arguments in favor of birth control and environmental protection don't get much of a hearing. To worry about the good of the nation as a whole, let alone the entirety of mankind, is, for someone engaged in a daily struggle to survive, a luxury he cannot afford.

Above: Mutual assistance in the Philippines – a house being "transplanted." Right: Dressed in their Sunday best.

"Typically Filipino"

William Howard Taft, the first US Governor of the Philippines, used to describe the "little, brown brothers" as humorous, polite, brave and generous. Other foreign "experts" consider Taft's judgement too patronizing, but overlook the fact that such views are only based on western criteria. Anyone who seriously comes to terms with the Filipino mentality will realize that it has positive and negative aspects, which are two sides of the same coin.

In general Filipinos have a fatalistic view of life. They are enormously long-suffering and accept even the most severe misfortune with stoical equanimity. The negative side of this attitude of *Bahala na* (God will look after things), can be a lack of initiative. Patience often turns into plain inertia and lethargy.

Filipinos show a sensitivity and genuine courtesy, the like of which would be hard to find anywhere else. But sometimes it is only a short step from courtesy to dishonesty. To give an unambiguously negative answer is the sign of bad up-bringing. A truth which could be hurtful is better left unspoken. Similarly, the high self-esteem of a Filipino can suddenly turn into what seems like unwarranted touchiness, which is sometimes accompanied by a desire to get back at his interlocutor. Often, Filipinos come across as bad losers. They are very fond of jokes, but only at someone else's expense.

Travelers in the Philippines are often surprised at how clean and relatively well dressed even poor people appear. This conscientious personal care, which is taken seriously as a precaution against illness and infection, is part of their self-respect, but can easily degenerate into vanity.

Age and authority generally command respect. While the regard shown for old people is exemplary and genuine, deference to superiors is purely an outward formality. For outside the hierarchical structure there is a tendency toward lack of self-control. For this reason, foreigners often criticize the Filipinos for only paying lip-service to moral principles. They shake their heads at criminals who claim to be deeply religious, or upright family men who gamble away their hearth and home at a cock-fight. This contradiction can only be explained as the difference between form and content, between appearance and reality.

Filipinos are anything but stolid or stubborn. They quite frequently change their mind, especially about other people, and this lays them open to the charge of unpredictablility. In politics and in other matters, they prefer to sit on the fence until they see which way the wind is blowing. A foreigner, who considers himself single-minded and purposeful, and likes things to be clear and straightforward, often has a hard time trying to build a friendship on shared values.

When it comes to judging these and other "typically Filipino" qualities,

which, like everywhere else, contain many exceptions to the rule, it must be remembered that they have evolved over thousands of years. Things also become more comprehensible when you realize that these people live in a tropical region, where a life of apparently blissful simplicity is frequently shattered by the most appalling natural catastrophes. No wonder they have a developed a special kind of mental flexibility to cope with this.

It is all the more surprising then, when foreigners who have lived for many years in the Philippines, find little good to say about the country and its people. What life has to offer here is something the western visitor is only aware of once he is back home again – in the industrialized west, where despite, or because of, affluence, one's existence is governed by a fear of death and dangers of all kinds. In the Philippines, enjoyment of life is the important thing. And the western traveler, if he can forget his materialism for a while, will agree that the friendly Filipinos can teach him a great deal.

209

STRANGERS IN THEIR OWN COUNTRY
– The Minorities –

There is not enough space here to introduce the 30 or more ethnic groups, classed as "minorities." Some of the Philippine peoples, such as the Muslim groups, have been described in the travel section. It seems best to give some examples of the situation of present-day descendants of the pre-colonial inhabitants of these islands.

The people whom the Spanish found here were simply called *Indios* for 400 years. The colonial masters proceeded on the well-tried principle of "divide and rule," just as they had done in Latin America, though without the same harsh and systematic brutality. This meant that an effective political and cultural hierarchy was established on the *Islas Filipinas*, in which the true inhabitants

Above: The Ati ("Negritos") still live predominantly in and with nature.

were right at the bottom, labelled *Indios*, below the *Mestizos* (half-breeds), the *Insulares* (Spanish born in the Philippines), and the *Peninsulares* (the Spanish born in Spain). The basic pattern of this socio-political scale still remains intact. The descendants of the christianized *Indios* now call the six million of their fellow countrymen, who were bypassed by the colonial integration, "cultural minorities" or "tribal Filipinos," a bureaucratic euphemism. Although these "minorities" are, from an ethnological point of view, the ancestors of a majority of the present-day population, they are frequently the victims of blatant discrimination. The technological and – at least outward – cultural differences that divide the "civilized" from the "heathen" Filipinos, are simply too great. Just as in many ex-colonial countries, the co-existence of different population groups in the Philippines is threatened by the common problem of post-colonial ignorance. The so-called "civilized" majority claim for themselves the prerogative of the Christian converts, which was taught by the Spanish monks, but identify more with the ideals of American Wild West pioneers than with their own Malay roots, and are ever more ruthlessly driving back the "tribes." On the wall-maps of international human rights watchers and conservation groups, the Philippines have been highlighted for quite some time.

From time to time, the world's press has taken up the cause of the Philippine ethnic groups. In the early 1980s, the Kalingas in northern Luzon came under serious threat from the Chico River Dam project, which was going to make vast inroads into land which not only provided their livelihood but was also sacred to their ancestors. After the fall of Marcos, it was the Tasaday from southern Mindanao who grabbed the headlines: until then these "stone-age men" had been completely cut off from the world. Finally, the eruptions of Pinatubo brought the plight of the Aëta, living on and around the volcano, to international attention.

Many of the 60 or so ethno-linguistic groups and sub-groups live in a permanent crossfire between rebels and the army. In the course of the military search-and-destroy campaigns they are harrassed and driven from their homes. Should they have the misfortune to live in the rain forest or over mineral deposits, they are always the first to pay for gold, copper or hardwoods, with the loss of their homeland and not infrequently their lives. Many of the tribal Filipinos are unable to resist the blandishments of the modern world and allow themselves to be swindled out of their land with dubious contracts. Admittedly, they are welcome as crowd-pulling representatives of national diversity in tourist ads. More and more hotel and resort-managers are building a "cultural show" into their entertainment program.

If there is one supreme example of the discrepancy between ethnic needs and reality with regard to the minority situation

in the Philippines, it is the *Ati-Atihan Festival* on Panay.The famous spectacle in Kalibo would be nothing without the long-established Negritos. But these are only imitated by the performers. Meanwhile the the real Ati tribesmen stagger about the village, rootless, drunk and begging.

There are still about 15,000 "pure-blooded" Negritos on the various islands. They are thought to be the most ancient population group in Southeast Asia, and are more numerous in the Philippines than anywhere else. There is no clear evidence as to the origins of the diminutive (never taller than one-and-a-half meters), frizzy-haired and dark- to black-skinned people. All we have is their own names for their individual clans: *Ati, Atta, Agta, Alta, Ita, Aëta.* However, anthropologists have established a possible relationship with the Papuas of New Guinea, and similarities with the Australian aborigines and with the Weddides of the Indian sub-continent. Any connection with the pygmies of Africa has been ruled out. Apart from the Dumagat, who live as fishermen on the coasts of north and central Luzon, the Negritos have, under pressure from the rest of the population, withdrawn ever deeper into the forests of the interior. They are not a homogeneous ethnic group, and their languages have been influenced by those of neighboring peoples. Wherever they continue to live their traditional, semi-nomadic aboriginal life, hunting in the forest with bow and arrow, and gathering wild fruit, their existence is still fairly tolerable. They build themselves simple shelters and wear clothes made from cow hair. Their religion focuses on the nature spirits around them, sometimes ruled over by a divine Creator. At the same time, most Negrito groups have come to terms with their Christian neighbors, living as settled rice- and vegetable-farmers, and working as laborers and household help. As exotic strangers in their own country,

with a skin color that "modern" Filipinos are not particularly fond of, they are bound to be hardest hit by the pressure of a growing population.

The Mangyan of Mindoro are more like a nation. There are great differences between their eight groups: Iraya, Alangan, Tadyawan, Nauhan, Pula, Batangan, Buhid and Hanunó-o. The 18,000 or so Hanunó-o – the "true" Mangyan, as they describe themselves in their language, live in the south of the island, where they have developed pottery, weaving, embroidery and basketweaving to a high skill, and use a pictorial script which was formerly found in other parts of the country. Yet, further north, the Alangan still live in almost stone-age conditions, roaming as hunter-gatherers through the forests of Mount Halcon.

Since 1971, the Philippines has been thought to be the last country in which genuine neolithic people could live un-

disturbed. These were the Tasaday tribe from South Cotabato province on Mindanao, around two dozen men, women and children, all dressed in aprons made of leaves, and living only on plants, fish, frogs, river-crabs, and other small animals – that is how they were described in the textbooks of the world. There they remained – apparently – untouched, in their closely guarded cave territory. Until the spring of 1986. Then some journalists and ethnologists claimed they had uncovered an elaborate fraud, said to have been dreamed up by the late Manuel "Manda" Elizalde, who at the time held the post of Presidential Assistant on National Minorities (PANAMIN), and was the self-appointed protector of the Tasaday. The main charge was that the tribe which had been "discovered" had long since ceased to be isolated and that "Manda" had bribed and bullied them into remaining in their "primitive" state. The motives for this "Stone-Age Swindle" included a desire for publicity and to get his hands on government funds

Above: Alangan tribesman in the interior of Mindoro. Right:T'boli girl in South Cotabato.

212

and donations from overseas. Eventually an official enquiry was held into the "Tasaday Case." Witnesses who would have given evidence to support the charge of fraud were threatened, bribed, and in at least one case, murdered, in order to ensure their silence.

Elizalde fled the country, but as a member of a powerful industrial clan, he continued to fight for his "life's work" and reputation. For his part, he accused his opponents, including anthropologists from the University of the Philippines, of self-publicity, and claimed they were deriding an innocent minority group that had helped to bring the country to world attention. Suddenly, national honor was at stake. By the end of 1987 the affair was, for the moment, closed. Official Philippine sources declared that the Tasaday were probably the last people on earth to have lived in an unchanged way ever since the Stone Age. At least up to the time of their discovery.

Respected scientists, at home and abroad, many of whom had been quick to accept Elizalde's "noble savage" story back in 1971, now declared that, despite rigorous protection, the Tasaday had very probably been subject to certain cultural influences, absorbed from their more developed neighbors like the T'boli and the Manobo-Blit.

It all leaves a nasty taste in the mouth. The fact that the rest of the world has been laughing up its sleeve at this "Philippine farce" has hardly been helpful to the native peoples of these islands. However, Cory Aquino has since closed down the doubtless corrupt PANAMIN office and entrusted the fate of the tribal Filipinos to two state agencies, the Office for Northern Cultural Communites (ONCC) and the Office for Southern Cultural Communities (OSCC). At the same time, provincial representatives of the Office for Cultural Minorities and Muslim Affairs, and the Department of Social Welfare and Development are protecting the interests of the aboriginals.

No such painful epilogue followed the sudden fame of the Tau't Batu ("Rock

213

People") of south Palawan. It was in 1978 that people became aware of a group of 80 hunter-gatherers, who lived mainly in caves in the inaccessible Singnapan valley. It is not exactly true to say that "20,000 years of history had left no mark" on the Tau't Batu. There had been frequent contact with the ethnically related Pala'wan, but this had not robbed them of their identity. In order to protect them from more harmful influences, the government nominated an area of 23,000 hectares near Mount Matalingajan as a tribal reserve. Alas, this did not prevent lumberjacks from encroaching on the Tau't Batu's protective forest.

In the South Cotabato Province of Mindanao, the steady advance of immigrant settlers from the Visayas has come up against organized opposition by the T'boli people. The Ilonggos and Bicolanos put up hand-painted signs saying "Do not buy the land of our ancestors" in the hope of reminding all Filipinos of the values which they should in fact share. But Christian Filipinos consider that their "civilization" entitles them to teach the more primitive people how to adapt to modern life. Supported by development programs, partly financed from overseas, and aimed at getting the economy of southern Mindanao into shape, these pioneers feel justified in occupying other people's native soil.

It is a sad fact that, for many of the 150,000 T'boli in South Cotabato, the future seems to hold only two chances of survival: Either they will be driven still further into the interior, or they will share in the development process, which sooner or later will destroy their own cultural identity. Ilonggo merchants have already taken over the marketing of the T'boli's highly valued textiles. The laboriously woven *T'nalak,* a brown cloth

Right: A living fossil – the arrow-tailed crab is still caught today by on fishermen on Palawan.

214

made from abaca fibers, with patterns in red and beige, can now be bought in western boutiques, made into purses, shoes and hairbands – a fashionable travesty of the traditional T'boli costume. The Santa Cruz Mission, based at Lake Sebu, has helped the T'boli to set up and run a *T'nalak* shop in Manila's tourist belt, as an exercise in self-help. But the mission has made itself unpopular with the new Catholic settlers by standing up for the rights of T'boli and against the "development" of the region. There is big money behind the plans for progress. The Dole Fruit Company needs more land, because the world demand for fruit is growing. Local administrators and economic strategists see new opportunities and are already trying to tempt the hitherto self-sufficient T'boli into becoming contract farmers, by offering credits and fancy profit forecasts. And ever since the first glint of gold deposits in the area, at the beginning of the 1990s, troubled times have loomed for the peace-loving T'boli people.

By now it cannot be denied that awareness of the problem of the primitive peoples has became more acute in the Philippines. Newspaper reports about the ethnic groups and the threat to their territory, are seen more frequently on an international scale. The Filipinos are continually rediscovering their multi-layered cultural heritage.

Yet the fears that were expressed by Philippine anthropologists at the time of the Tasaday affair, are justified in many parts of the world: "There is too much at stake. The problem of minorities is like a microcosm of our society as a whole, where the process of democratization continues to fall victim to naked power." When, as has happened in the Philippines, so-called civilization takes over the destiny of its minorities, there is always the danger that it will not only lead them astray, but also – as in the Tasaday case – make a fool of itself.

VULNERABLE MIRACLES
OF NATURE

Studies carried out by geologists and paleontologists indicate that the Philippines began life in the early Tertiary Period, probably in the Eocene or Oligocene age. Between 38 and 55 million years ago, the archipelago must have had an entirely different shape, and was connected to the Asiatic mainland by a land-bridge to Taiwan. While this bridge was sinking under the sea for the last time, new land connections were being created by the violent tectonic activity in the region. In the Pleiocene age, two to five million years ago, Mindanao must have bordered on Celebes (Sulawesi), which in turn was joined to the Moluccas and Australia. Palawan and the Calamian Islands were part of an ancient sub-continent, which we call *Wallacea*, and which extended across Borneo and the Great Sunda Islands as far as mainland Asia.

Still in prehistoric times, the Philippines underwent continuous changes during the Ice Age. At one time you could walk dryshod between what are islands today, while areas that are now joined, were then separated by expanses of water. In the age of early human settlement, people living, for example, on what is today the Bay of Manila could paddle straight up to the northern Gulf of Lingayen, since the present Zambales region was then an island. In view of climatic global warming, it is quite possible that a similar situation could soon recur as the sea level rises.

It is principally the evidence of living or fossilized fauna and flora that enabled scientists to piece together the remote past in this way. The various land links and migrations have brought the present-day Philippines plant and animal species that originated in Australasia, Celebes, Borneo, Java, Malaya, mainland Asia and even the Himalayas. In addition, there is a large proportion of species which are endemic, in other words they are found nowhere else but in the Philippines.

The World of Plants

The flora of the Philippines is astonishingly varied. Well over 10,000 species of tree, shrub and fern have been listed, 75 percent of which are found nowhere else. The primeval forest alone, which once covered almost the whole country, possesses between 2500 and 3000 types of tree. On the slopes of a single volcano – such as Banahaw, where the jungle is well preserved – more different species of tree grow than in the entire United States. Among the trees that thrive here are the Narra (*Pterocarpus indicus*), a type of mahogony and the country's national tree, as well as the Molave (*Vitex paniflora*) and Apitong (*Dipterocarpus grandiflorus*), both sought after for their wood. Giant hardwoods tower into the sky, lianas hang down, often as thick as a man's arm.

Above: The Narra, national tree of the Philippines. Right: The rare mouse-deer can be found on Palawan.

Tree-ferns spread out luxuriantly, and rattan plants defend themselves with long thorns. At higher altitudes, above the lush tropical vegetation, pine forests, oaks and rhododendrons cover the slopes. The wide range of plant life is further enriched by over 900 species of orchid, many entrancing in their beauty. The "queen of the indigenous orchids" is the Waling-Waling (*Vanda sanderiana*). The scented Sampaguita, with small jasminelike blossoms, is the much loved national flower. The fire acacia, hibiscus, frangipani and bougainvillea all contribute their vibrant colors to the landscape of the Philippines.

Many cultivated plants are important to the diet and the economy of the country, including, of course, rice, maize, sugar cane, abaca, tobacco, and a wealth of fruit such as pineapple, mango, durian, rambutan, many types of banana, cocoa, and coffee. Other cash crops are rubber and a large variety of palms. The coconut palm grows on about 10 percent of the land area and its many exploitable products feed millions of Filipinos.

The Animal World

The unusually varied ecosystem of the rain forest supports at least 230 species of mammal. About 200,000 years ago even the mammoth and the rhinoceros lived here, but now the tendency is more towards small creatures. The rare mouse-deer (*pilandok*), one of the smallest species of deer in the world, is only found on Palawan and grows no bigger than a hare. Although it is as fast as a hare, the animal is threatened with extinction, because its meat is much coveted by hunters. Prospects are not much better for the *tamaraw*, a kind of miniature buffalo. A few specimen still survive in the interior of Mindoro. Equally rare is the dwarf lemur or *tarsius*, a tiny prosimian, never taller than 15 centimeters which is said still to live on Bohol, but is more likely to

be found in south Mindanao. Wild boar, deer, flying-squirrel and several species of monkey also live in the forests. Domesticated pigs, from the familiar European sow, to the Asiatic pot-bellied variety, rootle happily around the villages. There are large populations of horses and cattle, but "the farmer's best friend" is the *karabao*, the phlegmatic water-buffalo.

The large and impressive Philippine eagle has the Latin name *Pithecophaga jefferyi*, which means "eater of monkeys" – but it only resorts to this diet in the absence of other delicacies. The bird is also on the verge of extinction. Altogether the Philippines can boast well over 500 species of bird, including the hornbill, peacock-pheasant, parrots and many sea- and water-birds. Many are endemic, others migrate here from Siberia, China and even Alaska.

Among the many thousands of insect species are some particularly impressive examples, such as the enormous ghost-locust, a good 30 centimeters long and

the largest insect on earth. Butterflies with unbelievable wingspans flutter through the forests, while millipedes and worms wriggle about on the ground. Everywhere in the Philippines you will find insects on the move. Mosquitoes of many varieties, some carrying malaria, can make life misery even in the big cities. The *nik-nik*, a tiny sand-fly, often chooses the most beautiful beaches for its blood-sucking expeditions. Equally numerous and often in very exotic forms, spiders can be found from sea-level right up to the mountain peaks. Seemingly ineverlasting, cockroaches have inhabited the earth for aeons. Here they are called *ipis,* and can grow as long as a finger.

The reptile family is represented by well over 200 species. They range from the little house-lizard, which even the smartest villa is happy to accommodate, to the noisy gecko and the one-meter-long monitor lizard. The mighty crocodile was prematurely declared extinct in the islands, but was then rediscovered on Palawan and Mindanao. In addition, at

least 35 species of snake have been counted, ranging from the giant python to tiny wormlike creatures. About 15 of the species, including the very common cobra, are poisonous – as are all sea-snakes.

The biosphere on land is matched by a marine one, with a positively overwhelming variety of species. This world of islands includes over 34,000 square kilometers of living coral reefs, as well as countless sandbanks and fishing-grounds. This huge area provides a habitat for about 2,000 species of fish of all sizes, including predatory sharks and barracudas, and the harmless whale-sharks. Nowhere in the world's oceans are there so many species of mollusc as in the Philippines; they number at least 5,000 and possibly more than 10,000. Over 350 species of coral and invertebrates complete the underwater fauna. Apart from

Above: Philippine virgin forest is threatened – lumberjacks in East Mindanao. Right: Vulnerable underwater glory, near Palawan.

some very unpleasant jellyfish, seen occasionally, you may find turtles, although the waters are unsafe for them, and dolphins, porpoises, whales and manatees.

Man and the Environment

The problem for the flora and fauna is that they have to share the islands with about 72 million humans. This is at least eight times the number at the beginning of the century, and the trend is continuing upward. Even in 1900 and right through the American colonial period, the environment suffered serious damage. Yet the wounds were still tolerable. At the beginning of independence, the country could still be described, with a clear conscience, as ecologically sound. Every year scientists were dicovering new plant and animal species. The primeval forest flourished over vast tracts of land, in the 1940's probably half the entire country. But then greed and faith in the almighty dollar proved too much for the virgin forest. The demand from overseas was,

218

of course, very great, and buyers of the valuable tropical hardwoods received generous export licences. Under Marcos, they sawed away at the rain forest like the very devil; but people are still trying fig- ure out where all the revenues went. Under Aquino's administration the forests fared not a whit better. Her strict embargoes never got beyond the desks of her officials into the heads of those re- sponsible. Things only began to improve under President Ramos. In 1988, a meager 25 percent of the pre-war forest acreage was (officially) still standing.

By the year 2000, experts estimate that no more than 10 percent of the original forest will be left. True, there is some re- planting taking place – but it is just a drop in the ocean. For tropical rain forest needs centuries in order to evolve once more to its previous richness. Without strict controls the land could be com- pletely denuded of forest, leading to the creation of a limestone desert, and a rapid increase in the number of environmental refugees; indeed in some part of the country this has already occurred.

The greatest threat is posed to the underwater world. Many coral reefs have been bombed with dynamite or poisoned by chemicals and sewage. There are ac- tually islanders who scarcely eat fish any more, but only non-nourishing fast- foods. If they can get fish at all, it is im- ported in cans. It is all too easy to shake one's head over this and raise a warning finger. True, a lot of the despoiling must be put down to the timber barons and fish tycoons. Huge tracts of land have been cleared to make way for grazing or monoculture farming, which as a rule only benefits the few. Yet often it is sheer poverty and aching hunger which drive the have-nots to indulge in the destruc- tive *kaingin* (slash-and-burn) or to dy- namite fishing. Anyone who has looked in despair at a stretch of ruined coral, or stood by the smoking remains of a jungle, finally realizes that the Third World is

certainly no sanatorium for "refugees" from industrialized countries.

Yet there is a little glimmer of hope. Recently actions have been launched by the public against the despoilers of na- ture. Even the Catholic church has recog- nized the signs of the times; now and again appeals for a "green" conscious- ness are made from the pulpit. Operators of tourist resorts increasingly insist on their guests behaving with respect for the environment. Some priests have paid with ther lives for their courageous inter- vention for the forests. The timber lobby hits back with brutality. Yet, in the con- flict between environment and economy, the government seems always to give prioritiy to the latter. Significant that the areas of environment and natural re- sources are still handled by one ministry.

It remains to be seen what the green version of People's Power will achieve. A mass-movement to protect nature? That would be more sensational than the fall of Marcos' in 1986, which was greeted by world-wide jubilation.

WOMEN OF THE PHILIPPINES
Caricature and Reality

The Filipina presents two sharply contrasting images to the world today. The first is an upper-class composite – an extravagant Imelda Marcos, the world-class musical singer Lea Salonga (Miss Saigon), and of course patrician Cory Aquino as her country's first woman president.

The other, much more obscure image is of a nurse, a maid, a mail-order bride, an entertainer legally and illegally roaming the world, in thousands. The Filipina immigrant is no longer just the typical nurse in a US hospital: she now attempts to make her living, which at home would be so meager, in other overseas contries such as Hongkong, Japan, Australia, the Middle East, and many European countries. Together with her colleagues from

Above: Women gathering sea-salt on the south coast of Panay. Right: A woman selling Christ-child figures in the town of Cebu.

the "Third world," she is filling both understandable and less normal needs in the industrial world – in places where local labor is expensive and males complain that their wives are becoming too emancipated.

"I do favor an Asian woman," an American in his sixties says, justifiying his marriage to a Filipina in her twenties, selected from a mail-order catalogue. "There you still find real women: they are more faithful and just have that something special about them."

Whatever that may be, the word *Filipina* has become a global cliché for "devoted, undemanding wife." In Honkong and the U.K., *Filipina* is a synonym for "maid," a status symbol, liberating fellow-women from housework and to bring in a second salary. She is often a sought-after employee because she often has a good school or university education, which means she can tutor the children. In Rome, a politician praises his "Filipina" as being a devoted Catholic governess for his offspring. In Saudi

Arabia, the servant from Asia adapts better than most to the elegant, but also feudal social system.

So it is not surprizing that in the 1980s, cunning agencies in Europe, Japan, the U.S.A. and Australia began offering "exotic Philippine dream wives". In most cases it is actually trading with "hospitality girls" and "trial wives." On the Philippine side the cooperation in this modern slave trade is anything but passive. Frequently managed by women, partner agencies advertize among city and provincial girls, promising a "future abroad." For some girls the bars in Ermita are a springboard to a marriage bed abroad. The media and even the tourist authorities know well how to use the image of the striking Filipina to their advantage.

Then in the Philippine news headlines such as the following cause furore: "Filipina raped in Iraq, Hongkong! Philippine girl arrested in Tokyo police raids! Executed in Singapore! Forced into prostitution in Athens. Found dead in America. In despair in the Australian bush!" In 1990 Cory Aquino introduced legislation against mail-order brides, but there was continuing anger at the Japanese government's leniency with the *yakuza*. It is well-known that this mafia-like syndicate forces Filipina mail-order bride applicants into prostitution, enticing them with prospects of marriage or a folkloric tour.

Still, the balancing act between seeking one's fortune in a foreign land and exploitation continues in a country with 20 percent unemployed and in which overseas contract workers are a major source of foreign exchange. A deep wound on national dignity is the memory of the earlier status that women enjoyed: the Filipina's ancient place of honor in a society that today leaves her no option but to go abroad.

Doubtless the dilemma began with colonisation. Before the *conquista*, a woman in these islands could administer her own property, divorce her husband, or keep her own name. In the Philippines of pre-

Hispanic times there were matrilinear societies, in which it was the custom that newlyweds settled in the woman's birthplace. Significantly, a woman was also her animist society's means of contact with the spirit world. Most *babaylanes*, the shamans and religious leaders were women. Then the Spanish monk replaced the *babaylan*, and the proud, free creature now called "Filipina" became a chattel, obliged to bear her husband's name. She was no longer permitted to independently enter into contracts or to make major decisions. The church had turned an adult back into a minor. Even though divorce is now also prohibited for men, not only was (and is) the Filipina forced to suffer the classic mistress syndrome in silence, she was also punished more harshly for adultery than her husband.

Above and right: For centuries Philippine women have subordinated themselves to the church and their family. Today they are on the way to a completely new self-confidence.

In southern parts of the Philippines where Islam determines society, royal women in the ancient families of the sultans on Maguindanao and Sulu have continued administering their own properties to this day, and sometimes still have the political leadership of their clans. Divorce and remarriage are permitted for both sexes – but in the case of polygamy, only the men have the right to more than one wife.

After suppressing the Philippine revolt, the Americans at least relaxed some of the social constraints on the Filipina. Higher education, formerly dominated by *Madre España* was upgraded, bringing about a minor social revolution. Soon, more women than men were enrolled in teaching, law and medical schools as growing numbers of Filipinas traveled to America on generous scholarships.

With universal suffrage in 1936, new opportunities opened up for women. As the writer Sionil José described it, they had slowly moved from "300 years of convent school to 50 years of Hollywood." Whole generations of Filipinas who grew up under U.S. rule and cultural influence have learned to live simultaneously in two different worlds, caught between divergent, often clashing, values. One set – derived from Catholicism – celebrates the image of the sweet virgin and obedient daughter who becomes an ever-faithful, long-suffering wife and mother to the most useless of husnbands. Even today many Filipina prostitutes ascribe their fate, caused as much by poverty as by premarital loss of virginity, to this "Maria Clara Syndrome," as it is called by feminists, in reference to the faint-hearted tragic heroine of a novel by José Rizal.

Meanwhile, American culture, imbibed in school, but even more powerfully projected by the movie industry presents a different set of values: "equal rights," which perhaps have led Filipinas to a certain reality, but have not yet been able to lead them out of the resulting inner tensions.

On this long trek towards self-determination, which restores to women of the Philippines some of their status from pre-colonial times there has never been a lack of males, prepared to disparage female professional achievement as "masculine." However the Philippine culture does not allow much room for maneuver. The educated Filipina who has refused burial by marriage has until recently juggled a family and a career only at the cost of great tensions. The combination of the global liberation movements, with the pill, mass communications and deepening economic crises could be considered the modern Filipina's real loss of "innocence."

The Filipina, if she is not concerned with earning a living abroad, is now surging to the forefront of the media, government, business and civics at home. Though under-represented even in the Cory Cabinet, women make up 14 percent of the judiciary, 10 percent of Congress and close to 42 percent of the

foreign service. Recently, the first Filipina general was sworn in by the first woman president. A woman now heads one of the two stock exchanges in the country. Female jounalists, no longer trapped in the society pages as they used to be, now outnumber the men in that profession.

Then there was the time when the Communist Party of the Philippines attracted as many young women as men into a "national liberation movement" that gave the Filipina a new role as gun-toting "amazon." Now a considerable number of Filipinas fight for national issues, without violence, at the head of various organizations: for agrarian reform, population control, environmental conservation and the vital cause of peace in a country still torn by insurgency and injustice.

These women want to remind their sisters, including the mail-order brides of the ancient wisdom that, it is not only up to the men, but that "women hold up half the sky".

PHILIPPINE CUISINE

Anyone in the Philippines expecting to find the hot and spicy dishes typical of Thailand or Indonesia, will be initially disappointed. After all, this is a country where the blend of colonial cultures has influenced what goes on in the kitchen, just as it has all other aspects of life. Indeed, Philippine cuisine represents a journey through the history and geography of the islands. The basic Malay ingredients were seasoned through brisk trade with the rest of southern Asia, cooked slowly in a Spanish oven for three centuries, and garnished with five decades' worth of American ketchup – to produce the "Mang Pinoy" menu of the Philippines today.

Sadly, the culinary aspirations of many Filipinos are overshadowed by the things brought in by "Big Brother:" hamburgers, soggy white bread, tooth-rotting soft drinks, insipid spaghetti and tired instant coffee. But if you can draw them out again you may be in for a gastronomic adventure. You must track down the *lutong bahay,* the delicious home cooking. Surprisingly, unless you have contact with a family, you are more likely to find this in the cities than the country. Even the supermarkets in Manila offer a wide variety of dishes from different provinces, which, with the exception of those from the Muslim regions, share *baboy*, pork, as a common ingredient. Here *lechon* is king: suckling pig roasted over a coconut-shell fire, preferably with an imported apple in its mouth, and served crisp, on banana-leaves with liver sauce. No celebration meal, be it a birthday or graduation, is complete without *lechon,* the age-old Malayo-Polynesian delicacy.

However, the true national dish is undoubtedly *adobo*, a word which refers rather to the preparation than the ingredients. Depending on the region, *adabo*

Above and right: "Lechon" – crisp suckling-pig, and fish in all shapes and sizes, form the basis of Filipino cooking.

can be made from pork, beef, poultry, fish or vegetables, steamed and braised with vinegar, garlic and soya-sauce or coconut milk. The *inihaw* dishes, with grilled meat or fish, are also delicious. In the Visayas they are called *sinugba*. Another dish popular all over the country is *tapa*, air-dried, salted beef, eaten braised or grilled, with nipa-palm vinegar (*suka*). Stewed oxtail and peanut sauce are the chief ingredients of *kare-kare*, a dish from Luzon. The *lumpia* is a small version of the Chinese spring roll. All over the islands large quantities of the pastry rolls are served, stuffed with meat or vegetables. You can buy them fried, but the variant made in the Ilonggos is a work of art, served fresh with slivers of palm heart and doused in a piquant sauce. Long noodles mean a long life, which is why *pansit*, a Chinese contribution, is a must at every birthday dinner.

Another national dish is *dinuguan*, a stew made of pork cut into small pieces with offal added, and cooked with peppercorns in fresh pig's blood. This is a

great favorite, accompanied by drinks. If you still have any doubts about the exotic taste of the Filipinos, you should try *balút*. This is a duck egg that has been hatching for about three weeks and is eaten with the feathers and bones of the embryo to increase potency.

In this island nation, fish and seafood are, needless to say, a basic element of the diet, and a regular item on any good menu. Whether grilled, boiled, baked or, as *kinilaw* (or *kilawin*) – raw, marinated in garlic, ginger, onions and chili – fish (*isdá*) is an indispensable part of Philippine life. *Lapu-lapu* (various types of perch, named after the chieftain who killed Magellan) is honored as the top-ranking fish, and usually served in a sweet-and-sour sauce. *Tanguingue* (Spanish mackerel) tastes equally good and is best when marinated as *kinilaw*. *Bangus,* the "milk-fish" from the lakes, is a favorite when stuffed with vegetables and potatoes. Squid, *pusít,* is eaten in a variety of ways, included in its own ink. Crab, prawns and crayfish are among the

most exclusive and costly seafood dishes. On the other hand, shell-fish and sea-snails are served in every fishing village, to fill the stomachs of the poor, but can also be found on the menu in good restaurants. All these are found together in *sinigang na isdá*, the Philippine version of the Mediterranean *bouillabaisse*.

The list of regional dishes is a long one. There are many different sauces and types of vinegar, various soups and preferred kinds of rice, which must be on the table for every meal, including breakfast. *Bagoóng* is the very spicy reddish paste, made from small fish or prawns, which the Filipinos even like to eat with fruit, such as green mango. *Keso putíh,* a mild white cheese made from buffalo-milk, also has its advocates. Sweets made from rice, eggs, sweet poptato, *búko* (young coconut) and *kassáwa* (Manioc) round off the meal.

Above: Shiny sweet mangoes at the San Andres market in Manila. Right: "Man with carabao," a Palawan wood-carving.

Only the rich can afford to drink imported vintage wines. For the rest of the population pure water is the usual drink. However, light sparkling beer like the world-famous "San Miguel" is very widely drunk. In the countryside, local people swear by *tubá*, the fermented juice from the fruit of the coconut palm. Spirits distilled from rice or palm (*lambanóg*) and mild rum are more sophisticated forms of alcoholic beverage.

The water from a young coconut is not only thirst-quenching but is good for the kidneys. Your quota of vitamin C can be obtained from the freshly-squeezed juice of the *kalamánsi*, a small variety of lime. Unfortunately, most fruit juice is poured out of cartons or cans and has to compete with cheap soft drinks. Tea is made only with teabags; huge amounts of of coffee are swallowed, but nearly all of the powdered kind, and, what is worse, served in insultingly small one-cup packets. But in good city restaurants, and at market stalls in the country, you can get *native coffee* or the strong, roasted *baráko*.

ART AND CULTURE

Roughly shaped stone tools from the palaeolithic era, neolithic axe-heads and banded pottery, proto-Malay rock-paintings, valauable burial gifts from the Bronze and Iron Ages – these are the few but unmistakable clues to the prehistoric creativity of the islanders. About 2,000 years ago, cultural influences from outside began to overlay and replace the art of the earliest indigenous inhabitants. The Indianized empires of of Sri Vijaya and Majapahit left behind not only their syllabic script, but also influences on the ancient literature of the Maranao, and a style of ornamentation which survives to this day in the metalwork and weaving of the peoples of Mindanao. At least 1,700 year before the arrival of the Europeans, the Chinese were spreading their artistic skills throughout Southeast Asia. Porcelain dating from their great dynasties has been found in massive quantities in the Philippines and today keeps local dealers in business. The influence of Islam can be traced not only in the language but also in the music, dance and handcrafts of the Muslim peoples of Mindanao today.

The Spanish employed a form of "cultural cleansing" and adaptation, which only permitted art that was suited to sacred and Christian purposes. They left behind the first great stone buildings in the country, the churches and forts which are in the truest sense, indestructible. Built in the "earthquake-Baroque" style, these stongholds were to protect them against natural perils and also against Islam and other foreign powers. The church of the colonial period was both a producer and a patron of art. The architecture of their sacred buildings was on the one hand strongly influenced by the highly developed Baroque style of Mexico, with which the Philippines had close contacts, and on the other it incorporated elements of Spanish-Moorish and oriental or Asiatic design. Unmistakably Islamic characteristics can sometimes be seen, and even the Chinese, who were employed chiefly as craftsmen, have left their traces behind. While the Spanish did everything they could to destroy indigenous art, they did promote the techniques of painting and sculpture which were then little known in the Philippines. But here, too, the religious imperatve prevailed. From the 17th century onward it was mainly Filipnos and Chinese who painted religious subjects on canvas and church ceilings. The ritualistic figures in wood, clay or stone were replaced by *Santos,* statues of saints carved from stone, ivory and, principally, from hardwood. Originals and reproductions of these are equally popular in today's art market. But apart from this the blending of religion and art has lost its importance. To the outsider the Philippine cultural scene appears rather westernized and commercialized, and ruined by standardization. Yet, since 1986 there has been a tendency for music, literature, film theater and graphic arts to seek inspira-

tion by rediscovering its roots. There is the beginning of a national awareness of the native culture, but it is as yet far from being a mass movement.

At first glance it certainly seems that the only things shown in cinemas and on TV are films of sadism and violence, soft porn and endless American series. The soap operas and quiz shows which flicker in the slum huts represent an unattainable dream world for the poor. At village festivals ephemeral American hits blare across the island, and the literary appetites of millions are quickly satisfied with schmaltzy romantic novels and comic books. Since the advent of People's Power, especially, a number of artists have declared that Filipino culture, which has admittedly emerged from centuries of being interwoven with many different strands, must continue to have a life of its own. These people feel they are still in

Above: A 17th century painting in the church at Baclayon, Bohol. Right: Traditional crafts-manship. A T'boli Bolo (sword).

the same position as the socially critical film directors of the Marcos era, for example, Kidlat Tahimik or Lino Brocka, who died in 1991: their work is given more recognition abroad than in their own country. Writers such as F. Sionil José, Nick Joaquin and Gregorio Brillantes also had their doubts about the values of the "New Society," but at the time they wrote mainly in English and for a small group of foreign-orientated intellectuals.

A Healing in the Arts

Juan Novicio Luna has been considered the first world-famous Philippine artist since his oil painting, *Spoliarium* was awarded the gold medal of the Spanish Crown in Madrid in 1884. As Luna's leading biographer, Nick Joaquin emphasizes, with him, the *Indio* artist who enriched sculpture, poetry, music and dance with an expressive form "borrowed" from Europe began to emerge.

Close to four centuries years of "Europeanization" were without doubt a major influence on the Malayo-Polynesian tribes of the Philippines. It was, however, only one among many cultural flavors history threw into the rich cauldron that brewed today's Filipino. It needed only the 20th-century addition of the new world-conquering English (if in a hybridized American variant) to further widen an already impressive cultural circumnavigation of the world. Conquest first by Spain, and then by America, was a double-edged sword: on one hand it interfered with natural cultural evolution, on the other it opened the tribal Filipino to an early experience of individualism and a wider world than was possible, for instance, in feudal Japan, which had closed itself off artificially from outside influence. This may be the reason why today's Filipinos are notably at ease in global fora. It is may however also be the reason for so many cultural tugs and

pulls; how to deal with the issue of a "national identity" has remained one of the recurring tragicomical problems of the Filipinos. It is in their arts – ancient and indigenous, global and contemporary – that Filipinos are dynamically and creatively resolving tensions.

A Musical Beginning

It is striking, for instance, how the most avant-garde Philippine music today is also the most ancient. In the same manner as Japanese jazz is played on the traditional Japanese *koto* and *samisen*, for example, the group *Maguindanao Lilang-Lilang* uses indigenous bamboo flutes, clappers and xylophone with brass gongs and wooden drums. They have revived magical-religious rhythms from the early periods of Asian music and by the integration of guitar and violin even transpose them into "modern" sounds. The better-known compositions of *ASIN* ("Salt") and Joey Ayala with his group *Banong Lumad* ("New People of the Earth") follow a similar method. Traditional melodies and instruments, similar to those of the Indonesian *gamelan* orchestra have influenced contemporary rolk, folk and pop music and with this musical synthesis have conquered churches, universities and ballrooms. The harmonic combination of east and west fuses exotic tribal sounds with Spanish melodies, *Indio* songs with Rock'n Roll, Calypso and Reggae. A reconciliation between the present and the long-denied tribal past seems to be on the way. The artists see this rediscovery of the tribal sounds as a critcism of the colonial arrogance which led to the polarization of art into "high" and "low" art forms.

For too long a distinction was made between *fieles* (faithful) and *infieles* (infidels), "learned" and "ignorant," and between a Christian majority and a cultural minority. These wounds need to be healed. One way to this healing is when they different streams all meet on the stage of the Cultural Center of the Philippines, more thoroughly "native" since the

revolt of 1986. Now *Indio* musicians now perform on a par with classical soloists or a madrigal choir. They work with the composer Feliciano Francisco, the pop-star Freddie Aguilar or the jazz great Bobby enriquez. The dances of the *Indios* have been made famous by folklore groups such as *Baynihan*, *Filipinescas* and the group connected with Ramon Obusan – and this has happened first in the west.

Oh, How They Dance

Whether educated or uneducated, the Filipinos assimilated the conquerors' arts better than their political forms. This had as much to do with their second-class status as with their natural inclination. The Spanish friars recognized this early and promptly harnessed it into church choirs which became the core for Western music schools all over the colony.

Above: A performance of the "Singkil" a Maranao dance from Mindanao.

The monks also noticed that dance, too, was as natural as breathing to the "child-like" *Indio*. Possibly this had to do with the fact that "art" for him had never been separated from his life and worship. Whether in dance or in music, the *Indio* simulated Nature in order to live in harmony with its spirits. As a result the monks concluded, and were proved right, that music and dance were indeed the best media for conveying their missionary activities.

Gradually tribal rituals were incorporated into the liturgical system; church celebrations were frequently held at sites considered sacred by the old animist religion. Where the natives did not protest or run away, they were brought *"bajo las campanas"*, under the church bells in the villages *(pueblos)* and the Filipino Christian *fiesta* was born. In the confusing variety of both secular and religious dances from the rural settlements, the *barrios* and *poblaciones*, the *fiesta*, that astute invention of the friars, can clearly be seen to have had its origins.

Modern disco music, which has taken over from other music, has even in small villages distorted the character of the fiesta, but now and again you may still have an opportunity to enjoy a particularly curious presentation of Phiippine cultural history. You may experience an unexpected performance of a sprightly folk version of the polka, made popular in Asia by the Spanish monarchy, who were descended from the House of Habsburg. Varations of the lilting *habanera* borrowed from Havana, Cuba, are popular as dance music with the older generation. or they like to swing their hips to the measures of the Andalusian *jota*.

At the other end of the spectrum are intriguing events such as the dance ritual called *subli* performed for the Feast of the Holy Cross – accompanied by drums, castanets and guitar sounding all rather Indian. It is similar to the somnolent *pasyon*, a sung play meditating on the Passion and Death of Jesus Christ which is performed in antiquated langauge in Holy Week. It is closer, in fact, to the centuries-old epics sung by a vanishing breed of indigenous bards. New Filipino scholarship surmises that this nativized *pasyon*, which would surely interest Oberammergau, became a powerful vehicle for political resistance. Identifying a conquered nation with a suffering Christ, it reversed the friars'teachings during later Spanish centuries. This is typically Filipino. The *kundiman*, originally a warsong called *kumintang*, was transformed into plaintive music of unrequited love, and was then rediscovered as a war song in the late-19th century.

History Repeats Itself

Nearly 100 years later, the assassination of Ninoy Aquino created another historic *kundiman. Bayan Ko* became the all-weather glue of a national protest movement that was to depose the Marcos dictatorship. In those three years a "parliament of the streets" became a stage for art harnessed to the Filipino's political protest. Many new *kundimans*, like Freddie Aquilar's *Luzviminda* in waltz-time, turned rallies into live concerts. Other political songs with obvious American influence sang of love for the fatherland in folk, pop and rock tones.

With military dictatorship as a formidable common foe, artists dug deep into musical memory for their weapons. The most effective certainly was the *ati-ati-han*, the percussion festival, which commemorates the barter trade of the aboriginal inhabitants of Panay with the Malays from Borneo, who were trying to acquire land from the Negroid aborigines in the Visayan island of Panay. The pulsating rhythm of the dancers was also adpoted by the protest movement which ultimately swept Aquino's widow, Cory, into the presidency. Who could then be surprized that the jubilant celebration of the revolution ended in such a pot-pourri of cultures, with pre-revolutionary Spanish marches and Tennessee waltzes, sung with a breaking voice, while on the main thoroghfare, the ESDA, in Manila huge floodlights illuminated a wild mass-disco event.

Changing Eras

After World War II a new struggle commenced, ushering in a new era: the controversy between conservative and modern artists which took place during the 1950s gave rise to many acrimonious, debates, and led to a boycott of the first post-war art competition, and a to-do in the media. With Picasso's *Guernica* in at the back of their mind, progressive Filipino artists wanted to portray the heritage of war in a way more appropriate to its ugliness. They experimented with cubist distortion, in order to better depict the changing scenes of an era without fixed values. The conservatives reacted

231

with indignation. They had enjoyed the patronage of American and Filipino colonial buyers who paid well for provincial still life paintings and portraits of bare-bosomed "native women."

In spite of an almost traumatic effect, which the moderns first provoked, it was the effect of the glowing colors of a Carlos Francisco, the impressionism of Victorio Edades, the geometric cyclists of Arturo Luz, the transparent cubism of Vicente Manansala, the stylized coutry women of Anita Magsaysay-Ho's, the dadaist experiments of someone like Galo Ocampo and the vibrant organic shapes of Hernando Ocampo, which captivated the imagination of a nation which was at long last achieving independence.

Above: Movies – like TV, provide millions of Filipinos with a cheap form of "cultural" entertainment. Right: Contemporary "People-Power" art, "Tertullia" by Noel Cuizon who has created a kind of "Peoples' Altar" with his moveable figures.

232

More barriers fall

More debates surfaced in the 1960s and 1970s – nationalism against internationalism, art for art's sake against art for the masses, commissioned versus committed art. All these discussions were the reflection of the inner tensions of a society which was absorbing a new global spirit, the stability of which was also increasingly threatened by insurgency and the militarization of the state that would one day climax in martial law.

In the rebellious, psychedelic years of the late 1960s and throughout the 1970s, the Filipino *zeitgeist* experienced yet another transformation. Now the visual and plastic artists took their turn in wedding animist roots to contemporary expressions. The painter and sculptor, Abdulmari Imao, from Mindanao broke with the religious law against the portrayal of the godly in human shape, while the sculpter, Napoleon Abueva, infused traditional Igorot design and lowland Christian culture into dynamic abstract sculpture. Meanwhile, painters were turning from oil to tempera, acrylic, aquarelles and experimenting with new printing techniques. Soon, they broke away fully from the two-dimensional surface of a canvas itself. Then came Roberto Feleo who by spreading several layers of paint on wood, progressively blended painting and sculpture. His works which represent images like tatooed tribal *pintados* or the ceremonial spirit boat of the ancestral dead resemble, in an ingeneously witty syncretism, the miniature folk altars of the Christians. Equally impressive are the mosaic-like paintings by Imelda Cajipe-Endaya; she began by depicting details of tribal decoration, worn by aboriginals and then later used larger panels, which were overlaid with fibers, woven fabrics and other ethnic artifacts.

Besides good examples of conventional art forms, the new generation is proving itself in its admiration for all things "indigenous." In the 1990's the painter-scuplter Roberto Villanueva has gone further and has declared art to be a shamanic ritual. His maze of bamboo stalks leading to the Igorot's circular stone *dap-ay* portrays an ancient ritual place: Earth Mother's womb, familiar to all tribal shamans from Delphi to New Guinea.

As a climax to its presentation at the Bagui Arts Festival, Villanueva had planned to partially burn his art work, an act in which he, as artist-shaman would almost have been burnt to death himself. Villanueva represents the passion of the movement, which wants to drastically break down barriers between art and nature, between religiion and life.

In the 1960s, a sudden fever broke out for translation of classic Greek drama, Shakespearean, contemporary French and American theater. This was followed by a highly successful revival of folk drama forms, which unfortunately has long since been displaced by Hollywood

and Broadway plays. The *Zarzuela*, a well-loved pre-war form of musical, began to enjoy new successes. *Walang Sugat*, a comedy about lovers caught in the confusions of the revolution against Spain, has entered its 20th year of continuous popularity. Today, advocates of the "high" art form, want to transpose the old Italian operas into typical Philippine settings.

Meanwhile, modern ballets have been staged beside waterfalls, in churches and on city plazas. Ballet is turning literature, poetry and lately also painting into dance. Song and dance become interchangeable in the dance drama *Encantada*, performed by the *Ballet Philippines* – to loud bravos from the audience, showing that art is now returning to its original function.

It will take some time longer for everyone painfully caught in the battle for survival to share this new vision. But more and more Filipinos are responding to the deepening environmental crisis by turning to art in all its forms.

FIESTA FILIPINA

Good grief, look at that. They must be going crazy! A herd of water-buffalo, real monsters, thundering down the muddy racetrack, making the earth tremble with their hooves. On their backs crouch half-naked figures, howling like dervishes and urging their unruly mounts on to maximum performance. There is a deafening roar from the crowd while at least three brass bands try to outblast each other. Firecrackers explode, car horns hoot, and church bells jangle. Wandering guitarists frenziedly strum their instruments, drums roll and harmonicas wail. Ah, it's another typical fiesta getting underway, just as the Filipinos like them!

A Spanish fiesta is a kind of fair, like the German or American kermis, which sometimes develops into an outright car-

Above: Parade of the "tribes" at the Ati-Atihan festival in Kalibo. Right: Cockfighting – an old passion among the Filipino menfolk.

nival. Then all hell breaks loose, as in the *Ati-Atihan Festival* in Kalibo, the *Sinulog* in Cebu and the dramatic *Moriones* festival in Marinduque.

Just so that nobody misses out, the fiestas are nicely spread over the year and throughout the country. Not even the smallest village gets left out. So you can bank on there being some hectic celebrations going on in at least one place in the Philippines on every day of the year. The fiesta calendar serves as a vade mecum to these long-running parties, which is of particular interest to hawkers, showmen and versatile pickpockets. For at the fiesta, according to ancient custom, the guest gets to eat and drink for nothing. In the cities this golden rule has long been reversed: The guest pays, quite a bit in fact. On the other hand, out in the country the law of hospitality survives, which nevertheless can have its disadvantages for foreigners. You have to keep up with the locals, whether you want to or not – and when it comes to alcohol this can seriously damage your health. As you

might guess, the Spanish introduced the custom of the fiesta, and even after the end of colonial rule the popular institution lived on in this country. Today, more than ever, it is lived out as a basic element of Philippine culture. With regional variations, of course.

Religious motivation is still predominant. A fiesta generally begins with some sober singing in church in the morning, and many a hasty prayer is offered up to heaven, that the fiesta and the coming year may be successful. But in the afternoon, if the stubborn *karabao* refuse to budge from the starting-line, then the air is thick with the darkest and most un-Christian oaths. Forgive me, Saint Isidore! For in spite of all my good intentions, I have gambled away half the house-keeping money on a cockfight, and now my wife will give me a good scolding. But when it comes to the fiesta Derby everyone just has to place a bet. It only comes round once a year, and tomorrow it's back to the stony fields, or off to sea again.

In the 1960s a moralistic senator had the notion of abolishing fiestas by law. "We simply cannot afford them," argued the politician, and he was perfectly right. For during the days of the fiesta a host is obliged to splurge, regardless of how much or little money he has. To turn away a guest means to lose face. And no worse fate can befall a man in Southeast Asia. Therefore he must go into debt, even take out a mortgage. *Bahala na –* what the hell! Tradition requires it, and respect is the important thing. Even if it means eating plain rice for the next month – the last guest to leave still has the fare pressed into his hand, so that he gets home safely.

Abolish the fiesta, forbid cockfighting, deprive the Filipinos of their indulgence in betting? No way, never! No politician would be able to enact such a law and get away with it. Admittedly those in power are well aware that these extravagant celebrations are a strain on everyone's purse, today more than ever. Nevertheless there is a lot of sense in the strife-

weary country sticking to these old, deeply engrained traditions. The majority of the population are small farmers and fishermen, with large families to feed. That's hard work, without the paid holidays and leisure time that the city-dwellers enjoy. So the fiesta no doubt fulfils a valuable function as a safety-valve and a means of recuperation.

The truly bewildering "Party Calendar" begins on the very first day of the year, literally with a bang. In the provinces people use home-made bamboo cannons to shoot the old year out of and the new year in to their humble lives. In the cities, *Bagong taon*, New Year, is celebrated with fireworks and hooting horns. This explosion of joy exacts its tribute, however. In Manila alone every New Year's Eve, about 2000 people end up in hospital. The celebrating crowds however do not care in the least about such dangers. With renewed energy the

Festival of the Three Kings is celebrated on the first Sunday of the year. It is especially colorful on Marinduque.

On 9th January comes the *Procession of the Black Nazarene* in Manila's suburb of Quiapo. Thousands of men parade through the streets with the lifesize statue of the *Nazareno*, which dates from the 17th century. Women can watch, but they are not allowed to take part. The event draws enormous crowds, since touching the statue is supposed to produce miraculous effects. In the course of this, a number of the faithful usually collapse in a faint, and people have even died in this pious throng.

This is followed by harvest and sacrificial festivals among the mountain tribes, and on the third weekend of January comes the really big pub-crawl, when the *Ati-Atihan Festival* breaks out on Panay. This began as a feast of reconciliation between the immigrant Malays from Borneo and the resident Ati. But with time it acquired Catholic elements, when the Spanish ascribed magical qualities to the

Above: Crowds around the cross, in the procession of the Black Nazarene in Manila.

Christ-child that would keep the Muslim pirates at bay. But today this three-day event still looks more like a colorful tribal feast than anything else. It is a gigantic dance and masked ball, in which all inhibitions are thrown to the winds. "*Puera pasma! Hala Bira! Viva Santo Niño!*" The rousing cries echo through the little town of Kalibo, until the drums fall silent and everyone collapses exhausted.

The drums rumble on for a whole week during the *Sinulog* festival in Cebu, which takes place at about the same time as the one in Kalibo. The word *Sinulog* means something like "flowing" and refers to the dance movements of the crowds: two steps forward, one step back – so that the fiesta should not come to an end too soon.

In February it is the Chinese who paint the town red. The Chinese New Year is celebrated with as much pomp and noise as in Hong Kong or Shanghai. And in all the big cities of the Philippines the hotels are booked solid, since this is an occasion for the far-flung Chinese familes to get together for elaborate festivities. The Filipinos, of course, do not want to be left out of things.

A series of smaller festivals follow, building up to *People's Power Day*, commemorating the momentous revolution that took place between February 22 and 25, 1986. Millions of people still flood the streets of Manila each year, in order to relive the events which finally spoiled Marcos' election party.

The *Moriones Festival*, along with Passion Plays in other regions, is the high point of March or April. The *Semana Santa* or Holy Week, is the most important event in the cycle of festivals and the most religious in nature. You can witness the pious, perhaps sanctimonious fervor of which the Philippines, the most Catholic country in Asia, is so proud. The Easter festival is honored right across the country, and almost all worldly activities,

including air and surface transport, are halted.

On the religious front, however, no effort is spared: processions, ceremonies, christenings, birthdays – in the *Semana Santa* everything takes on added significance and involves three times as much work. As if this wasn't enough, there are some who feel it necessary to purge their sins by flagellating themselves with barbed wire and whips made of razorblades; or, as in the case of the courageous men of San Fernando/Pampang, by allowing themselves to be nailed to the cross.

The recreation of historical events is always well received, for instance on the island of Limasawa to the south of Leyte, where the landing of Magellan is re-enacted in a colorful fiesta on March 31. The attempts of narrow-chested local actors to turn themselves into burly *conquistadores*, provokes a lot of mirth. But the gales of laughter from the spectators are meant in good heart. What does it matter if they cannot afford a spectacular *Son et Lumière* show?

On April 9 comes the *Araw ng Kagitingan*, Day of Courage, when the last desperate defence of the Bataan peninsula by American and Philippine troops is honored. The survivors of this bloody World War II slaughter certainly have reason to celebrate, and apart from this the day of remembrance is an occasion for speeches about honor and freedom. In April people also remember the jeepney, that smelly, uncomfortable vehicle, which was born out of the ruins of war and of which hundreds of thousands now jolt about the Philippine roads in various modernized forms. How often has its demise been prophesied, yet every year the most beautifully painted example and the one equipped with the most powerful stereo equipment is awarded the title of "King of the Road."

In May, the *karabao* is king. Homage is paid to the usefulness of the water-buf-

falo at many provincial fiestas. In San Joaquin on Panay, these sturdy animals are allowed to fight each other as early as January for the honor of their breed, while in Pulilan in Luzon's Bulacan Province, even the most miserable-looking *kalabaw* is awarded a special prize. Its owner is given a whip, with the exhortation to use it unsparingly on himself.

The most important month of all for fiestas is May, when many of the celebrations have the unmistakable character of a harvest festival. When the weather is getting unbearably hot and the fields have been tilled in expectation of early rainfall – what better season to celebrate? May is also the time when a great many flowers are in bloom, which provides an opportunity for the four-week-long *Flores de Mayo* or *Santacruzan,* a gentle and esthetically pleasing fiesta. Every

Above: Women dancing at the Sinulog festival in Cebu. Right: Joy and abandon at the 120th anniversary of the city of Puerto Princesa, Palawan.

day, little girls in festive costume present fresh flowers to the Virgin Mary in church, and at the end of the month the May festival culminates in processions and parades. Most of the pilgrimages also take place in May. All over the country, in picturesque spots, on a mountain, in a cave or any place where some miraculous event is once said to have occurred, a shrine awaits huge crowds of devout pilgrims. The patron saint of the Philippines is St Mary, May is her month and millions go to receive her blessing – conveniently during the nationwide school holidays.

However, saints are not the only reason to have a fiesta. In Cagayan de Oro, on Mindanao, there is a festival in May, where kites are flown and water-buffalo race through the streets of Pavia, near Iloilo on Panay. In Obando, central Luzon, unmarried and childless women dance in the streets for three days in the hope of a wedding ring and numerous offspring. And everywhere the fair sex of all ages competes for the title of Beauty

Queen, a distinction which can open a door to social success to many a Filipina.

On June 12 Independence Day is celebrated with pomp and military parades. But soon afterwards more mundane matters are the theme, for example, when the *Parada ng Lechon* is held in Balayan, in Luzon's Batangas Province. This celebration on St John's Day makes the visitor's mouth water as large numbers of roast sucking-pigs are carried through the town, admittedly protected by barbed wire to stop anyone taking an unauthorized nibble.

In July, with the beginning of the rainy season, big river processions take place in Bocaue and Bulacan, Luzon, and in the Manila suburb of Pateros. In September, as the typhoons are raging, the famous river parade of the *Peñafrancia Festival* is held in Naga, south Luzon. In 1972 a bridge collapsed and 138 spectators were killed, but not even a disaster like that could dampen the enthusiam of the Bicolaños for their fiesta. It still gets more magnificent every year.

It is after all the declared aim of any mayor and his townfolk – from the capital down to the smallest island village – to achieve new heights with every year's fiesta. Powerful amplifiers are, needless to say, brought in to shatter the eardrums of the crowd. But the more noise the better. That way even the most distant settlement will know that the big day has come. So if you have come to the Philippines in search of peace and quiet, you should study the festival calendar carefully and look for gaps. But as you can see, there aren't that many.

October is the month when the towns of Zamboanga on Mindanao, and Bacolod on Negros, come to the fore. During the *Zamboanga Hermosa Festival* in the "City of Flowers," Badjao Vintas compete in a sailing regatta, while not only is *Nuestra Señora del Pilar* onored, but also the most beautiful Zamboangeñas are chosen. In the sugar capital of the Philip-

pines, smiling masks are worn for the *Mass-Kara Festival.*

At *All Saints* the cemeteries are full to capacity, and at the end of November the Igorot tribespeople provide the main attraction of the *Grand Canao* in Baguio, north Luzon, by which time you begin to hear Christmas carols across all the islands. Jumping-jacks hop through December, until, with an earsplitting din, they shatter the silence of Holy Night night and announce *Pasko*, or Christmas, the feast of feasts.

But after the smoke has cleared, a pause for contemplation intervenes in many places. People sit down together and discuss this and that, including of course the many fiestas of the departing year. Do you remember when the mayor was flung off the water-buffalo? Or when Uncle Pepe had too much to drink and fell head-first into a cowpat? How we laughed. Everyone agrees. And soon, Saint Isidore willing, fiesta-time will come round again. That's the best thing about life in the Philippines...

239

METRIC CONVERSION

Metric Unit	US Equivalent
Meter (m)	39.37 in.
Kilometer (km)	0.6241 mi.
Square Meter (sq m)	10.76 sq. ft.
Hectare (ha)	2.471 acres
Square Kilometer (sq km)	0.386 sq. mi.
Kilogram (kg)	2.2 lbs.
Liter (l)	1.05 qt.

TRAVEL PREPARATIONS

Entry requirements

On arrival in Manila or Cebu, visitors from all countries with which the Philippines maintains diplomatic relations (including most European states, the USA, Canada, Australia, New Zealand, Japan and ASEAN states) are issued with a visa entitling them to stay for 21 days. To qualify, you must have a passport valid for at least six months, and an outward bound ticket. Business visitors can stay for 21 days without a visa. Visitors from countries who are obliged to carry a visa (including Hong Kong and Taiwan) and who wish to stay longer than 21 days, must apply to their national embassy or consulate in the Philippines. There they will obtain, for a fee, a tourist visa valid for either 59 days or 90 days.

Anyone arriving without a visa and who wishes to stay up to 59 days or longer, must pay additional fees to the immigration authorities. (For addresses, see under Manila and Cebu), who will then issue an extended visa. If you are planning a stay of more than six months, the authorities may make the extension conditional on the result of an AIDS test. After residing in the country for a year or more, an exit tax, called Travel Tax, is payable. This is currently set at approx. US$ 60.

Money

The national currency is the Peso, officially called the Piso. It is divided into 100 sentimos (c). Now only coins of a new serioes are in circulation: 1c, 5c, 10c, 25c, 50c, 1P, 2P, 5P; and notes are 5P, 10P, 20P, 50P, 100P, 500P and 1,000P.

It is advisable to bring US dollars with you, for safety's sake in the form of Travelers Cheques. The well-known companies like American Express, Thomas Cook or Bank of America are recognized by practically all banks, even in the provinces, in any case in every branch of the PNB. However, you should also keep a reserve of cash in some safe place. You will not get far with Eurocheques, but the major credit cards (Amexco, Mastercard, Diners Club, Visa) are accepted by many hotels, restaurants, beach resorts and shops.

Any amount of foreign currency can be brought in, but any sum in excess of 3,000 US$ (or its equivalent) must be declared to the Central Bank when you clear customs. You must not leave with more foreign currency than you came in with, and you may only take out up to 1,000 Pesos of Philippine currency or bring in up to 5,000 Pesos.

Apart from banks, which have branches at Manila, Davao and Cebu airports, you can change money at the larger hotels and resorts, and at authorized moneychangers in Manila, Cebu and several other cities. Their exchange rates are usually more expensive than at banks, and large notes get a better rate than small denominations. Count these carefully!) Do not on any account do business with black-marketeers, who approach you in the street with tempting offers. You will inevitably lose out on the deal and have no redress.

Always have small change ready in taxis, buses and small restaurants. That way you will save time and avoid unnecessary tips. Filipinos are happy to bargain: whether you are renting a car, hiring a guide, booking a room several days ahead, or buying in souvenir shops or markets. Taxi drivers who want to keep the fare for themselves, rather than for their boss are often willing to do a deal with you. In general it is true that a good bargain is achieved by insistent, but friendly negotiation, meeting somewhere between the two positions, thus allowing both parties to save face.

Health

Inoculations are only compulsory if you are arriving from a zone of infection in another country. However, the Philippines is not entirely free of serious health risks. You should therefore take medical advice about getting injected against hepatitis, cholera and typhus. If your polio and tetanus inoculations are due for renewal, it is advisable to have this done. After traveling in Palawan and other humid regions (such as the forests of Mindanao and the Sulu Islands), you may come away with a nasty souvenir from the malaria mosquitoes which are very common there. Before going, you should obtain the appropriate prophylactic pills (from an institute of tropical medicine, or public health office) and swallow them conscientiously. Do not scratch mosquito bites, but put eucalyptus cream on them.

It is useful to have the necessary disinfectant, dressings and bandages at the ready, to deal immediately with any wounds. The word "hygiene" is certainly not unknown in the Philippines, and personal cleanliness is given a high priority, yet often the sanitary facilities are not up to western standards. In the cities, tapwater is treated with chlorine to make it drinkable. The sale and consumption of mineral water from plastic bottles are widespread. In cheap hotels and restaurants caution is obligatory. In these places you can, if necessary, ask for drinking water that has been boiled for at least 15 minutes. In any event, and especially if you have a sensitive stomach, you should pack water-sterilizing tablets such as Micropur.

Any medication you need for malaria, diarrhoea, infections and chills, can be bought, even as individual tablets, at the numerous pharmacies and drugstores, sometimes called *boticas,* in the larger towns, so there is no need to bring them with you. Philippine doctors have a good reputation and are experienced in tropical diseases, even though the nation's health service is in a parlous state. In case of serious illness or injury, always make for one of the hospitals listed in the chapters on Manila and Cebu. You don't need to head straight to a controversial faith healer, if you are feeling a little out of shape. Usually a reputable massage is enough to put you back on your feet. .

Mosquito repellant and sun lotion are rather hard to find. The latter often has the message "Guaranteed not to tan" on it, since Filipino tourists chiefly belong to the upper class who place great value on a light skin.

Climate and clothing

The Philippines offers the entire spectrum of tropical weather conditions. That means it is generally warm right through the year, and sometimes oppressively hot. In Manila, the mean temperature varies from 25°C during the cool, dry period (December-February) to over 35°C in the second half of the dry period (March-May). In Mindanao and the Sulu Islands you can tell you are close to the equator, even though the maritime climate on the coast provides cooling land- and sea-breezes. Rain and humidity can occur outside the rainy season from May to November, and you should always allow for regional variations from the general weather pattern.

This all means that your selection of clothes should be based on light, but strong and quick-drying materials, especially cotton. You should also bring

241

something to keep off the rain, and warmer items of clothing (anorak, pull-overs) for when you are in the mountain regions or for windy journeys on land or water. Strong, hard-wearing shoes are necessary for trekking, though flip-flops or sandals are all you need for the beach or indoors. You should wear bathing shoes as a protection against coral and sea urchins.

Some of this equipment can be bought in the shops in larger towns, but if you are especially tall or heavily built, you should be warned that in Asia clothes sizes, and particularly shoe sizes, are a good deal smaller than the typical Anglo-saxon or European equivalent. You will have no problem, however, in buying hats and caps of all kinds, which are an essential protection against sunburn and skin cancer. Try to avoid too much exposure to excessively cold air conditioning, otherwise the warmest tropical night will leave you with a stubborn cold.

GETTING TO THE PHILIPPINES

By air
Currently, tourists travel to the archipelago almost exclusively by air. The main airports are the Ninoy Aquino International Airport in Manila and Cebu's Mactan International Airport. It is also possible to fly from Manado, on the Indonesian island of Sulawesi to Davao City in Mindanao. In 1997 an air route between Zamboanga City and Sandakan, in Sabah/Malaysia, on Borneo was introduced (one flight per week).

By ship
Until recently only passengers of cruise ships or cargo ships arrived by sea in the Philippines. The ferry connection from Mandao/Sulawesi to Davao City and the route from Zamboanga to Sandakan/Sabah (Malaysia) have once again made it an interesting way for normal tourists to travel between the three states.

TRAVEL WITHIN THE ISLANDS

By air
The preferred method of travel between the islands is by air for anyone who can can afford fares that work out at around 70 US$ per hour. The privatized Philippine Airlines (PAL) operates throught the country with modern jet and propellor aircraft. However, at busy periods (Christmas, Easter Week and the beginning and end of the holidays), you should allow for bottlenecks and always book well ahead.

Delays are not unknown, and timetables may be altered two or three times a year. On internal flights, there are only modest fare concessions: students up to 25 years old and people over 60 can get a small discount on return flights if they show the necessary document. You can find out more about this when you book your flight at home, or in the internal PAL offices in all the towns and cities they fly to. (You can get the addresses at the airport or in hotels).

About ten other airlines, such as Pacific Airway, Grand Air, Air Cebu Pacific, Air Philippines, Air Ads and Soriano Aviation now serve a large sector of the monopoly previously held by PAL. It is worth comparing prices and booking early.

By ship
A few years ago, the whole world was made aware of the dubious reputation of Philippine ferries by a series of accidents culminating in the sinking of the *Doña Paz* with the loss of 4,000 lives. Since then, the big shipping lines have improved safety standards on their ships. William Lines, Gothong Lines and Aboitiz Lines together form WG&A, the most modern concern and, like Negros navigation, now use safer and faster ships on the routes between the islands.

In calm weather and with an attentive crew a sea voyage in deck or cabin class can be a restful experience, once you get away from the crowds on the dockside. The big ships have restaurants and even discos, though on the smaller ferries you have to bring your own food.

In the city center or dockside offices of the shipping companies you can find out about timetables and whether tickets have to be bought ashore or on board ship. Early booking is necessary at most times of the year. Short trips between the islands are usually covered by motorized outriggers (*pumpboat, banca*). The watchword here is: in bad or stormy weather, stay ashore!

By train, bus and jeepney

The only journey you can still make by train, with the Philippine National Railway, is the ten-hour long south Luzon route from Manila (Tayuman Station) to Bikol (at present to Ragay, 60 kilometers before Naga). The section of the route to Legaspi is being modernized. You have a choice between the very basic economy class and air-conditioned tourist class.

The fastest form of public transport on the larger islands is the bus. The most comfortable are the big express buses, equipped with air conditioning and usually video as well. The regular buses do not provide meals. However, they stop several times at restaurants, and in larger towns every stop is accompanied by an invasion of hawkers selling drinks and food. Luggage is placed not only on the roof, but in the passenger space, under seats and in the gangway, beside the driver and in the boot. You can buy your ticket before departure or on the bus. Inspectors frequently come aboard, more to check up on the honesty of the conductor than that of the passengers.

The jeepney is the ideal transport for local journeys, as well as for longer journeys on roads that are too poor for buses. Riding in a jeepney is something that has to be learnt, especially the sitting position for long-legged westerners. It is no joke crouching for hours on low seats under a roof which bangs the top of your head every time you drive over a bump. But one is not alone. The fuller the jeepney is, the less each passenger will be flung from side to side, and the better is the revenue for the driver, who celebrates by hooting the horn and keeping a heavy foot on the accelerator.

Unlike the city jeepneys, the ones in the country do not set off until every last seat has been occupied, hens stuffed under the benches, and pigs or crates of fish tied on to the luggage rack. The seat on the right next to the driver is the favorite one, and if your are clever you will book this position the day before the journey. The jeepney's starting point and destination are written on or above the windscreen and on the sides. The fares are collected by a traveling helper. There are several of these, to look after loading and unloading, to act as a substitute for the missing jack when there is a breakdown, or to fetch water from the river for the overheated radiator.

If you want to ride on the roof to get some fresh air and enjoy the view, you should be aware that you will have to come down again at the next town, since the driver will not be happy about paying a fine to the police, who regard this as an additional source of income and deliberately pick on jeepneys.

If you want to board a jeepney during its journey, provided they have seats still vacant, jeepneys stop anywhere when you give them a hand-signal. Once aboard, if you want the jeepney to stop, so that you can get out, give an audible knock on the roof or emit a loud hissing sound.

Looking like a smaller relation of the jeepney, the tricycle is a rattling, smelly moped with an adjacent passenger cabin welded on to the back. And like the jeepney, the tricycle is pure *joie de vivre* on wheels. Colorfully painted, and decorated with cheeky slogans or pious mottoes, this vehicle can be found operating in the most remote provincial areas. Regional design variations are even more imaginative than with the jeepney. But what they all have in common are their iritating engine noise and a remarkable loading capacity. These fragile-looking machines are capable of transporting large families, house removals and livestock over unbelievably bad roads.

By rented car and taxi

Hotels and travel agents will arrange for you to rent a car with driver. If you prefer to drive yourself the international Avis Rent-a-Car company has offices in Manila (several addresses including the Manila Pavilion Hiloday Inn, Ermita, tel. 5252206, Cebu (Archbishop Reyes Ave., Lahug, te. 2317317) or Baguio (Harrison Rd., tel. 4424018). The Hertz company and various local agencies also rent cars. International drivers licenses are not recognized, but your national drivers license is normally accepted.

In Manila there are thousands of taxis, many now with air conditioning at your disposal. At the start of the journey the driver should switch on the taximeter and leave it to run without interference. Unfortunately this is often not the case, and the traveler arriving for the first time at the airport may be caught out, not knowing any better. This can put you off the country. It is true that at NAIA Airport a few years ago they decided only to allow official Aircon taxis into the arrival terminal. These charge an expensive all-in fare. This arrangement may fall into disuse and regular taxis, which have dropped their passengers off at the departure terminal (one floor above), could then collect passengers from the arrival terminal.

The alternative is awkward: walk with your luggage up to the departure terminal and try to find an empty taxi there, then negotiate a fare. The larger hotels have their own courtesy buses at the airport.

Philippines Airlines runs a shuttle bus-service between the international and domestic airports for passengers who have an immediate connection with an internal flight.

Taxi fares in Manila and Cebu City consist of a basic charge of 16 P, covering the first 500 meters, plus 1 P for every additional 250 meters. If a driver claims that his meter is not working, either do not get in at all or else get out out as soon as possible.

If you are familiar with the price-distance ratio for a particular trip, you can negotiate a deal that will satisfy both parties. In other cities (e.g. Iloilo, Bacolod, Zamboanga) the taxis are called P.U. (Public Utility) or simply "cabs," and some of them still run without taximeters. There are two fares: one for the city and one for the outer area.

DEPARTURE

Before you leave the Philippines you should check the validity of your visa and confirm your flight at least 72 hours prior to departure (this also applies to domestic flights). On international flights an airport tax (*Passenger Terminal Fee*, 550 Pesos in 1999) will be charged at the airport.

PRACTICAL TIPS

Accommodation

There is a very wide choice of accommodation on offer, especially in the tourist centers. The grading of facilities and hygiene also covers a considerable range. The selection runs from cheap, and none too clean crash pads, through pleasant family pensions, and simple but functional hotels right up to luxury palaces.

The descriptions can sometimes be misleading. Terms like "Lodge" or "Inn" are used in the American sense and do not indicate rustic charm, whereas a "New Plaza Hotel" can be pretty seedy.

The accommodation listed in this book as "budget" ranges in price from £3 to £12 (US$ 4.50 - US$ 18 per day, "mid-price" covers hotels, pensions and resorts between £ 12 and £ 40 (US$ 18 - 60), and "luxury" covers everything above that price that merits the description. This rough classification does not make allowances for local differences. In a remote provincial place, a "budget" lodging for £ 10/US$ 15 can be much pleasanter than a room in a mid-price hotel in a big city or even a resort hotel in some tourist trap.

Wherever you stay, as soon as you have looked at the room, you should note the location of the emergency exit. Because of the risk of fire and earthquakes, the rooms lower down are safer.

Check the lock on your door and security of the hotel safe. Even private householders who let rooms are not above helping themselves to a financial or material "present."

Alcohol

The range of drinks available is wide and, at least as far as local products are concerned, not expensive. Local beer is drunk all over the country. It can be a lot of fun to have a few rounds of drinks with Filipinos you make friends with, but you should be careful about trying to keep up with them, for the sake of "honor." It is precisely when you are drinking with people you don't know that you should keep a clear head, or make a polite deaprture at an early stage, since alcohol can quickly lead to trouble.

Business hours

Government offices and banks are open from Monday to Friday, but many commercial offices work on Saturdays as well. Shops are generally open every day, including Sunday, from 8 or 9 am until 7 pm. Smaller shops shut for a siesta from about 1 pm until 3 pm, but are open until 9 pm. Business offices work as a rule from 9 am until 5 pm, but stop for a siesta, as do government offices. Diplomatic missions shut for the day as early as 1 pm. Banks are open for business between 9 am and 3:30 pm.

Contacts

Hospitality is a Philippine virtue which you generally find is practiced everywhere. But take care, especially in big cities or tourist centers, if a Filipino man or women, hitherto unknown to you, invites you home or to the home of a friend or relative who "happens" to live in the neighborhood, and tries to offer you refreshment, some gambling, a massage or a family party! Beware of knock-out drops in your drink! These touts usually base their approach on some supposedly shared experience such as: "Weren't we on the same plane/ship/bus?" or "Didn't I see you at the airport?" Even the reference to a sister working overseas can be used to inspire confidence. All they are after is your money which afterwards will be missing, or at least some of it. If you should be seeking intimate contact, just remember: the number of people in the Philippines infected with AIDS was estimated at around 50,000 in 1998!

Customs duty

You are entitled to bring the following into the Philippines, duty-free: 400 cigarettes or 50 cigars, or 250 grams of pipe tobacco, and up to two liters of alcohol. It is forbidden to import fire arms, or to export protected shells, coral and parts of certain endangered animal species, such as tortoise shell. There are restrictions on the export of antiques.

Eating and drinking

Even if they are not listed in the regional tourist information leaflets, you will find one or more places to eat in every small town. Most of the places to stay listed in this book have their own restaurant. People will be happy to tell you about local specialities. In country districts they will often be surprised that a foreigner should take an interest in such things – since they will tend to assume you probably will only be interested in steak, chips and fish fingers. In many cases the dishes served are better than the service, for although your order will be taken with a charming smile, it will get confused with other orders taken on the way back to the kitchen. Be prepared for the fact that Filipinos do not necessarily eat their food hot. If you want to eat a really hot meal in a little eatery, you should go there in the morning, as then the food for the whole day will is being cooked.

Cutlery was first introduced by the Spanish, and even today simple people still eat with their right hand. Now, even educated Filipinos have rediscovered the traditional eating style, *kamayan* ("with the hand"). This name is given to many special restaurants in the cities, where delicious hand-to-mouth dishes are served on banana leaves in a basket.

For service, you should call "waitress" or "Miss," or "waiter," as the case may be. In simpler places it is acceptable to attract attention by snapping your finger or hissing. The bill is a "check," which is usually pronounced "chit." You ask for it by drawing – with both hands – an imaginary bit of paper into the air.

Electricity

The current throughout the country generally is 220 volts, but in a few places it is still 110 volts. The sockets are of the US type, so European plugs need an adapter. Even in big cities, there are often blackouts lasting for hours.

Guided tours

It can enhance your appreciation of museums and historic sites if you take a qualified guide. For climbing mountains or exploring caves, it goes without saying that you should have a guide with knowledge of the local area. It is also advisable, when visiting ethnic and social minorities, to procure the services of a native guide.

Handicrafts

Traditional handicrafts are practiced by the ethnic minorities. Their textiles and wood carvings can be found in the places they are made, or in specialist shops in the cities, especially in Manila and Cebu. A lot of the products that were originally utilitarian have, under the influence of tourism, become fashionable ethnic art. Popular souvenirs are textiles (shirts, blouses) made from pineapple or abaca fibers, the hard-wearing materials of the mountain people ("Lepanto cloth"), brass and bronze ware from Mindanao (Moro brass), the abaca mats of the Samal, and wood-carvings from Ifugao and Paete (Laguna). You can also buy decorative basketwork made from bamboo, nipa and rattan (including furniture). Cebu is the main source of fashionable jewelry, in constantly new creations from shells and coral. But it is all too easy to forget that the great demand for these poses a threat to marine life.

Media

Commercial TV from almost 30 stations (including 10 in Manila) is spreading ever futher into the provinces, where TV sets are often run off a generator. The mainly western-angled program content is of little cultural interest to foreigners. Broadcasts are in English and Tagalog.

The national press comprises a good two-dozen daily and weekly papers, e.g. *Free Press*, in English and Tagalog; a few serious periodicals and pulp magazines are bilingual. In many provinces English-language local papers are published. Important papers include *Manila Bulletin, Daily Globe, Manila Chronicle, Malaya* and the *Daily Inquirer*, which, because of its sound, critical reporting is also respected abroad. International publications can be bought in all the larger hotels, airports and bookshops.

Photography

The Philippines is a very photogenic country and easy to photograph. And the people all seem anxious to have their picture taken. You should respect the usual exceptions: military facilities and personnel, as well as private individuals if they do not invite you to photograph them. You should also be reticent with old people and ethnic minorities. Film and transparency film are obtainable in all cities, but the best selection is in Manila and Cebu. Make sure they have been kept in a cool place.

Telecommunications

The postal service is not without its snags. True, every sizeable town has a post office, but the transport routes are often very long and not always reliable. Within the country a letter will often take longer to arrive than one posted to or from abroad. Packets that look interesting frequently disappear. Even so, Filipinos abroad often send money to their relatives by letter, and postal employees get greedy around Christmas time. Make sure the stamps on letters are franked. Local phone calls, also collect calls, all go through the operator and can take quite a while. You can telephone abroad, using the offices of the cheaper PLDT (Philippines Long Distance Telephone Co), from better hotels and, in Manila, by direct dialing. Telephone numbers change frequently; the current telephone directory or directory inquiries (tel. 114) can help.

Theft and narcotics

Tourists are always classed by the locals as rich, and attract envious looks from the sort of people who are no respecters of property. So never leave your luggage unattended, be sure it is locked when you deposit it or dispatch it, and use the hotel safes for valuables. The pockets in the front of your clothes are a safer place for money than the back, as pickpockets are most frequently active in crowds. The Philippines has a serious narcotics problem, especially in the cities. There are severe laws in force against importing, exporting, producing, possessing and dealing in drugs. Really serious offences can lead to life imprisonment or the death penalty. Never ever accept any little packets for safe keeping or as a "present" for friends or relatives, without first inspecting the contents. The police make random searches.

Time

The Philippines is 8 hours ahead of GMT and 7 hours ahead of British Summer Time. The figures for continental Europe are 7 and 6 hours respectively.

Weights and measures

In general the metric system applies. However, Anglo-American units such as Fahrenheit, inches, gallons and feet are still in common use.

ADDRESSES

Embassies in the Philippines

Australia: 104 Paseo de Roxas, Makati, Tel: 8177911. **Canada**: Allied Bank Bldg., Ayala Ave., Makati, Tel:8108861. **Great Britain**: L.V. Locsin Bldg. 6752, Ayala Ave., Makati, Tel. 8167116. **Indonesia**: Indonesian Embassy Bldg., Salcedo St., Makati, Tel: 855061. **Malaysia**: Tordesillas St., Makati, Tel: 8174581. **New Zealand**: Gammon Center Bldg., Alfaro St., Makati, Tel: 8180916. **Singapore**: ODC Intern. Plaza Bldg., Salcedo St., Makati, Tel:8161764. **USA**: 1201 Roxas Blvd., Ermita, Tel. 8322003.

Tourist Offices/Diplomatic Representations Abroad

Australia: c/o Consulate General of the Philippines, Wynyard House, suite 703, 301 George Street, Sydney 2000, Tel. 92996815. **Great Britain**: Philippine Embassy, 17 Albemarle St. London

W1X 7HA, Tel: 4995443. **Hongkong**: Philipp. Consulate General, 6/f United Centre, 95 Queensway, Tel: 28666471. **United States**: Philippine Center, 556 Fifth Ave. New York, N.Y. 10036, Tel: 5757915. Philipp. Consulate General, 3660 Wilshire Blvd., Los Angeles, CA 90010-1717 USA, Tel: 4874527.

LANGUAGE GUIDE

The following list is a brief glossary of Tagalog, which, in spite of nearly 90 regional languages, is understood more or less everywhere. The accented syllable is stressed in speech.

Welcome, cheers . . . . *mabúhay*
Good morning . . . *magandáng umága*
Good day . . . . *magandáng tangháli*
Good afternoon . . *magandáng hápon*
Good night . . . . . *magandáng gabí*
Goodbye . . . . *paálam / adyos / bye bye*
What's your name?(inf./formal) . *anóng pangálan mo/anóng pangálan po?*
My name is . . . . . . *ang pangálan ko*
How are you (sing.)? . . . *kumustá ka?*
How are you (plural)? . . *kumustá po / kayó?*
Where is the..? . . . . *saán ang (saán si for persons)*
Where are you from? . *saán ka gáling?*
What country are you from? *tagásaáng bayán ka?*
Where are you going? *saán ka pupuntá?*
What is that? . . . . *ano itó?*
I would like to eat/drink . . *gustó kung kumáin/uminum*
I would like to pay . . . *magbabáyad na akó*
What time is it? . . . . *anong óras na?*
How much does this cost? *magkáno itó?*
I . . . . *akó*
you . . . . *ikáw*
he, she, it . . . . *siyá*
we . . . . *kami / táyo*
yes . . . . *oó*
no . . . . *hindí*

thank you . . . . *salámat*
thanks a lot . . . . *maráming salámat*
OK, let's go . . . . *síge*
good . . . . *mabúti*
bad . . . . *masamá*
big . . . . *malakí*
small . . . . *maliít*
today . . . . *ngayón*
tomorrow . . . . *búkas*
yesterday . . . . *kahápon*
day . . . . *áraw*
week . . . . *linggó*
month . . . . *buwán*
year . . . . *taón*
hot . . . . *maínit*
cold . . . . *malamíg*
clean . . . . *malínis*
dirty . . . . *marúmi*
room . . . . *kuwárto*
bath, bathroom . . . . *bányo*
mosquito-net . . . . *kulambó*
toilet . . . . . . *kubíta (comfort room)*
expensive . . . . *mahál*
cheap . . . . *múra*
rice (uncooked/cooked) . . *bigás/kánin*
fish . . . . *isdá*
zero, nothing, no/none . . . . . . *walá*
1 . . . . *isá*
2 . . . . *dalawá*
3 . . . . *tatló*
4 . . . . *apát*
5 . . . . *limá*
6 . . . . *ánim*
7 . . . . *pitó*
8 . . . . *waló*
9 . . . . *siyám*
10 . . . . *sampú*
11 . . . . *labing-isá*
12 . . . . *labing-dalawá*
20 . . . . *dalawampú*
30 . . . . *tatlumpú*
40 . . . . *apatnapú*
41 . . . . *apatnapú't isa*
50 . . . . *limampú*
60 . . . . *animpú*
70 . . . . *pitumpú*
80 . . . . *walampú*
90 . . . . *siyamnapú*
100 . . . . *isáng daán*

Pronunciation

The letters *p* and *f* are often inter-changed, even when English words are spoken or sung, e.g. "Hey, *fretty* woman!" The letter *w* in the middle or at the end of a word is pronounced as *oo*, e.g. áraw = ára-oo, Banáwe = Baná-oo-ay. The words that are written *ng* and *mga* are pronounced *nung* and *munga* respectively.

AUTHORS

Albrecht G. Schaefer, project editor of this book, is a journalist, photographer and ethnologist specializing in South-east Asia and Melanesia. He writes for German and international media about his experiences in this fascinating island world. His long stays and extensive travels through the Philippines, and the invaluable assistance of his wife, Maria Lourdes Perlas, made this book possible. He contributed the chapters "Land and People," "Luzon" (except Southern Luzon), "The Visayas" (except Samar and Leyte), "The Mysterious Sulu Sea," "Western Mindanao" and the features "The Minorities" and "Philippine Cuisine." He was the co-author of "Manila," "Mindanao, the Troubled Southern Island" and "Art and Culture."

Wolf Dietrich taught philosophy and psychology at the De La Salle University in Manila. He often tries to share the simple life of the islanders. He wrote the chapter "The Living Past" and the feature "A Mixed Legacy." He is the co-author of "Manila."

Sylvia L. Mayuga lives in Manila, where, she works as a journalist, writer and maker of video-films. She is well versed in the artistic achievements of the Philippines. She wrote the feature "Women of the Philippines" and is the co-author of "Art and Culture."

Roland Hanewald arrived in the Philippines as a ship's officer in the 1960s. He stayed for about 25 years and ex-plored, described and photographed the archipelago on land and water. His writings have been published in a number of different countries and languages. For this book he contributed "Southern Luzon," "The Middle Islands" (Mindoro, Marinduque, Romblon Archipelago, Masbate, Samar, Leyte) and the features "Vulnerable Miracles of Nature" and "Fiesta Filipina." He is the co-author of "Mindanao, the Troubled Southern Island."

PHOTOGRAPHERS

Archiv für Kunst und Geschichte, Berlin — 25R, 32

Cuizon, Noel (Hiraya Galley) — 233

Fajardo, A. — 45, 101, 106, 126, 234, 238

Hanewald, R. — 16, 75,79, 88, 115, 200

Höbel, Robert — cover, 10/11, 14, 21,23, 27,46/47, 48/49, 73, 78, 81 99, 100114, 123, 130, 150/151,184, 202/203, 208, 230, 232, 236,236, backcover

Jones, E. Michael — 219

Kiwitt, Eckhardt — 34, 35, 50, 80, 121, 127, 135, 144, 157, 165, 192, 209, 216, 227

Kunert, Rainer E. — 57, 71, 74, 90, 117

Riethmüller, Robert — 36, 37, 55, 56, 60, 64/65, 84, 87, 104/105, 119, 164, 166

Schaefer, Albrecht G. — 8/9, 12, 18, 19, 20, 22, 25L, 28, 29, 30, 31, 39, 40, 41,42, 43, 59, 66, 72, 76, 85,89, 91, 93, 96,97, 110, 111, 112, 118, 120, 122, , 126,128, 129, 131, 133, 134, 136, 137, 139, 140, 146, 152, 156, 159, 161, 162, 167, 168, 170, 171, 173, 176/177, 178, 1 80, 182, 183, 186/187, 188, 194, 195, 196, 197, 198, 204/205, 206, 210, 212,213, 215, 217, 218, 220, 221, 222, 223, 224, 225, 226, 228, 229, 235, 239

Explore the World

AVAILABLE TITELS

Afghanistan 1 : 1 500 000
Argentina *(Northern)*, **Uruguay**
 1 : 2 500 000
Argentina *(Southern)*, **Uruguay**
 1 : 2 500 000
Australia 1 : 4 000 000
Bangkok - *and Greater Bangkok*
 1 : 75 000 / 1 : 15 000
Burma → *Myanmar*
Caribbean - **Bermuda, Bahamas,
 Greater Antilles** 1 : 2 500 000
Caribbean - **Lesser Antilles**
 1 : 2 500 000
Central America 1 : 1 750 000
Central Asia 1 : 1 750 000
Chile 1 : 2 500 000
China - *Northeastern*
 1 : 1 500 000
China - *Northern* 1 : 1 500 000
China - *Central* 1 : 1 500 000
China - *Southern* 1 : 1 500 000
Colombia - **Ecuador** 1 : 2 500 000
Crete - Kreta 1 : 200 000
Cuba 1 : 775 000
Dominican Republic - Haiti
 1 : 600 000
Egypt 1 : 2 500 000 / 1 : 750 000
Hawaiian Islands
 1 : 330 000 / 1 : 125 000

Hawaiian Islands – **Kaua'i**
 1 : 150 000 / 1 : 35 000
Hawaiian Islands – **Honolulu**
 - **O'ahu** 1 : 35 000 / 1 : 150 000
Hawaiian Islands – **Maui - Moloka'i**
 - **Lāna'i** 1 : 150 000 / 1 : 35 000
Hawaiian Islands – **Hawai'i, The Big
 Island** 1 : 330 000 / 1 : 125 000
Himalaya 1 : 1 500 000
Hong Kong 1 : 22 500
Indian Subcontinent 1 : 4 000 000
India - *Northern* 1 : 1 500 000
India - *Western* 1 : 1 500 000
India - *Eastern* 1 : 1 500 000
India - *Southern* 1 : 1 500 000
India - *Northeastern* - **Bangladesh**
 1 : 1 500 000
Indonesia 1 : 4 000 000
Indonesia **Sumatra** 1 : 1 500 000
Indonesia **Java - Nusa Tenggara**
 1 : 1 500 000
Indonesia **Bali - Lombok**
 1 : 180 000
Indonesia **Kalimantan**
 1 : 1 500 000
Indonesia **Java - Bali** 1 : 650 000
Indonesia **Sulawesi** 1 : 1 500 000
Indonesia **Irian Jaya - Maluku**
 1 : 1 500 000
Jakarta 1 : 22 500
Japan 1 : 1 500 000

Kenya 1 : 1 100 000
Korea 1 : 1 500 000
Malaysia 1 : 1 500 000
West Malaysia 1 : 650 000
Manila 1 : 17 500
Mexico 1 : 2 500 000
Myanmar (Burma) 1 : 1 500 000
Nepal 1 : 500 000 / 1 : 1 500 000
Nepal Trekking **Khumbu Himal -
 Solu Khumbu** 1 : 75 000
New Zealand 1 : 1 250 000
Pakistan 1 : 1 500 000
Peru - **Ecuador** 1 : 2 500 000
Philippines 1 : 1 500 000
Singapore 1 : 22 500
Southeast Asia 1 : 4 000 000
South Pacific Islands 1 : 13 000 000
Sri Lanka 1 : 450 000
Taiwan 1 : 400 000
Tanzania - Rwanda, Burundi
 1 : 1 500 000
Thailand 1 : 1 500 000
Uganda 1 : 700 000
Venezuela - Guyana, Suriname,
 French Guiana 1 : 2 500 000
Vietnam, Laos, Cambodia
 1 : 1 500 000

FORTHCOMING

Bolivia, Paraguay 1 : 2 500 000

Nelles Maps are top quality cartography!
Relief mapping, kilometer charts and tourist attractions.
Always up-to-date!

Explore the World

NELLES GUIDES

Nelles Guides – authoritative, informed and informative.
Always up-to-date, extensively illustrated, and with first-rate relief maps.
256 pages, approx. 150 color photos, approx. 25 maps.

Welcome to

• GENIE STREET •

Join Daisy and Tom on their Genie Street adventures by visiting them at Ladybird's Genie Street website.

Find out about the latest Genie Street books and meet all your favourite Lampland characters!

www.ladybirdgeniestreet.com

Written by Richard Dungworth

Illustrated by Sarah Horne

A catalogue record for this book is available from the British Library

Published by Ladybird Books Ltd.
A Penguin Company
Penguin Books Ltd., 80 Strand, London, WC2R 0RL

001 – 10 9 8 7 6 5 4 3 2 1
© LADYBIRD BOOKS LTD MMXII

LADYBIRD and the device of a Ladybird are trademarks of Ladybird Books Ltd

ISBN: 978-1-40931-240-6

Printed in England

THIS LADYBIRD BOOK BELONGS TO

Sesha
....

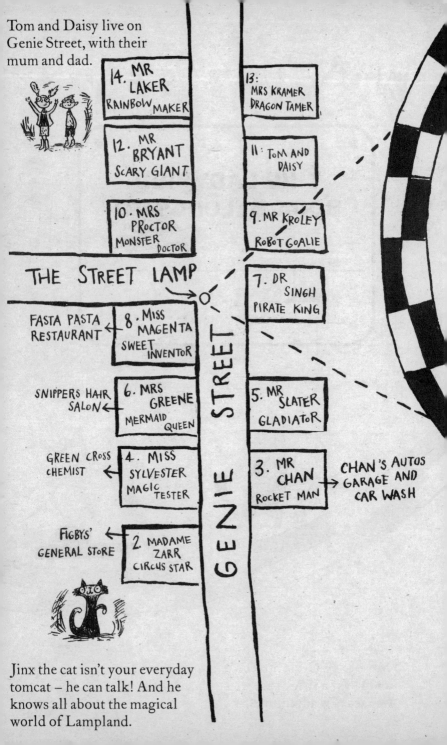

LAMPLAND

Wild Isles

to the Noom

Launch pad

the eventh Sea

Sweet Factory

Rainbow Meadows

Techno Town

City of Ancients

castle Kinghold

to Rossbone Island

Mermaid Reef

Red Dragon Hills

Fairy Forest

Land of the Giants

Monster Mountains

Mr Mistry, Genie Street's postman, gives Tom and Daisy a special parcel which sends them on each new adventure!

GENIE STREET

Mr Chan
ROCKET MAN